LOUISVILLE STORY PROGRAM

If You Write Me a Letter, Send It Here

VOICES OF RUSSELL
IN A TIME OF CHANGE

LOUISVILLE STORY PROGRAM

Copyright © 2023 by Louisville Story Program

Louisville Story Program
851 South 4th Street
Louisville, KY 40203
www.louisvillestoryprogram.org

ISBN 978-0-9914765-8-9

Library of Congress Control Number: 2022951832

Book design by Shellee Marie Jones

Edited by Joe Manning, Althea Allen Dryden, and Darcy Thompson

Front cover: Quante Woods, corner of 19th Street and
Muhammad Ali Boulevard, early 1980s (courtesy of Joyce Woods)

Back cover: Grandchildren and great-grandchildren
of Joyce Woods, same location, 2022 (photo by Darcy Thompson)

Printed in Lithuania

Contents

Introduction

We frequently hear that the Russell area of west Louisville was once "the Harlem of the South," or "the heartbeat of Black life in Louisville." People may talk about growing up in the Walnut Street business corridor surrounded by a thriving Black working and middle class. If their family had not achieved the affluence of their neighbors in the big houses on "Oatmeal Avenue," folks might describe growing up on "Cornbread Alley" in houses that were more modest than the larger homes on Walnut and Chestnut Streets. Of the more recent past, people discuss the splintering effects of Urban Renewal, the divisions it fostered, and the persistence of poverty and housing inequity that resulted. There's a conflicting mixture of pride and disappointment as residents recall past glories, difficult times, uncertain futures, and renewed commitments that have been a long time coming.

Like an old song we think we know very well, but whose verses may be elusive, Russell has many facets, identities, and histories which frequently run deeper than our surface understanding and recollection. Whether considering the heroes of the civil rights movement who lived there, the vibrant club scene of Russell's heyday, the disharmony of hard times, Black excellence in high society or Black excellence on the front porch, folks in Russell—from City View Apartments and Beecher Terrace to Elliott Park—remember what came before them, and have hopes and skepticism about what lies ahead.

In 2015, Metro Housing Authority and Metro Government initiated the Vision Russell plan which, along with additional public and private development endeavors, will culminate in nearly a billion dollars of financial and structural investment into the Russell area of west Louisville. It's a once in a century moment whose agendas and potential outcomes differ depending on who's being asked. What are the opportunities and risks of this moment? What will be gained or lost? The extent to which these investments will address some of the historic injustices visited on the Russell area and its residents during the eras of redlining and Urban Renewal remain to be seen. Whether this city can invest its way out of past missteps, and what effects this will have on the families, culture, and lived experience of Russell is yet to be determined. In the words of Rev. David Snardon in this book, "Time will tell if promises given will be promises kept." Change is coming, though. Inarguably.

It seemed important, self-evidently so, that this moment in our city's history be documented by people with the most at stake and with the authority of lived experience in Russell. So, we spent three years partnering with the twenty-six authors of the book in your hands, and they have documented a piece of their lives in Russell in their own words. Their voices are clear and resonant in these pages and—like so many stories worth telling—the value of these stories lay both in their singularity and their universality.

Even if you have never been a Motown trumpeter like McDaniel Bluitt, you have likely spent quiet moments in earnest entreaty for guidance. Even if you have never lived in public housing, you have navigated sharing space with neighbors and have likely learned to admire and rely on a few of them as described by Lamika Jordan, Rameriz Reed, Jane Grady, and Manfred Reid. Though you may not have ever been a gang violence interrupter like Demetrius McDowell or Rev. Geoff Ellis, you have likely asked others or been asked to consider the far reaching consequences of decisions made in haste. And while you may not have lived on the same city block for eighty years, you may find a sense of familiarity in the title chapter of this book in Ms. Joyce Woods' fond recollections of childhood, of the ways the neighborhood has changed, or what it's like to know, with confidence, that she's centrally important to the community right outside of her front door.

What these authors demonstrate is that we and our communities are always changing, all the time, and that in order to recall ourselves, our homes, and our neighborhoods with any clarity, we must reflect thoughtfully and ask each other, "What do you remember?" and, "What is it like for you now?" The impressions of Russell offered here are not and could not be comprehensive. But the outline traced by this book—1.5 square miles, from Ninth Street to 32nd Street, from Broadway to Market—is somehow much bigger than the lives and neighborhoods discussed herein. This is an historical record that stretches out as wide as two centuries spent learning how to be neighbors in this community, in this country. It's the microscopic view of something immense and very important: an understanding that the only thing cementing the past in place is how we talk about it, and that to create a common vision and a shared future, what is required is deep listening. So listen to the voices of Russell in this time of change. Listen for similarities amid the differences, for the universal in the unique. The tune is familiar to all of us. We only need to learn the words.

—Althea Allen Dryden, Christine Gosney, Joe Manning, and Darcy Thompson

Never Felt Whole Until I Helped Someone Else

PAM HAINES

I started out at Sweet Peaches in February 2014. I've been here for almost eight years. I used to go to the beauty shop next door; that's how I found this little spot. I had no idea it would become a full-blown restaurant. Sweet Peaches started because I was working on my Ph.D. and couldn't hold a full-time job. I had to travel to do interviews and research for my Ph.D. I decided to sell cookies out of this little spot. It was convenient for me.

I received a double master's degree in business management and business from Indiana Weslyan. I knew I wanted an education but never knew exactly what I wanted to do with it. I'm grown, though. I have to do something. So I just kept going to school until I found my place.

When Sweet Peaches first opened, I just thought I would sell some cookies, get my Ph.D., and go forward with my own business and my own agenda. But the longer I stayed, the more I felt like I was needed by the community. The Russell neighborhood is one of the poorest neighborhoods in the city. It's financially unstable, and it has a high crime rate. I was a little afraid of this neighborhood when I first opened the restaurant. I would sometimes think, *Do I really want to go over there? I'm scared.* But that didn't deter me because I knew the neighborhood needed it. I got to know the people; all people wanted was to be understood and for somebody to be kind to them. I felt like the people in this neighborhood, whatever the situation that they were in, deserved to eat wholesome food where they lived and worked. Sweet Peaches is not just some little restaurant. We're here for our community.

One time, a little boy asked me if he could sell my cookies at school so he could afford his school uniforms. I started asking the city and surrounding businesses for money to buy school uniforms for this neighborhood. Then we started giving away Christmas baskets, Easter

On the Lily Pad

Giving out food on the Lily Pad

baskets, school supplies, and uniforms for the kids in the neighborhood. For the little kids, we do art classes. The city gave me some land behind the building, and I turned it into the Lily Pad. I wanted it to be a place where the kids could hang out in the summertime, eat lunch, have birthday parties, and watch movies. We have educational movies and hot dogs on Friday nights out on the Lily Pad. So the longer I stayed, the more involved I got, and the more I felt like I was needed. They didn't have anything down here.

Pam, Tony, and Alana

Pam and her son Tony

I used to sit in the window at Sweet Peaches to study, and I could see prostitution, drug deals, fights, guys packing guns. I never thought I would fit in. But for some reason, I do. I fit right here where I'm needed. And I need these people to make me whole, and that's what this neighborhood has done.

There was this one time when I was sitting in the window at the restaurant and a young lady knocked on the window. It was kind of late at night, and I was a little bit afraid. She knocked on the window over and over. I opened the door, and she said, "Ms. Peaches. Can you help me?"

I said, "I'll try. What is it that you need?"

She said, "I want a different life. My kids are hungry. They don't have no school clothes. And I don't like the job that I do." It was obvious that she walked the street at night. If she felt comfortable enough telling me all that personal stuff, it meant that I was not a stranger here; I belonged here. I helped her. I got her kids together. She's gone to school, and she's not reverted back to the way she used to be. It made me realize that this is where I belong, and this is what I wanted to do. From that day forward, I've invested everything I have.

I'm the baby girl in the family and was always kind of spoiled. I always had somebody to look after me and give me what I wanted. So I had to learn how to change my personality and be a giving, more loving person. And that's what I learned here. I could say, "You don't like it? Get out." But now I say, "If you don't like it, is there something else I can help you with? You want me to make you a different type of cookie? I can't do it today, but come by tomorrow and I'll have some oatmeal cookies with some extra raisins in it." I learned how to be more diplomatic and gentle and kind and understanding. Working here has been good to me.

Being selfish and uptight got me nowhere. I didn't know what people had been through. Now I bend over backward if I have to for my customers because I feel like they've gone through enough heartache and pain and misery. If you come off the street and you're not as clean as you should be, other people might not want you in here, so I wait on you personally and get you going. I tell you next time you want something free, knock on the back door: that's where the free stuff comes from. I don't tell them, "Come back here because you're dirty." I say, "I gotcha now, but if you want something free, you ain't got no money, just knock on the back door, and I'll give it to you. It ain't gotta be nobody's business." I've

From left: Tony, Pam, Alana, and Jasmine

had about seven people today, and we're not open. They want a peanut butter and jelly sandwich and something to drink, and I give it to them. It's not gonna make me or break me.

Toward the end of the month is when people really start saying, "I spent all my food stamps. We need dinner for one day." I say, "Okay. How many kids you got? Give me a couple of hours and come back later." I cook them a vegetable, meat, and bread. Something easy to cook. A meatloaf is always easy to cook. So are green beans, or I always got fresh greens frozen. Just give them something. Some of the older people in the building over here can't get out to get something to eat. Well, if they send somebody over here, I'll send some food. I budget for it, and most of the time, I'm over the budget.

I beg my family something terrible. My sister says, "Pam, you're just like another bill." I say, "So what? I got kids that need some tennis shoes." And she says, "Well, when I get my retirement check, I'll help you buy three pairs." If a little guy that's going on a job interview needs a tie, I'll call my brother and say, "You got a hundred ties. I need five of them and a clean white shirt because these guys got job interviews." I have eight brothers, and they know if I ask for something, it's the last resort. They'll figure out a way to get it to me. They know that it feels good.

Say I got six little boys that need a pair of Nikes. I ask Ms. Barbara Sexton Smith who was on Metro Council, and she'll turn me on to somebody. I ask the mayor, and he'll turn me on to somebody. I ask Sadiqa Reynolds at the Urban League for anything. I just ask

uniforms, and I'll wash them for you. Not only will I wash them, I'll give you enough for the whole week. And you ain't got to worry about it." So I did that. I started doing that for other kids too. I taught them how to wash and fold the clothes. When they need to wash, they come upstairs, and we wash the clothes. Mamas started coming over and washing stuff too. I told Barbara Sexton Smith I needed another washer and dryer, and she said, "I'm gonna ask my husband." I met him at Lowe's, and he bought me a washer and dryer.

After a while, I decided to give one of the machines away to a family who needed it. I gave a washer and dryer to a girl who had four kids. I said, "You can have it. I have another one." Then I donated the other washer and dryer to another family. Now when I have to wash clothes for somebody, we go to the laundromat. I teach them how to fold the clothes up without wrinkles in them and show them how to iron. We sit and talk and figure out what's really going on. It's my opportunity to talk to them and see where they are at and try to get some of them registered for the GED. "Get your GED. I will help you. I will show you how to pass the classes and stuff like that." People need a job; you need your education. You need your feet on some solid ground, not just on some food stamps that's going to help you for a little while.

So, if they come, then I make time. If they come and ask me for something and I don't have it, I figure out how to get it and how to make time for them or turn them over to somebody that'll help them. Then they'll report back to me, and I know that they're getting help. I know where to send them for help if I can't do it. So I make time.

I've had the best of the best. I had the best cars. Lived in a big fancy house. I had the fancy red bottom shoes, the fur coats; I had it all. Doesn't mean anything

for what I want for the kids, and people see that I get it. It makes me feel good to help somebody, but that's not why I do it. I want them to have what they need. I want them to be lifted up, to stop selling drugs, to stop not having a job, to get a paycheck, and to help their family.

One day I saw a kid at the restaurant during school hours. I said, "Why ain't you going to school? Isn't your mom and dad gonna get you?" He said, "My uniform is dirty. And the kids talk about me." I said, "We're gonna go upstairs. We're gonna wash them. Bring your

to me any more. I don't need that stuff. I sold all that stuff to take care of my kids in this neighborhood and give them art lessons and everything. All my red-bottom shoes? I can't fit my big toe in them. I got one pair now, but I used to have fifty. I used to have thirty Louis Vuitton purses; now I got one. I'll sell it if I have to. I just did what I did for the people in the community. I had everything I wanted. If something was going on and I came up short for the Thanksgiving giveaway, I'd just sell my stuff. Sometimes, Kroger would give me turkeys. When I wanted to give everybody a cake at Christmas, Kroger at UofL sold me cakes for three dollars when they usually cost ten. I bought 150 of them, made the icing, and gave everybody a cake.

It's very fulfilling. Not only am I doing good for those people, but it's good for me; it's making me whole. It's giving me strength to do more and figure out how I can help somebody else. I feel blessed to be able to come up with the resources to help families. I've never felt so good about me. And I never felt whole until helping somebody else. It's not that I got a whole lot of money or anything, because I don't. I'm one of them. I'm probably poor, but that's okay. Because it's not material things that I need, it's me being here, knowing that on Sundays, I'm not feeding my people unhealthy food. It makes me feel good. We all come together, and we have a good time.

My first job was managing a restaurant at the Hyatt Regency. Later I was the food and beverage manager there. I worked at Popeye's and Taco Bell as manager and as a district manager at Rally's. When I was working for them, I never thought that I would be opening up a restaurant and working for myself. I learned a lot at those restaurants that I use at Sweet Peaches, such as getting the cleaning chart done, how much money I should be making, the food costs, doing the reports, hiring the right people, setting the schedule, and what to expect from customers. I learned quite a bit from those restaurants during both the good times and the bad times.

I come from a big family. I have eight brothers and three sisters. I'm number seven. My parents worked, so we all had to learn how to cook. I learned how to cook from my mom and my oldest sister, Wanda. They'd show me how to cut up a whole chicken and how long to cook the green beans before I needed to cut an onion up and put it in there. I was making biscuits and fried chicken when I was about nine years old. When I was about ten, I'd bake a yellow cake with homemade chocolate icing. My mom loved that icing. I didn't want to cook, though. I wanted to be outside playing with my girlfriends or playing with baby dolls. I never thought that I would own a restaurant.

I started reading cookbooks—Betty Crocker or whatever I could find—and learning more and more. I distinctly remember learning that when you're cooking a roast, you should cut the roast up into little squares and let that cook, then add the potatoes, and *then* the carrots because they cook quicker than the potatoes. Before I knew it, I was good at it. Now, every other Sunday, I do roast, potatoes, and carrots here at the restaurant, and it turns out really good. I put the roast in the oven in a roasting pan and let it cook on low for at least six hours until the meat's so tender. Then I cut the meat into little squares, add the potatoes, carrots, onions, and all the seasonings and put it in a bag with some onions and salt and pepper. I tie it up, put it in the roaster and let it cook, and it's so tender and juicy. And then I pour the juice off of it and make the gravy, put the potatoes, carrots, and onions in the gravy, and let it cook for about another hour. Then we're good to go. Just keep it simple. It's one of our specialties.

I'd like to have an advertisement on a bus and one of the billboards to let people know that we're

Before remodeling in 2019

open on Sundays and we have soul food. Things like smoked ribs, baked chicken and dressing, oxtails with gravy and carrots and potatoes, salmon croquettes, white fish, fried pork chops with macaroni and cheese, sweet potatoes, potato salad, cabbage, pasta salad, green beans, and fresh greens. I do strictly collard greens. I buy two cases of collard greens from the Restaurant Depot every Friday, and then we pick them and cook them fresh Sunday morning. I don't open till 12 p.m. on Sunday, so I put the collard greens on at 6 a.m., and they cook, and cook, and cook. We just season them and boil them for six hours. I don't put any kind of meat in. I just use some pepper, some salt, and then some secret seasoning.

We also have sweet potato pie, blackberry cobbler, peach cobbler, pound cake with caramel icing, carrot cake with burnt butter and cream cheese icing, and sherbert cake with orange glaze. My son Tony made the sherbert cake, and I made the glaze for it. Tony cooks here. He runs the kitchen. We complement each other. It is both difficult and pretty rewarding sometimes to work with my son. I have three children. Tony is thirty-four, Jasmine is thirty, and Alana is twenty-eight. They're grown up. Thank goodness! The girls don't want to work in a restaurant. They don't want to cook for nobody else. Alana has a beauty shop upstairs, and Jasmine works from home for a stock and bond company.

On Sundays, we expect about at least a hundred people. It's a lot of food, and we sell out of everything. But I would like to serve 175 to make it worth my while. Back when COVID first hit, I went to being open three days a week instead of five. It slowed down a lot. I had to change the price around a little bit, but we gave away five hundred bowls of soup every Wednesday. And then, when I wanted to make soup for folks in the early days of the pandemic, Barbara Sexton Smith

Pam and Senate candidate Amy McGrath

Prepared meals given out during COVID

bought the food. She's been a true friend. All the soups had eleven ingredients to boost the immune system: thyme, garlic, sage, fresh ginger, fresh cilantro, black beans, and others.

The lady that drives the TARC—I never knew her name—would stop right across the street and let people off the bus to come in and get their soup. Five or ten of them would come in, then she let them back on, and then they'd go on. Somebody would come down from Park Hill and take about forty soups and give them away up there. And a lady and her friend came over to get about twenty-five soups and cornbread and give it to the people on Hemlock Street. It made me feel good that they would come. I may do that again this fall, maybe a good old potato soup with fresh herbs and spices. I don't know who it'll help, but it might help keep somebody healthy. I like to think it may have helped boost somebody's immune system. I didn't make as much money during the pandemic—we just made it—but the people in the neighborhood came out. They were out of work, and they suffered a little bit, but they came to the restaurant, and I made friends with a whole lot of them. It was hard, but the neighborhood came together.

My business has survived by the grace of the Lord and the grace of the people that I asked stuff of. I don't know why they don't recognize the magnitude of how much is needed in these neighborhoods. The thing that I'm hoping and wishing for is that they're going to do what they say they're going to do for this neighborhood. There's a lot of stuff going on in Russell, a lot of investment, but I don't think the money is going where it should go. All that money that's supposed to come down to the West End, I still don't see it. What about the little people that maybe want a mom-and-pop store that could use some money? Or some of the families that could use their houses fixed up? If more businesses

Pam, Torrie, and Tony

After remodeling

Pam cooking for a television program

are coming down here, are they going to cause the little people to leave? They say they have money to uplift this neighborhood, beautify it, and to bring jobs to the people who live here. Don't keep talking about it. Just do it. Find a way. If you have a long-term plan, it could take ten years. Some of these people won't last for ten years. They're not gonna last for five years. Stop playing and just do it.

The people in the neighborhood thought money would come to this part of town because they said it's for the Russell neighborhood. But what has happened in the Russell neighborhood? Nothing. People don't believe it. They just think it's a way for somebody to get them to sell their house so they can move out. I get text messages all the time about my little raggedy house. "What do you want it for?" They don't stop. I told them it's raggedy; I owe back taxes. "What do you want it for? We gonna take care of all that." These people want to stay here. Help them fix their house up, spruce up their land. Give them money to open up a business down here where they live. People should be able to eat and play where they live.

The Russell neighborhood gave me a place where I felt like I belonged. Not only did they need me, but I needed them to complete who I was. And that's what this restaurant has done for me. It has completed me. It made me whole. I never thought that I would find that here on this corner. ✦

Mr. Red's Grandson

HAVEN HARRINGTON III

As a kid, I never really called it Russell. I never even knew the neighborhood had a name. It was just a place where I grew up. In my twenties, I got this book from the Western Branch Library called *Life Behind a Veil: Blacks in Louisville, Kentucky, 1865–1930.* I read that thing like three times. I recognized some of the names in the books and their connections to people I knew through my grandparents. And that's when it hit me: "Oh, *this* is Russell."

I remember hearing stories from my grandfather, his friends, and my dad about Russell back in their day. I could imagine what it was like when they were younger and how much more vibrant Russell must have been. Their stories inspired me to start doing research. I used to go to Dr. Blaine Hudson, who lived across the street. I'd say, *Tell me about this. Tell me about that.* When I transferred to the University of Louisville, I took one of his Pan-African history classes. In every conversation I ever had with him, he would take off his cap slowly and with his left hand and brush back his long, flowing hair. He was one of my favorite people and one of the reasons I started learning more about the history of Russell. That's when I became a junior historian of Russell, I guess.

Growing up, I spent most of my time at my grandparent's house at 24th and Madison. That house was the cornerstone of our lives for so long. Especially my cousin William Perkins and me because that's where we would go every day after school. We spent all our summers and pretty much all our free time there. It was a typical little white shotgun house with a stone porch and six trees surrounding it. The guy who built Central High School at its current location was a friend of my grandfather, and the hardwood floors from the old Central High School basketball court ended up as the floor in my grandparents' house.

Haven in the second grade in Wilmington, Delaware

My grandfather built his barbershop on the side of the house, and for many years Mr. Red's Barbershop was my world. It was just this neighborhood place. Everybody from three generations got their hair cut at my grandfather's shop: all my friends, everybody in my dad's age group, then all of my grandfather's friends who would be there for hours. Even when they got to be in their eighties, his friends would still come by to get their haircuts. Those guys had like one hair. He just took the scissors and—*clip*—they were done. They would sit in the barbershop, talk for a bit, and take a two-hour nap before their grandsons picked them up and took them back home. Next week, they would do the same thing again.

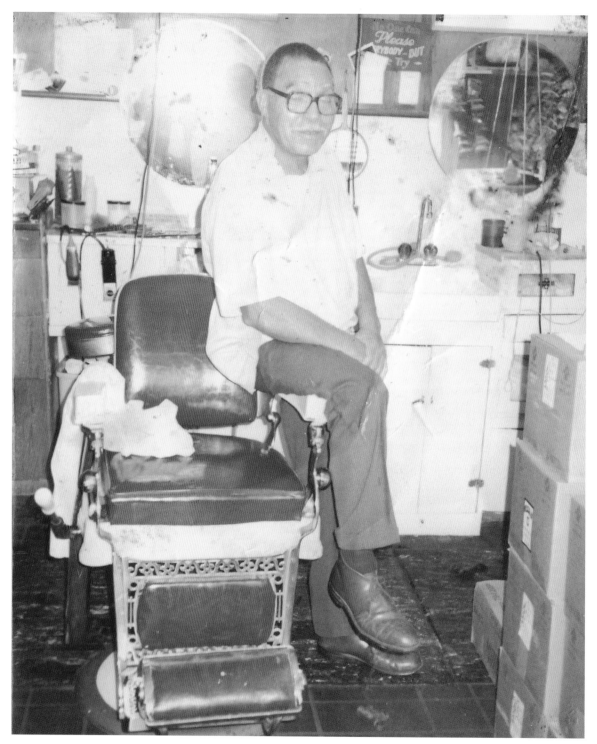

Haven D. Harrington, Sr. in his barbershop, December 1982

Everybody knew Mr. Red. I'm almost fifty years old, my grandfather passed away over ten years ago, and people still call me "Mr. Red's Grandson." There were tons of barbers in the area, but he was an icon. Like all the barbers of the day, he would loan people money and sell candy and spring water out of the barbershop. All these little kids from the neighborhood would come in and out all day, getting haircuts and buying candy. My grandfather would give them a little money or a free haircut if they could show him a report card with good grades.

He had old-school porcelain barber chairs with the crank. He had straight razors, the leather strap you sharpen the razor with, and the little foam machine for shaving. Every Black barbershop had this poster of hairstyles you could get, and his was from the 1970s. I remember one of them was called "The Watusi." The clippers he used were ancient and heavy—like ten pounds apiece—but they were great for cutting. You wouldn't think a seventy-year-old guy could cut a high-top fade, but he was one of the best faders. He could do the Gumby with the little part down the middle. I had no control over how I got my haircut, though. He cut it *his* way—really short—and that was it. But I would never complain.

My cousin and I would spend hours listening to my grandfather and his buddies at the barbershop. They'd tell us stories about World War II and what it was like growing up in Black Louisville. My grandfather told me he did not want to go to World War II when he was drafted. He hadn't been in Louisville too long and didn't want to leave his wife. Like a lot of Black men in his day, he felt conflicted. He knew that if he returned from the war, he would still face the same injustices. Yes, you're fighting for freedom, but you're fighting for someone else's freedom. He waited until the last possible day before he left.

Haven D. Harrington, Sr. "Mr. Red" in his barbershop

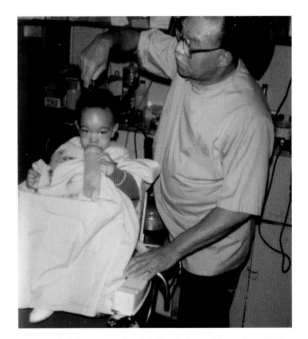

Mr. Red giving Jason Cox his first haircut, November 1985

He told my cousin and me stories about the time five hundred men went into a battle, and only five or six came out. Or when his squadron captured some German soldiers. The Black soldiers in his unit were told to move out of the barracks and pitch tents. They wanted to house the German POWs in their barracks. The Black soldiers were like, "Yeah, that's not gonna

Haven D. Harrington, Sr. "Mr. Red"

happen. Here's what's gonna happen. We're gonna stay in these barracks or fight this out." While the Black soldiers knew they could be killed, they let them know they would kill a whole bunch of them too. Needless to say, the German soldiers were the ones pitching tents.

They called him Mr. Red because when he would get mad, he would turn red like a beet. My grandmother used to call him Strawberry for that same reason. Lyman T. Johnson, who integrated the University of Kentucky in 1949, used to come to my grandfather's barbershop, and apparently they used to get into hellacious arguments. Lyman was all about, "We need to integrate. We need to move out to St. Matthews." My grandfather was like, "We don't need them. We can do this on our own." He had strict beliefs about what Black folks should do for themselves. I was told that he and Lyman used to get into this argument on a monthly basis. They'd stop talking to each other for a few days, but Lyman would always come back.

My grandfather used to order his shoes and suits from a catalog. I thought that was the weirdest thing until I got older and he started talking to me about more adult things. When he moved to Louisville, he used to shop at Byck's Department Store like everybody else. But Byck's didn't let Black folks try on shoes or clothes. "If they won't let me try anything on, I'm not gonna buy anything from them." He refused to buy his shoes and suits from them. He was really upset when they renamed James Bond Middle School to Dann C. Byck. That infuriated my grandfather to no end. He questioned why they would name a school in west Louisville after a guy who wouldn't let Black people try on clothes at his store.

When I was a kid, we used to shop at Sears on the corner of Ninth and Broadway before it was the LG&E building. We also shopped at Consolidated on 15th and Jefferson, which is now a halfway house. I used to go

Haven and his cousin William Perkins

there and buy clothes all the time. It had this department store smell like old, musty hardwood floors. My cousin William and I used to get our suits and shoes at the Hub Clothing Store on 17th and Jefferson. He was my right-hand man. From the time we were born, even up to now, we have done almost everything together. He's like my brother. They used to dress us alike, which annoyed the hell out of us. We had the same outfits. We got the same stuff for Christmas—little striped shirts, and identical little suits for church. It was annoying.

My grandmother would make breakfast for William and me on a typical summer day. My grandfather wouldn't let us sleep in even if there was no school. He'd come in, turn the lights on, and say, "Get up."

"We're not doing anything today," we'd say.

"Get up."

We would start our day by eating my grandmother's pancakes and watching Nickelodeon. On Tuesdays, we'd get in the car, run errands with my grandfather to the bank, and then buy candy and other items for the barbershop. Afterward, we'd go outside and play with all our friends who lived down the block.

Haven and his cousin William Perkins

We would play with Travis Hudson, Dr. J. Blaine Hudson's son, who lived across the street, and my buddy Steven Reynolds, who looked dead-up like Prince. We used to ride our bikes all over. We were supposed to stay on our side of the street, but that never stopped us. We were all over the place and always in trouble because my grandfather had spies everywhere who would rat on us. My grandfather would know everywhere we went. Those were good times.

My grandfather didn't leave the barbershop for anything. That's the last thing you wanted because if he had to leave, you were getting it. If we were being too noisy in the house, or if we weren't practicing the piano, we could hear him scream through the walls.

He'd come out with the paddle, and we quickly got in line. You didn't want my grandfather to come out because it would be swift and instantaneous punishment. We took piano lessons at the Bourgard College of Music and Art from Aunt Joetta, William's mom. If we didn't practice for at least an hour a day, my grandfather was coming for us. We also had to read the Bible every day after school. We'd take turns reading Bible verses until we finished a whole chapter. I have read the Bible almost three times, cover to cover. Then, we did homework. And finally, we'd go outside and play.

My grandmother had a brother who lived on Chestnut next to Stith Cleaners. You could always tell when they were pressing clothes because the steam

From left: Haven's paternal grandmother, Harriet Harrington, her sisters Dorothy Matthews and Francis Howell, and his great-grandmother Ella Robinson

would shoot out the side of the building from the old press. One of my favorite people was Aunt Birdy. She was the most religious person in the entire world. She would pray for us *all of the time*. She'd pray before we left the house for us to have a safe journey back. I was like, "Dude, we're going two blocks. We're literally just going from 24th and Magazine to 24th and Madison. Come to find out, Birdy had been a flapper back in the '20s and '30s. She ran off with one of the big bands and she just popped back up a few months later.

My grandmother sometimes made us go with her to Bacon's on Dixie Highway. It seemed like we would go at least once a week. One day Aunt Birdy came along. It was raining, and she prayed the whole time.

"Lord, don't let us get in an accident. Lord, *be* the tires. Stick to the road." I'm in the back seat praying, "Lord Jesus, let this ride be over quickly." That was one of the longest trips to Bacon's ever. On the way back, I just pretended to be asleep.

My grandfather was a very religious guy too, a churchgoing man, but he wasn't one of those people who say, "We're gonna be at church all day." That was never him. By 2:00 p.m., he was like, "I'm out. Let's go." We went to Broadway Temple AME Zion, on the corner of 13th and Broadway, designed by the renowned Black architect Samuel Plato. That was one of the prominent Black churches at the time. Going to church was fun because the church was vibrant.

The men of Broadway Temple AME Zion Church on 13th and Broadway in the early 1980s

There were hundreds of people there. We loved it to death. Church service was always boring, but I was there with my cousin. We'd sit there drawing on church envelopes and eating Hall's cough drops like candy. We used to talk and giggle, but you couldn't get too loud because Mrs. Pleasant, the Sunday school teacher, had a fly swatter, and she'd appear out of nowhere: *Smack!* It was amazing how fast this eighty-year-old woman could slide down the pew, hit you, and then slide back like she never even moved. She was like a ninja. If you saw that flyswatter come out, you'd better get quiet as a church mouse because she wasn't playing.

We'd go to church at 10:30 a.m., leave around 1:00 or 2:00 p.m., go to my grandparents' house for Sunday dinner, and then go back home. That was our Sunday ritual from the time I got to Louisville to when I went to Morehouse. It would be me, my cousin William, his sister, Amanda, Aunt Jo, her husband, Uncle Bill, my grandparents, and my dad. It was a big family, and we were thick as thieves.

I spent almost all my time with them when my dad worked at DuPont. When we moved back to Louisville, my dad would drop me off at Aunt Jo's house in the mornings, and I'd ride with my uncle to school at Stonestreet Elementary. Then they'd drop me off at my grandparents' to wait for my dad to get off work. For middle school, I went to St. Denis on Cane Run Road. My dad would drop me off in the mornings, and after school, I would ride the TARC to my grandparents' house. Dad traveled a lot for work, but we were inseparable. We did everything together. It was always him and me when I wasn't at my grandparents' house. Whether going out of town to the Air Force Museum in Dayton, going to D.C., riding Amtrak, or going to New Orleans for a convention, we did everything together.

As a father, he struck the perfect balance between friend and parent. We were really good friends, but I always knew the line. He was not as strict as my grandfather, but you always knew where you stood. He let you be a kid, make mistakes and learn from them. He rarely said, "I love you, son," but there was no doubt because we did everything together. We loved watching movies. He indulged my love of horror movies. He took me to see *Nightmare on Elm Street* and movies like *Revenge of the Nerds* that probably weren't appropriate for my age. I guess that's where I get my love of movies.

He was a human resources manager with DuPont for what seemed like forever. I don't think I remember him working anywhere else. He's still on the board of the NAACP, a deacon at Broadway Temple AME Zion, and very active in the community. You can drop him off anywhere, and he will make a friend. He's my best friend and still one of the coolest guys I know. My dad has next-level people skills, and everybody knows him. I'm a mini version of him. We talk or text almost every day. I was always "Mr. Red's grandson" or "Haven's boy." I wanted to be my own person. It took me thirty years to grow out of being in their shadows, but then I realized I loved being in their shadows.

My dad's generation, the baby boomer generation,

Haven, his dad Haven Harrington, Jr.
and his cousin William Perkins

was very prosperous. My dad and his friends all ended up as managers and principals or with good jobs in state and city government. My cousin Chico used to tell me how he moved from New York to Louisville in the 1970s because Louisville was the place to be. "This place was happening. I could work at Philip Morris. I could work at International Harvester. I could work at Brown-Forman. I can come out here and just make good money. Housing was cheap." They had tons of things to do. You still had a Black business district. There was a roller rink, ice cream parlors, and a ton of little restaurants where people could hang out. You had all these nightclubs like the Top Hat and Joe's Palm Room where Count Basie and all those guys would come into town and hang out. The neighborhoods were vibrant with parks. Listening to the stories from other folks, you see the decline, and it just hurts.

A lot of my friends tried to get me out to the suburbs, but I'm an urban guy. I lived in J-town, but that's not me. I like the noise, commotion, density,

Haven and his daughter Marley, August 2022

walkability, and bikeability of "the Bricks," as I call urban neighborhoods. My daughter Marley is the same way; she's an urbanist. I think Louisville may be a little too small for her. I think she wants something bigger. I don't think she will be an activist like me—that doesn't appear to be in her DNA—but I think she'll be an urbanist like me. That keeps me in Russell. We go on bike rides all over Russell and downtown. We ride downtown across the walking bridge, get our fro-yo, and ride back. My relationship with my daughter is a lot like mine with my dad. I drag her with me all over town to hang around with all my little rabble-rousing friends as we talk about gentrification, economic development, and how we're going to change the city and make things better.

By the 1980s, the decline in west Louisville was setting in. When it declined, it declined quickly. The effects of Urban Renewal, Reaganomics, and Black folks leaving urban neighborhoods en masse for a "better life" in the suburbs interrupted traditional Black neighborhoods in the inner cities. Families used to own their houses. All my grandfather's friends started dying off one at a time, and their kids wouldn't take the houses. They would let them just fall apart. You started seeing house after house abandoned. They'd get torn down, and you get these vacant lots. Then the decay sets in, and you just watch the decline.

Some years back, my grandfather and grandmother passed away, so my dad and aunt sold the house. He just didn't see the need to hang on to the property. He'd previously been a landlord and didn't like the idea of renting it out or fixing it up. So he and my aunt decided to sell the house. My cousin and I were upset, but I understood why they did it.

My dad still feels it was the right decision, but my aunt regrets that we sold the house. She wishes they had kept it for the memories—generations of memories. They were both born in that house on the dining room table. Four generations have been in that home at one point, counting my daughter. It was very bittersweet when I found out that they had sold it and we no longer owned that house. I still drive past it quite a bit. It kind of makes me sad. But it is what it is. It's somebody else's home now.

There are not a lot of places to move into in Russell right now. I recently tried to purchase one of the two micro houses behind my grandfather's house. Both of them are pretty small, around seven hundred square feet. They are both three-room houses with a living room, bedroom, kitchen, and nothing else. No hallways. Literally just three rooms in an L shape with a door to the kitchen and the living room, and that's it. Unfortunately, the purchase did not go through. It was just bad timing, but I think it was for the best. Being right behind my grandfather's house, seeing it every day, would have been kind of unsettling.

Now you have large-scale developers coming in and buying large swaths of west Louisville. I heard three hundred houses recently sold to one out-of-state developer. Getting back local control of those houses is gonna be damn near impossible. Those will be rental units permanently. For most of the newer properties being built, you have to be at a certain income level to purchase them. As a single person, I make too much for properties that are income-based, and I don't make enough to build a brand new $200,000 house, so I've been priced out on multiple levels.

Housing availability at all income levels is definitely a hurdle Russell must overcome. Another is Louisville's Black brain drain. When I grew up, we all pretty much went to things like Black Achievers. And when I was in high school, you'd have what seemed like thousands of kids every other Saturday at the West Chestnut Street YMCA on Tenth and Chestnut for Black Achievers. It was mostly middle-class kids. We all hung around each other. All went to the same places. We all had grandparents in west Louisville, so we all still hung around west Louisville quite a bit. In the early '90s, when it was time for us to go to college, many of us went to UofL or UK. I went to Morehouse in Atlanta. However, a vast majority of them who left never came back because they just didn't see any real opportunities here. It was not only a Black brain drain; the Black community also lost a lot of wealth.

Louisville has a glass ceiling, and my peers realized they would never have the same opportunities in Louisville as in other places. Because even in the mid to late '90s, you could feel Louisville's economy shrink. If you didn't work for Humana, Brown-Forman, or Tricon (before it became Yum! Brands), those middle-income, middle-class, middle-management jobs weren't here. If you wanted to make between $60,000 and $100,000, that kind of economic vibrancy wasn't here. It still isn't. Louisville can't keep pace with places like Atlanta, Houston, or Nashville.

Of course, Louisville's Black neighborhoods suffered because that would've been the next generation of middle-class folks that could've kept their houses and stayed in those neighborhoods. Now, the vast majority of them left, and they're not coming back. Economically, there's no reason to be here. A lot of my friends would like to come back, but they can't because they would actively lose money by moving back. I have friends in Houston and other places who want to come back to be near their aging parents but won't because they would lose too much money. Why leave where they are now to move to Louisville and take a $40,000 pay cut?

Ultimately, the problem that Russell is going to have is Louisville is declining as a whole and declining quickly. There just isn't enough money and wealth to

sustain needed changes in Russell. Louisville doesn't have that economy anymore. You don't have those jobs that will allow the community, as a whole, to build that kind of wealth. The kind of wealth where you could own a home, maintain it, have enough disposable income to donate to charities and patronize a wide range of local businesses.

However, with that said, all's not lost. There still is a ton of hope and opportunity. We're still here working hard to build things back. What you see now in Russell is the next generation of folks doing everything they can to build back Black wealth and rebuild our neighborhoods and communities. Kevin Fields at LCCC and Kevin Dunlap with Project REBOUND are actively trying to build back Russell. You have AMPED and their Russell Business Incubator building back Black businesses and other organizations like Tarsha Semekula's Buttafly Group. I'm on the advisory board of Russell: A Place of Promise, tackling the issue of creating generational Black wealth. A whole host of other institutions and individuals are actively working in the Russell community. It's hard to compete against a city that sometimes actively works against your interests, but we have good people who are in it for the long haul and are willing to fight.

There are instruments on the horizon that could transform west Louisville. Tax Increment Financing, or TIF, *could* be an utterly transformative tool for west Louisville. Harnessing all those tax dollars through a TIF district to fund businesses and other developments could be a game changer. But I don't think it's going to happen. What tends to happen in Louisville is that the same players get access to the vast majority of the resources, and everybody else gets what's left over. I think that's how the TIF will go. Hopefully, I'm wrong.

The days of cities like Louisville attracting large corporate headquarters may be behind us. So we need

Haven speaking at community meeting at Quinn Chapel regarding the proposed Walmart development

to think about what we can do to grow our community and city. We need to settle on an identity. We must figure out how to grow our communities from within and attract people back to these historic neighborhoods like Russell. I always thought we should copy Paducah's Artist Relocation Program. Their downtown was decaying until they came up with this program where, if you moved to Paducah and could prove that you could sustain yourself through your artistic pursuits, they would give you this dilapidated house and work with banks on loans to rehab the house. They completely transformed their downtown.

We should actively entice more Black artists to move to Russell and other parts of west Louisville, especially filmmakers, visual effects artists, and actors.

I've always thought Louisville should be more heavily involved in filmmaking. There is already a foundation here. We have the Kentucky Center for the Arts. Our public school system includes Lincoln Elementary Performing Arts School, Western Middle School for the Arts, and the Youth Performing Arts School. We have Actors Theatre with the Humana Festival of New American Plays and one of the largest dinner playhouses in Derby Dinner Playhouse across the bridge. We need to build on that. We just need to take it to its next logical conclusion.

Russell is in a unique position to be revitalized without displacing its residents or losing its identity. We just have to be intentional and honest about our efforts. ✦

Let the Beat Build

CHRISTIAN BUTLER

I've always liked my birth story because it aligns with who I am: I'm always on the go.

I was born on November 7, 1989, in the back of an ambulance on Brook Street. My name was almost Brook as a result. Mama had been through childbirth twice before, so she knew what to do, but the EMT in the back of the ambulance didn't know what was going on. It was his first day, and he was freaking out. For whatever reason, when I was born, he told my mama I was a boy. My mama said that it was the umbilical cord that had him mixed up. I guess he was nervous. My mama had planned for her baby girl, and she was like, "I don't have any boy names!" But, lo and behold, when we got to the hospital, I was a baby girl. I don't know who that man is, but I hope he got it together. To this day, I don't understand how that confusion happened.

I grew up in a very close-knit family. My mama and dad were married for most of my life. Together, they have three children. My dad has five: my sister Jakim, my brother Enriqué Jr., who we call Buddy, my sister Ashley, myself, and my baby sister Reonna. My parents brought us up as siblings and hated for us to fight and argue. They said, "Hey, all you have is each other, so you cherish that relationship, and no matter what anybody else is doing, you all make sure that you stay together." That's something that we've carried into adulthood and are teaching my nieces and nephews.

My dad's from Bloomfield, Kentucky. When his family came to Louisville, they kept that down-home sense of family and community. My greatest moments were spent over at my dad's mother's house. Nanny's place was a hub. We all went out there. She stayed in an apartment in Norfolk, which is Newburg-adjacent. If you're from down here in the West End, people think it's the same, but there's a difference. Most of my time out there was spent with my cousins, aunts, and uncles.

Christian and Nanny, Thanksgiving 2009

It was a very country, down-home upbringing.

I got that real-life experience of cooking with my mama and my nanny, Lord rest her soul. My mama never would buy me a Playskool kitchen set when I was a child, but what I did get was so much better, so much more. Growing up, there were times when everybody else was doing other things, and Nanny and my mama would let me help in the kitchen, and we'd cook together. I remember being in the kitchen with them and asking, "Why are you doing that? What is that process for?" My fondest memories were sitting in the middle of the living room floor, picking greens with Nanny while she watched her stories. The stereotype is that Black people eat collard greens. I did not grow up on collard greens. My Nanny loved kale greens and mustard greens. That's what I grew up on.

I have always had positive female role models, strong Black women in my life. Nanny was close with her sisters. They all stayed physically close to each other too. Her sister Bernice lived right upstairs from Nanny. Aunt Bernice's couch was right there in the window, and she'd be hanging on the back of her couch out the window, having a full-blown conversation with my Nanny downstairs. She was like Pearl in that show *227* sitting in that window. She knew everything happening

Enriqué and Enriqué Jr. (Buddy), 1998

Nanny and Aunt Bernice

really close, so we spent a lot of time with her family growing up. I had twin cousins, Joy and Jazzmine, who were around the same age as my brother Buddy. We're all close in age. We were always together because my mama and Aunt Contrainere were always together. My grandmother on my mama's side, Wilma Keene, had thirteen kids. She's so little! My granny is about four feet tall. But honey, she pushed out those kids, and she always had this mighty, mighty voice. She is a minister and a very spiritual person. She's a strong Black woman. But then she always had this comfort as well.

My mama was a very strong woman too. She was very sweet and soft but very mighty. She did not play no games. When I was in second grade, I had seasonal allergies, and I kept getting up in class to blow my nose because the tissue was on the teacher's desk. She told me I was using too much tissue, so of course I told my mama. I was very emotional, so I was probably crying. My mama set up a meeting with the teacher and the principal. Now, my brother had had this teacher a couple of years before, and he had been a lot to handle. My mama felt she was taking that experience and making me pay for it. My mama told the teacher, "She makes good grades and does her work. I bought tissues at the beginning of the year. You're not gonna scold her for simply having to blow her nose." Those types of situations happened often. That's part of the reason I am who I am today. I don't allow people to mistreat kids. I speak out against injustices and unfair treatment. I want to support people's agency.

I grew up in the Newburg area and eventually in Hikes Point, where my parents bought a house. I appreciated them showing me home ownership. They stayed together for most of my childhood until eighth grade when they separated. I moved out to Prospect with my mama the summer before my freshman year at Ballard. It was an adjustment, moving to this whole

on the street, who was doing what. She only came out to go to the store, get her cigarettes, and every now and then, come down and sit outside.

On my mama's side, they were raised in the West End. My Aunt Contrainere and my mama were always

new environment at a time when I was already going through so many transitions.

My sister set a high bar. She went to Central High School, was in Black Achievers, and had all these scholarships and opportunities. The idea of walking in her shoes was intimidating. I thought I had to go to college even though deep down I knew it was not for me. I ended up at Jefferson Community College, and I loved it. It was kind of like high school. It had smaller classrooms, everybody knew everybody, and I felt connected to my professors.

How it was *supposed* to work out was that I would go to JCC and switch to UofL. So I worked my butt off and was accepted to UofL. Against my mother's wishes, I got an apartment and ended up partying so much that I was put on academic probation my first semester at UofL. When I didn't do the right thing the next semester, they said, "Okay, you got to go." With that went all the money, and I had to get out of my apartment. My mama was like, "Well, I tried to tell you." My pride wouldn't let me move back into her place, so I ended up going to my dad's back in Newburg. I got a job working at a daycare and tried to find my path by focusing on things that I loved to do. I love children, so for the next couple of years, I worked in daycares a lot. I also worked in restaurants and catering because I always loved food. I always wanted to go to hair school and did that a couple of times; I still haven't finished.

But I've always been an entrepreneur at heart. The first business I started was inspired by watching Food Network with my mama. We loved *Cupcake Wars*. She said, "Christian, you can do that!" So, I started researching the cupcake business. That was when Gigi's Cupcakes came out, and she was popping. I made a connection with her because her last name was Butler. That's how my business Noopie's World was born. Noopie is a nickname my dad's side of the family gave me.

Cynithia and Enriqué

Christian, age four

Buddy and Christian with their mother, Cynithia, ca. 1993

Clockwise from left: Christian, Enriqué, Buddy, and Kim

My business was supposed to encompass cupcakes but also party planning and catering.

So, I was just figuring things out for eight or nine years in my twenties. Those times were like on-the-job training. I just tapped into all the things I love and the jobs I've had over the years reflect that. I tell myself that I went to "life school." I did not finish college, but working in daycares taught me about children. Working in restaurants taught me a lot about food and what we put into our bodies. Working in hair school

taught me about skincare and hair health. So, life has taught me things I could not have learned in college. I wasn't meant to be in institutionalized education. I'm more of a hands-on learner.

My journey with Play Cousins Collective is a good example. I was stepping into social justice and started seeking different spaces to be around like-minded people. I found them through Books and Breakfast Louisville. Once a month, they provide a space to learn about different types of social justice topics over free breakfast, books, and programming for families. Before one event, Books and Breakfast asked if anyone was interested in providing childcare at the next event, and I volunteered to help. When I got there, Kristin Williams asked if I had taken care of kids before. I said that I had, and she asked me to create a lesson plan around relationships for the kids in twenty minutes! So she sat back and watched as I ran the session. We had a group game where you introduced yourself in the form of a song, and then we did activities around self-love. The kids were engaged, and it was just beautiful.

At the end of the programming, Kristin told me she was starting this wonderful organization called Play Cousins Collective and asked if I would be interested in being a part of it. I didn't have a job then, so it was the perfect timing. Kristin, Torkwase, Shawna, and I met at the Waterfront and talked about her idea for what would become Play Cousins, and that's what got me boots to the ground in social justice work.

Play Cousins Collective provides childcare at pop-up play dates at community events with free games, activities, and food. Providing space where the Black community can participate in events and utilize resources without the barrier of finding childcare is a critical service PCC offers. They even create curricula for the children around the topic of the community meeting so it's at the child's level. It's an amazing organization. When I have children, a lot of the ways I will bring up my child will come directly from my time with Play Cousins.

Prior to working at Play Cousins, I moved around a lot. I tried to get apartments, but it just didn't work out. The money I made working in restaurants as a server was nice but unpredictable. It's not something you can count on. Working in daycares is just no money at all. I was living with Dad and ran that out. I lived with my brother and ran that out. Then my mama said, "Won't you come here? I need help." Me and my mama have always been close. That was my best friend. So I ended up moving in with her to Zion Manor Apartments in Russell. I had cooked for my dad when I lived with him. I had helped clean and watch my brother's baby when I lived with him. Now I would live with my mama and cook and clean for her.

Moving in with my mama at Zion Manor worked out. I was working at Play Cousins in the West End. I could save some money, and moving in with my mama empowered her to do more. She wanted to take care of her baby. My mama was always somebody who just wanted to do for other people. She was always on the go. She was adventurous. She was spontaneous. I didn't realize that her being in a wheelchair and unable to do those things was killing her spirits. My being there gave her a sense of belonging again. But it was an equal exchange. They say you parent your parents once you get to a certain age. It taught me a lot about myself.

I brought what I was learning while working at Play Cousins home to my mama. A lot of them were vegan, and we started talking about eating healthier. I got up and cooked her breakfast and made sure she took her medicine. I cooked her lunch and dinner, and it got to the point where she started feeling better. She said, "I'll cook today," because that's how me and my mama used to spend time together, in the kitchen. I

Clockwise from left: Destany, Christian, Buddy, and Marquese, ca. 1997

Christian at home in Newburg, Easter, 1994

look back at those times and realize I was where I was supposed to be. What seemed like the worst time of my life was the best time because of the relationship and experiences I could share with her.

From 2017 to 2019, I worked at Play Cousins, picking up shifts here and there. I also worked at a lounge and a restaurant. I heard Miss Lucretia of Lucretia's Kitchen needed somebody to do desserts for her, so I helped her off and on at the restaurant and at her kiosk in the mall where she sold desserts.

Christian and her niece, Jaiden, 2004

Miss Lucretia told me, "Hey, there's this great opportunity, and you have the perfect personality for this organization called Russell: A Place of Promise." I'm like, *What is this? If she's saying it's good, it must be good. I need a job where I'm making a little bit more money. So, let me go ahead and apply.*

In February 2020, I took the position at RPOP as a Community Outreach Specialist. The pay was fifteen dollars and fifty cents an hour, more than I've ever made. The expectations were high. It was the biggest opportunity that I have had in my career. Russell: A Place of Promise is a justice-based initiative focused on building Black wealth in the Russell neighborhood. Our job is to go out in the community and build relationships with the residents, the business owners, the faith leaders, organizations, and pretty much anybody connected to Russell. We ask people about their vision for Black wealth and how we can connect them to those resources.

Ms. Jackie Floyd took us through a crash course of all things Russell. She did not play! "Look," she told us, "Russell already has a rich history. It already has promise." I had no idea that Russell had that rich history. Russell used to be one of the richest Black communities in the South, period. Teaching people about that rich history, letting them know where they are and where they've come from, helps us preserve that history and create Black wealth. Honestly, I used to think I was too big for Louisville. *Oh, wow. This is such a small town. I can't believe I'm from here.* But once I learned about its history, I realized that Louisville is too big for me. If I had learned about that stuff when I was younger, my life might have changed.

Once I started with RPOP, I made some money and decided it was time to move out of my mama's place. Anthony Smith, the Executive Director of Cities United, got me connected to Russell Apartments. There were some negative parts to living there, but there are a lot of positives that go on. There was a sense of community I saw in Russell Apartments. We took care of one another. We took care of each other's children and made sure they ate. We often weren't getting the support we needed from New Directions, who managed the property. I lived in the Russell Apartments for a while, but I wasn't living the way I wanted to be able to live in that building. And the company just was not willing to make the appropriate changes that I thought the residents deserved.

I began looking for other places to live, but I was not willing to walk away from the community in Russell. I loved waking up where most of my neighbors, if not all, looked like me. I got used to that. With the work I was doing with RPOP as a Community Outreach Specialist, I wanted to stay in the neighborhood. But I had gone through evictions, and my credit wasn't the best. I had to have all of this money to even move in, like thousands of dollars. The median income here is pretty low, but the rent does not reflect it. A lot of the homes around here are not affordable. I was at a point where I was making enough money to pay my rent and maintain, but landlords would see me on paper and be like, *Oh, no, she's a flight risk*, or whatever the issue.

Ms. Jackie, who has been my angel since I met her, said, "Christian, don't give up yet. I'm gonna connect you with Butch Mosby. Give him a call. He's got this awesome organization, Sponsor 4 Success." Sponsor 4 Success rehabilitates homes to create affordable rental units. It targets people who are on the path to success but may have some barriers keeping them from moving forward. It's for people who do not qualify for public housing, don't have the best credit, or have evictions on their record that keep them from getting housing elsewhere.

Thanks to Sponsor 4 Success, I went straight from Russell Apartments to a house. You don't own a home from them, but the rent is lower than the market rate to help you save money so you can get back on your feet and then be able to excel to the next level. At that point, if someone is ready, Sponsor 4 Success

Fifth grade field trip, 1999, Christian and Enriqué with fish

Music/dance group RDC.
From left: Reonna, Destany, and Christian

also has a partnership with the Louisville Urban League to connect you to their homebuying resources and readiness program for when you are ready to be a homeowner.

I was the very first tenant in one of their refurbished homes. I love my place. It's a two-bedroom. It

Junior Prom, Christian and Dad

Christian, Buddy, Kim, Reonna, Enriqué Sr.

neighborhood. Since I was the first tenant, it came with a lot of attention. The local news came out and talked to me. I did a *Courier-Journal* article. I got used to talking to the news and being interviewed.

I was specific about wanting to be in Russell because I was working for RPOP, and I wanted to be a part of this community. It just worked out and also opened other doors. It was amazing.

Living in Russell has made me change my mind, not just about Russell, but about the West End, period. There's a narrative painted not only by the outside community but also by some people who live in the community that Russell is a dangerous place. Some of that is true, but I've experienced less crime living here in the West End than when I was living in the Highlands. Ms. Jackie always says that when something negative is put out about Russell, we should put out two positive things to counteract that, and I've started doing that.

You hear about people getting shot, but you don't hear about the Ms. Renees of Russell, for example. She's my neighbor who came over and introduced herself when I moved in, and now she checks in on me all the time. If I'm gone for a couple of days, she'll say, "Hey, where you been? I was worried about you." You might hear that our neighborhood is run-down, but you don't hear about the young people in the community who are buying homes and fixing them up. They put bags on their fences so that, instead of throwing trash on the ground, people walking by might think about it and say, *Lemme use this trash bag.*

You don't hear about Club Cedar, where everybody knows everybody like it's *Cheers*. The food and drinks are good. The bartenders are amazing. Or the Green Store, where you can get toilet paper, bread, or whatever you need when Kroger closes its doors. Every time I drive past the Green Store, it's the same people sitting outside, playing cards, drinking, and talking. It's

has a big kitchen, bathroom, and a nice living room. It's like a shotgun house, but the kitchen is off to the side. It has all new fixtures and this swiveling island spice rack. That was the highlight of my day when I moved there! Most of their houses are within the Russell

a hub. People don't hear about Joe's Palm Room, a legendary Black-owned club with a rich history. I like to tell people about Hip Hop Sweet Shop, a Black-owned fully-functioning bakery right there on the corner of 18th and Jefferson, or the Western Branch Library, the first library in the United States run by and for Black people, period. Right here in our city, in Russell. Going to a Central football game is lit! It reminds me of college football. It's amazing. People who don't even have kids attending the school come out for those games because of the community and the connection to Central High School. I share those different opportunities for people to come and experience something different.

These are good things that I see within Russell that I didn't know before I lived in Russell. And these are things that don't necessarily get highlighted in the news. So when you ride through, don't be scared, and don't listen to the narrative painted by people who wouldn't even step foot in that neighborhood.

Cynithia Butler

◇◇◇◇◇◇◇◇

My nanny died in February, and my mama died in March of this year. For my grandmother, it was completely unexpected. For my mama, I felt it coming over time. Their deaths are still really fresh. Last week, I was missing my mama. I just woke up, and I'm like, *I want my mama today*. I was missing that matriarchal comfort because my mama was gone and my nanny was gone.

Later that day, I went to the grocery store like I always do and ran into two strong women from my past that I had not seen in forever. Ms. Hinkle-Jones was my English teacher at Ballard High School. I didn't even know who she was until she pulled her mask down. She was like, "I just want you to know that I see you, and I'm so proud of you and that I'm praying for you." And then I saw my Sunday school teacher from Forest Tabernacle Missionary Baptist, my home

church growing up. She's like, "Christian! It's me, Ms. Hale! How you doing?" She said the same things, like "I'm still praying for you all," and told me how much she loved me.

I held it together in the store, but when I got in my car, I lost it. It was like my mama was sending angels. *I'm not here, but these are other women who have been in your life who will pray for you or give you a hug in the middle of the grocery store*. That morning I woke up needing to talk to my mama, needing a hug or an encouraging word. I don't know what it was that I needed, but I knew that I was getting it when I saw them.

Ms. Jackie checked in on me that day too. She checks on me every day, especially since losing my mama and grandmother. Everything I've learned over these past couple of years about Russell has come

RPOP Team members Maya White, Christian, Daphne Walker, and Doneah Marshall

from Ms. Jackie sharing her experiences, taking me on walks, and showing me the history. When my nieces and nephews come and stay at my house, I take them to different places in Russell and let them know these are safe places. "If you don't have anywhere else to go, you can pull up to Hip Hop Sweet Shop, and Lafeesa's gonna be there, and she's gonna love on you the same way I would." The same with Lucretia's Kitchen. I wouldn't expect them to go into Club Cedar, but that is a safe space for a lot of people in the community.

These are places I know I can go to. They're not going to trip about me using their Wi-Fi or being there for an extended amount of time. I'm just welcome to be my authentic self. I don't have to fake who I am. I don't have to code-switch who I am. I can be who I am authentically within this community. And they make me feel like I belong, like I'm valued and supposed to be here. That sense of community and welcome is how we work as Black people. That's how we were taught. It's how we were raised. I want to invest in this community because it's investing in me.

There's a Lil' Wayne song I've been listening to for a long time called "Let the Beat Build." It's saying to just let things happen as they are. Let things progress. Let things grow. Give yourself time to grow. I was an outsider when I moved to Russell. I had to step back from what I thought I knew about Russell and the West End. I have had to retrain my mind every single day. I'm from Newburg, and I'm proud of that. Those are my people. But I was reborn in Russell. ✦

Go Pastor My People

REVEREND GEOFFREY ELLIS

A few years back, my wife Deirdre and I came past 19th and Cedar, and there were about eleven new houses that had just been built there. We saw a sign that said, "Operation Rebound: build a new house." Rebound works out of the Urban League office, and they're buying properties and building new homes in the West End. We had lived in Shawnee for thirty years, but we said, "We're getting older. We got to get out of this house with all these steps." And so we built a house on Cedar and moved in in 2017.

Those of us who want to live where our parents lived in the West End, we need this type of housing to live in. We don't want to just live in what's already there. What's already there is a bunch of vacant houses and empty lots. I think it's 157 condemned houses in west Louisville. The next block west from ours? It's underdeveloped. Torn down houses, vacant lots.

For a lot of years, developers didn't want to develop in the West End. The developers don't want to build down here because they can't make a profit from the sale price they'll get. But they found out that African Americans *do* want homes. They wanted to create something reminiscent of the way African Americans lived in the heyday of Walnut Street. Brick houses, family homes, and the like. Deirdre grew up on the corner of 19th and Jefferson, and I grew up at 2108 West Walnut. So, we've ended up in the neighborhood where we started out.

I was the only child of my mother and father, and we lived upstairs in that house, which isn't there anymore. We all three slept in the same room. Downstairs was my grandmother and my great-grandmother. My uncle and his wife along with their three sons lived there, too. Then my cousin and his mother came to live with us. He was the same age as me, and we were raised together. My aunt didn't really live

Geoffrey with his parents,
Chauncey and Willie Mae Ellis, ca. 1942

there. She was a model in those days and came back and forth from L.A. We had a coal shed in the back where they dumped coal. Sometimes I'd go out and bring in the coal but only if they wanted two or three lumps. If they wanted more, my dad or my uncle would have to because it was too heavy for me. I don't think there was an indoor toilet. There was an outhouse. The kitchen was tiny and everybody couldn't eat at the same time in there, so we ate at different times. The banister on the stairs was good for sliding down.

My father and I were close. I was his only son. I remember going with him to Levy Brother's clothing store where the Old Spaghetti Factory is now. Levy's is where you bought good clothes. I was always an admired kid because my little suits, hats, and overcoats were relatively expensive. He made sure I was pretty sharp.

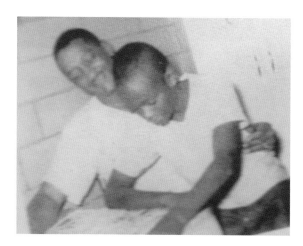

Chauncey and Geoffrey Ellis, ca. 1946

Geoffrey Ellis at St. Augustine Catholic School, ca. 1944

My father worked at the Green Turtle, a bar on the northeast corner of 20th and Walnut about a block from where we lived. He was a bartender and must have worked there for ten years. My mother used to make his lunch, and I'd walk over there and take it to him.

I'd walk in and all the people always greeted me, "Here comes Little Goody!" My father's name was Chauncey Ellis, but his nickname was Goody because he was such a nice guy. He was charismatic, and everybody knew him.

He was the house man for the Green Turtle and for another gambling place in the East End called Circle Bar. I could always go into the back room where everybody was smoking and hollering and gambling. My father ended up with a lot of silver dollars in those days; we called them Bo-Dollars. He'd have a stack of them on the dresser. One night we went to bed, and when we woke up those Bo-dollars were gone, and we didn't know who came in or how they got in and got them. I never figured that out.

He had an alcohol problem, and I always wondered why in the heck he was working in a bar. It didn't bother me because he wasn't a reckless alcoholic. I never saw him drunk. There would be times that he wouldn't drink for about six or seven months. He would go on the wagon. Then the rest of the year he would drink every day, and people would bring him home in cabs. They wouldn't charge him because he was Goody.

I got a picture of him somewhere, he and I are in the house and I'm sitting on his lap reading the paper with him. That is a good picture of our relationship. He was present in my life. He took me to football games, specifically Central High School's Thanksgiving Day games which were really important in the Black community. Central was the colored high school. Going to one of those games was a big deal. I got a picture somewhere of my father and me at the game together.

We were very fortunate to have my grandmother and great-grandmother living downstairs. My grandmother, Nellie, made sure my father and my uncle did right by my mother and my aunt. She'd tell them, "You

Kindergarten class at James Bond Elementary, ca. 1946

got to stop that drinking and stop fussing with your wife and carrying on." I never seen my mother and father fight. I think one time they got into a heated argument, and I got in between them saying, "Whoa, whoa, whoa!" But he never put his hands on her. Never seen anything like that growing up.

My grandma was a real light-skinned lady. She worked in the Old Walnut Street Chili Parlor during Walnut Street's heyday. The Chili Parlor was run by a white woman and her husband who was Mexican. That chili was so different from any other chili anybody ever had. My mother and I worked there also. That's three generations. My grandmother helped make the chili, my mother took it to the tables, and I stood on a box and washed the dishes. I was the only kid doing that kind of work in those days. The owner offered my mother the opportunity to take that chili up to Cincinnati to open a place. My mother said, "I ain't going to leave my husband and child. We ain't going nowhere."

My mother also worked at Zax Pharmacy on the corner of 12th and Walnut. I used to get brand-new

funny books. Other kids didn't have access to comic books until somebody had passed them on, but mine were brand new because she would bring some home every night.

From about the age of nine, I grew up in Smoketown in the Sheppard Square projects: The Bricks, we called it. In the 1950s my mom moved up to Finzer Street, and my grandmother moved to Beecher Terrace. That's how I got my Beecher Terrace roots. I used to stay with her while my mother worked at the drugstore. My great-grandmother and grandmother were really important to me. I loved them very much.

So my mother, my dad, and I lived in Sheppard Square, but we always went to church at Asbury Chapel AME down on 18th and Chestnut. I used to clean up the chapel for a little change when I was twelve or thirteen. One day, I was in the pulpit, wiping the place down when I just heard this inner voice—though it sounded like it was coming from outside—that said, "Go pastor my people." I said, *Whoa, whoa. No, no, no, no, no.* Then, I heard it again, but I denied the call from

ca. 1950

Geoffrey Ellis, far left

that time forward. From thirteen to fifty years old, I denied the religious side of me. I had some wrestling matches between being good and bad when I was younger. Just fooling around, trying to be a big-time thug like Superfly. Everybody wanted to be Superfly: hat on the side, Cadillac with the diamond in the back. That was my bad side. We were just the other side of being hoodlums. I cared, though. I always cared.

I went to Jackson Junior High School, now Meyzeek Middle School, and then to Central for high school. Back then, Central kids would get out of school and go down to Quinn Chapel to learn how to demonstrate. I went a few times and learned what to do if you got arrested. A lot of the civil rights movement came out of the church. Martin Luther King's brother was pastor at Zion Baptist on 22nd Street, so Dr. King came to town to visit him. He was here and started a movement for open housing so people could live where they wanted to. They took it all the way to Frankfort and marched and all that. But that wasn't where my head was at that time. I was more radical and always outside of the church's way of dealing with integration and segregation.

We respected Dr. King because he was a Black Baptist preacher and a doctor: *Doctor* King. But Dr. King's ideas and that movement wasn't always agreeable to all the people. A lot of people didn't believe that was the way to go. Not everybody wanted to *ask* for our freedom. *I ain't asking nobody to let me sit at a lunch counter, let me buy clothes. Let's get our own. Let's not try to be integrated, let's try to be independent.* That's where I was at. I wasn't into the peaceful thing. Did it mean we'd shoot somebody or blow somebody up? No, not necessarily. It meant if we take what is ours, eventually we'll have our own.

I joined the Navy in 1957, right out of high school. I had a scholarship to Grambling University, which became a major HBCU. My mother said I needed to go, but I didn't want to. So I joined the Navy. I got out of basic training in the Great Lakes, and they sent me to the Mediterranean right away and put me on an aircraft carrier, the USS *Forrestal*.

The first day I showed up, I'm headed to the aircraft carrier. I got my sea bag on my shoulder, and I'm walking down the dock to the ship. I asked a guy, "Where is the ship at?" He said, "Look up." I was walking *under* the deck of the ship and didn't know it. It's the first of the supercarriers, where they had an angled deck where you could land and take off at the same time. This was a monster carrier: 69,000 tons. I was walking under the angled deck. I'm a Smoketown boy. I hadn't seen anything like that. Had never been to a body of water larger than a swimming pool or the Ohio River.

All my time in the Navy, I was on the USS *Forrestal*. The ship's complement was about 3500 men, and then, when everybody was on the ship and we were going overseas, you had about 4000. There was another guy from Louisville onboard. My girlfriend Pauline wrote and told me, "Norman Brown is on the same ship as you." It was months before I found that guy. That's how big it was.

There were only two African Americans in my company, Company 270. Fifty-three guys all lived together, worked together, trained together. You recognize yourself as part of a group. It was my first time being away from home in that kind of an environment, and I did not feel segregated. I was a popular young man. They called me Howdy, like Howdy Doody, because I was always smiling. I spent four years in the Mediterranean. We'd be out to sea for two and a half months at a time. As an African American, I felt comfortable in Italy and Spain, where the people were almost the same color skin as us. But not so comfortable

From left: Willie Mae, Chauncey, Geoff, and Grandmother Nellie Ellis at an Asbury Chapel AME tribute for Geoff before he joined the Navy, 1957

Geoff, far right.
Great Lakes boot camp yearbook, 1957

in France. While in Germany, we experienced some segregation, and we couldn't go everywhere our white buddies went.

My job was to refuel aircraft. The most dangerous place to be on a ship is the flight deck of an aircraft carrier. It's exciting with planes landing and taking off

Writing a letter home from the common area
aboard the USS *Forrestal*

and so much going on, but you can get hurt real easy. We saw a lot of bad accidents and people getting killed. I saw a guy get sucked up in a jet engine. We got him out with a squeegee. I saw another guy get his head knocked off by an airplane propeller.

I wrote home, "Mama, I kind of want to come home. The things I'm seeing aren't good." She couldn't do anything about it though. I'd never been so far away from home, so getting letters from my mom and my sweetheart kept me grounded. Pauline and I had been dating since we were fourteen years old. I thought we would always be together, really. Not all the guys got letters, but I did. I was thrilled. Kept me knowing that I was special. Other guys look at you like, *Man, wish it was me.* So getting letters was a very emotional connection to home.

My mom wrote to me once and told me that she and my dad were splitting up. I never thought I would see them apart. I thought, *What the heck is going on?* That was a shock.

I came home to Louisville in '61 and a lot of things had changed in my family. My parents had divorced, and my mother was married to another guy. We found out that my dad had fathered some kids out of wedlock, a boy and a girl, so all of a sudden, I'm not an only child.

Plus, Pauline and I had some kids while I was in the military. I'd come home on leave from time to time when I was in the Navy. Between 1957 and 1961, we had two kids, Mark, and then Sheree. My mother and Pauline's family thought we'd end up together. They'd seen our love affair develop since we were fourteen, and they figured we would get married. But we never did. I wasn't ready for that. I was back from the military. I was footloose and fancy free. I had secured a good job with Delta Airlines making good money. So even though we had two kids, I didn't have a sense of getting married about it. I was too loose. I just wasn't around them or part of their lives as much as I wanted to be or should have been. Not until they were much older. I wasn't a bad guy. I just didn't understand family.

It was a pretty freewheeling time in my life. I was living in some apartments down on 44th Street. Had a car, a nice green Buick Riviera. I had girls running in and out. That's when I started dating Mary Ann. Later, we got married and had a daughter named Regina in 1964. Mary Ann and I were together for three or four years until she found out that Pauline and I had had another daughter, Zina, who was also born in 1964. Mary Ann divorced me and kept me away from Regina for a long time. She never let me have too much direct involvement because of the way I'd acted in our marriage. I didn't understand it then. It was very hard. I faulted her for it then, but she thought she was protecting her daughter. I understand that now. I had to get together with Regina years later and tell her why that happened, why I hadn't maintained contact over the years. That was a really rough conversation, but we're solid as a rock now. She went to law school and is a judge in Atlanta now.

I have a lot of daughters, and I'm very proud of all of them. It means everything to me that I have been able to have a relationship with all my kids in my life. My wife Deirdre, whom I've been married to for forty-two years, made sure of that. I have to give credit where credit's due. She's the one who has made that happen. We're all one big family with a lot of girls now, including Deirdre's kids, Tia and Terria, whom I adopted as my own, and our daughters, Kishya and Akia. It's a blessing.

My wife made that happen. I had kept everybody separate. I didn't want to mix everybody. I was always thinking, *Don't want to mix this daughter with this daughter because it brings up all this old stuff.* Silly stuff like that. For years I kept everybody separate. But Deirdre fixed that. She said, *No. These are all of your children. This is your family.* I have worked hard to repair these relationships, the ones I could. Now, when I text my family, I text all of my kids and grandkids at the same time. I was able to spend time with Mark and Zina and have relationships with them before both of them tragically passed. Later in my life, I've been able to have meaningful relationships with all my kids.

I worked for Delta as a skycap and later as a ticket agent into the 1970s. I took free trips anywhere on Delta Airlines if a seat was available. So I used to go back and forth to L.A. just because I could. That was the place to go. On one of my trips, I visited a shoe store that some gangsters had started. It was like a living room inside with a large couch and some chairs, a TV, and so forth. It was set up almost like a lounge. I said,

From left: Unknown Navy buddy, Norman Brown, and Geoff Ellis in Guantanamo Bay, Cuba, 1958

Geoff with Mary Ann Ellis, ca. 1964

Geoff Ellis in front of the Boot Gallery
near 15th and Broadway

Geoff Ellis as a Delta skycap with his mother (right)
and Aunt Creamery Evans, Standiford Field, 1965

That looks interesting. I had wanted to go into the shoe business, and so I said, *Let me go try that kind of thing in Louisville, that kind of decor, that kind of approach to selling shoes.* At the time, people were wearing high-fashion shoes: boots up to their knees and boots with heels on them. That was in the late '70s, early '80s. I got a loan from the SBA, and I put a shoe store together next door to Captain's Closet, a men's high-fashion clothing store on the corner of 15th and Broadway. We called it the Boot Gallery. We knew people that wore high-fashion clothes also wore high-fashion shoes, so we cut a door between our two stores.

The highlight of that time was when the Kentucky Colonels basketball team began to come to the shoe store to hang out. They were popular at the time. Artis Gilmore, Dan Issel, and the like. Artis Gilmore was seven foot two and wore size sixteen. It was incredible. People would come to the store just to see them and would purchase shoes while they were there. We were really at our height. The shoe store business was good then. People seemed to have an abundance of money because west Louisville was going strong at that time. Everybody had a job at either GE, American Standard, Phillip Morris, or International Harvester. They were going strong. All of that made for financial success, and we had a lot of success. People recognize it as the first African American shoe store in the West End or in the city of Louisville period.

We opened up a second shoe store in a shopping center in Newburg, out on Indian Trail and Poplar Level Road. I got myself on the night shift at Delta so I could run the shoe stores in the day. The shoe store lasted four years until people began dressing a little more conservatively. People changed the way they dressed, and we weren't ready for that change. We didn't have the funds to buy more shoes to keep up with the new trends, so we decided to let the store go.

One day before we closed, a guy came in and asked me if I had a job for him. I didn't, but that guy turned out to be Ross Jessup. We became inseparable for many years after that. He was such a brilliant guy. University of Louisville would eventually send him to get his degree at Harvard. They recognized him as a very highly skilled, intellectual individual even though he had very little college education and a criminal background. When I met him, he was just coming out of prison. He wrote some bad checks and went to prison for a couple of years. Odd thing about him is that he was wearing dreadlocks, and *nobody* was wearing dreadlocks at the time. People would look at him like, "Who's this guy? Is he from Africa or what?" So he came in asking for a job. My partner and I said, "We don't have a job." But something about him caused me and Ross to bond, so we began to run around together.

He moved next to where I was living at an apartment. We were into a lot of the movement then. A lot of the revolutionary kind of things were going on with Black folks across the country. Black Panthers and Angela Davis were popular. We had about five or six people that ran with us, and we called ourselves a family. At that time, we lived communally at one of the houses around 35th and Broadway. Ross and I were kind of the leaders. We listened to revolutionary music, wore dashikis, and called ourselves revolutionaries.

We might let some runaway kids come and stay at the house for a while to get their life back together. Anne Braden bought a house about three doors down, and that's the Braden Center now. Anne was part of the movement at that time, and that house used to be the headquarters for BULK, the Black Unity League of Kentucky. The Pan-African movement in Louisville was wrapped up in BULK. Sam Hawkins was the president, and I was vice president. We had about fifty, maybe sixty active members. Sam Hawkins and

Ross Jessup

Bob Kuyu, and some other members of BULK got charged with a conspiracy to blow up the oil refinery down in Chickasaw. They called them the Black Six. Law enforcement started breaking up BULK, trying to scatter it by charging them with insurrection or threatening the institution, something like that. They kept the charges on these people for years. I know for some guys right now, Manfred Reid and Sam Hawkins, it's only been maybe ten or fifteen years ago that they got out from under those charges. Meanwhile, they couldn't get jobs because their case was in federal court which hindered their opportunities.

Ross and I started dreaming up some programs together at that time. Ross was my philosophical leader, partner, and friend, and I hurt when I think about him being deceased. Conversations between me and Ross—and our friendship—were around saving young people, anybody really, from going into a life of crime. We always had a saying: *Crime does not pay, but you will, with your time.*

CETA, the Comprehensive Employment Training Act of 1973, was enacted, and we would write programs to work with young people, boys and girls, to try to give them another direction from gangs or from deviant activity. We began to write grants for programs like

Work Pays Too. We'd get kids jobs after school with companies, and we would pay them out of the CETA funds, pay our salary, and run the program. And that worked; the companies hired them to do not very technical work like stocking shelves, sweeping up, that sort of thing.

Mayor Harvey Sloane and the political part of the city appreciated us. We were always able to get whatever we needed through the Board of Aldermen and local business leaders. We always had political connections as we were trying to change our people's trajectory and their mindset. Kids were going to juvenile centers, and then when they got out, they had a messed up record. From there, they'd often end up in prison. But we began to write intervention programs. Ross was good at that, and I was good at writing the grants. We were a good team.

At that time, gangs were getting started because some of the community centers were being defunded or shut down. It was the beginning of gangs out in California. The Crips and the Bloods had popped up. Of course, you had people here trying to imitate those kinds of gangs. The Bloods were up in the East End, Smoketown; the Crips were down in the West End.

With Ross's background coming out of prison, keeping other people out of prison was his primary purpose. The politicians and the mayor approved of what we were doing. We had a good friend in the Commonwealth's Attorney, Ernie Jasmin. He was very supportive. He said, "You two need to get in contact with those guys so I don't have to lock them up and put a bunch of them in prison." People knew that we did that kind of work. The police came to us and said, "You guys know all these kids out here on the street. Why don't you all do something with them?" We said okay, and what we called "doing something with them" was going and interacting with them. We had another guy

with us named Chuck Cowan, a martial arts specialist who's still my tai chi instructor. His name is now Baba Serikali. The three of us single-handedly, and with no police, went out and stopped a major gang war in the early '80s between the Bloods and the Crips and some other gangs.

That was a pretty frightening thing for me. I grew up in a hard area, but this was a little different. When I was a kid we had our crew of boys, our gang, and we would go to another area to date girls or play basketball, or whatever. We might get into a tussle about something, but that was silly territorial stuff. These gangs were criminal-minded. They wanted to make some money now, and they knew the way to do that was to sell drugs, steal, or keep their territory clear of other kids coming in and wanting to do the same thing. They were getting ready to do a pretty serious shootout, and we went to them down in the California neighborhood and met with them in secret. We were at the middle of the table, and one gang head was on each end. We just told them, "You all can't do this. You can't kill each other. That ain't going to work." We tried talking to them and tried to turn them around. We said, "We can produce some jobs. Will you take them?" They said, "No, we ain't working no eight hours a day. We can make more money than that by doing what we were doing." We got them to postpone this purging they were getting ready to do, but some of them did it anyway. We lost two or three kids. We went to their funerals. That was a very sobering time. That violence was terrible. It made an empty place in our spirits.

We stayed with it for a couple of years and finally, some of those kids grew out of it, more or less. But right now, everything is right back where it was. It's the grandkids of the kids we were dealing with. You get in their territory and they'll kill you. It's crazy. It's mind-blowing that they don't take life more seriously than that. My God. I mean, *murder.*

Ross and I were able to walk both sides of the street with the gangs. We could be with the Crips and the Bloods. He wasn't a big guy, he was smaller than me, really. But they respected him because of his former prison life. If they respected me, it was because I was with Ross. So we got them to kind of calm down.

Ross and I had started off writing grants to intercede in the lives of young people prone to juvenile delinquency, kids moving from children's center to prison. When they got out of the juvenile center, we would go to the judge and say, "Let us supervise them. Have them come to us." The programs were about work, about changing their direction, their mindset, and their sense of self-worth.

Then, we started writing adult programming, and we got an idea about halfway houses. Guys were coming back to their neighborhoods when they got out of jail or prison. So some of them would go right back into crime. That's when we opened a halfway house at the old Allen Hotel, which had been the first and only hotel for African Americans in Louisville. That was always a place that soldiers from Fort Knox could come and stay during the segregated times in Louisville. It was iconic, and it was just sitting there. So we opened a halfway house there called Ervin House. When guys got out of prison—we only took guys—if it wasn't for sex crimes, we would give them a place to stay for sixty days, get them a job, and turn them around. Guys would get an individual room like they have in the prison, but they were free to come and go. We had work training and counseling, fed and housed them, and tried to get them jobs.

It had thirty-six rooms and took thirty-six guys at a time. While you were with us, you had to take job training and counseling. If you didn't have a job, you'd

go on parole and do what you're going to do. Still, we were pretty successful getting guys jobs because we knew construction companies, and they would always hire our guys. We had connections with the white community downtown and places like GE, American Standard, and International Harvester, so we could get guys good jobs. These guys would turn around. All they needed was a job, some self-worth, and a place to stay.

It was a great place. Everybody loved it, recognized it. We were rolling until we had a fire in the hotel. We didn't have any major capital to renovate. In the meantime, the Catholic community liked what they saw and gave us Flaget High School for two dollars a year. It was just me, Ross, and two counselors we had hired. We had this whole big building.

Geoff with Deirdre in Central Park, ca. 1977

Geoff and Ross Jessup, ca. 1974

It was perfect, tailor-made for us, because there were thirty individual rooms where the priests used to stay. Thirty rooms. Thirty guys. We got twenty-six dollars a day for every ex-offender we kept.

We were rolling, but the neighborhood wasn't convinced that our program belonged. Chickasaw and Shawnee were very nice neighborhoods, and the residents were concerned about criminal behavior there. Black people that lived in that part of town thought people in the halfway house would go back to their old ways. We kept saying, "These are *your* people. They are coming back to the community they left. When they get out, they ain't got nowhere else to go. So you may as well let us have them because we know where they are and what they're doing." But the people didn't want us there.

We had to get Darryl Owens as our attorney, and we went through court and won. We finally convinced the Black community in that area that we were all right, that we were doing the right thing. And they ended up supporting us. We really thought we had done something, because we really changed some minds. We met with the community at churches. Ross and I went out and talked up the process and the program. We sold the people on the fact that we knew what we were doing, and it worked because there wasn't recidivism with our guys. They didn't commit new crimes. Our record for rehabilitation was outstanding.

We ran Ervin House for seven years, until the state changed the way they released prisoners on parole. Ex-offenders were released to local jails instead of halfway houses, and we were no longer able to get state funds, and that was it. But we had made it really successful up to that point. We changed guys' lives. I still have guys out there who come up to me and say, "What's going on? Man, you changed my life." They'll come up and give me a hug, "Man, I was headed toward a life of crime."

After we closed, they changed the laws again and started releasing offenders to halfway houses again. Then mostly white developers started buying up houses in the West End and opening halfway houses.

These places are just doing it for the money they get from the state government. They don't have the same philosophical approach to halfway houses that we had. Ervin House was a community response to crime and to people's needs in terms of jobs and training and changing their trajectory and what they were thinking. These new places are taking people that don't fit in the African American community, or in a community like Russell. Most of them come from out in the state somewhere, and they get paroled to Jefferson County. They think they'd get a job easier in Louisville than they could somewhere out in the state. So you drop them in the middle of an urban environment in a halfway house that is not well managed? That's a conflict. And that's what the halfway houses are doing now.

But Ross and I were really proud of what we did at Ervin House. It was all because of Ross Jessup. He knew how to handle ex-offenders. I didn't, but I knew people, I knew politicians and all of that. I could always talk and always stayed attached to the political side of the community in Louisville. That's the advocacy and the type of relationships that I came to be recognized for.

After Ervin House, I worked in youth programs at the Presbyterian Community Center in Sheppard Square. I did a lot of volunteer stuff also. I was involved all over. National Council of Christians and Jews. I volunteered at the NAACP. I was sometimes too radical for the NAACP. Whenever the busing issue got hot in the '70s and the school system was debating it, the president of the NAACP at the time was pulled into the school system's side, saying we had to do the busing to get the kids integrated. Well, I didn't think so. I was of the mind that we *shouldn't* do it because Black kids were going to carry the bulk of the burden of being bused. NAACP President Maurice Sweeney and the lawyers for the school system were having a big meeting, and they wouldn't let me in. Maurice said, "Geoff, you're too radical. You'll tear the meeting up. You got to sit on the outside."

Later, I worked with the Kentucky Commission on Human Rights doing housing work. Looking at the way housing was segregated, investigating realtors that had broken the law, taking people's complaints about housing discrimination, and investigating them. And if it was proven, we would submit it to the state who would then adjudicate it.

That's around the time when I got tapped to go into politics. I became president of the local chapter of the NAACP in 1985, and I think I did a lot of good work there. The police wasn't treating people right in jail. They were beating them up. So I led a demonstration about police violence down on Fourth Street. My work at the NAACP was helping people get their jobs back and dealing with inequities that people went through. Also, I dealt with the school system and how kids were treated. Spending hours on the bus was so hard on kids that they would become disruptive in class and get kicked out of school. I was helping parents get their kids back in school.

The city-county government was split back then, and in the county police department, they found a KKK robe in an officer's locker. I asked that that officer's name be made public so we would know who was in the Klan and on the police force. They wouldn't do it. They sequestered the name. The NAACP marched about that. We wanted to know his name, wanted him convicted and kicked off the police force. They never opened up the file. Later on, when I was working under David Armstrong, this same guy began to work in the government beside me out of the mayor's office. He had quit the police force, and I found out he was the one. He said, "Yeah, I did that. But it was just a prank." I said, "No, man. You know what you caused?"

Chairing a Black History Month program in the rotunda of the Jefferson County courthouse, ca. 1985

Another big case we had at the NAACP years later was where a guy named James Taylor was in an abandoned house, and the police were trying to get him out because he wasn't supposed to be there. These two detectives said he came after them with a box cutter, and they shot him dead. That caused an eruption just about like Breonna Taylor. Nothing happened. Nothing changed. I took part in those demonstrations.

Another incident around that time was a guy they caught in a stolen car in an alley in west Louisville. They told him to get out of the car. He was a young guy, and he didn't get out immediately. They said he revved the car up to run over them, so they shot him all up in the car. They got a lawsuit out of that and the police had to pay millions of dollars. So when you look at that, you think, *has anything changed*? For some people, no, for other people, yeah, things have gotten better. But not where I sit. They just kind of repeated themselves.

I was still the president of the NAACP when I started working for the county government. The county judge executive at the time was Harvey Sloane who had been a very popular mayor. This is back when we had two governments: city and county. Sloane became the county judge executive in 1986. They were getting rid of Cotter Homes and Southwick back then, and Harvey Sloane put up Park DuValle Health Center. Ernie Allen was the chief of staff for Sloane, and he called me one day and said, "Geoff, would you come work for me? I want you to come and be my special assistant and keep track of the West End." I understood politics but thought that being a politician would take away from all the trust I had built up in the community as an advocate. I said no, but he didn't stop. He called me back about a week later and said, "I really want you to come and work for me to help me change this city." That kinda got me: *Change the city*. And the pay was good. So I said okay. I went and worked for him and that was a turning point in my life.

Sometimes there were issues between my work at NAACP and my job with county government. That got real sticky because Jefferson County would have one policy, and I'd be advocating for another kind of policy at the NAACP. Or I'd be issuing a response about people getting shot by the police and carrying on about housing getting denied to African Americans. Whenever something was happening I'd have to tell them, "I'm leaving. I'm going to be out for two hours. I will not be on government time." And then I'd go and do whatever NAACP work I was doing. Then I'd have to come back on the clock, so to speak. After a while the city said, "You can't keep doing this." So, I left the NAACP when my term as president was up.

I was proud of the work I did as Sloane's special assistant for the West End. I had a little budget, and people would come to me for little grants. I became very popular because I didn't play politics with things.

When somebody came to me and said, *I need a grant*, or, *I need some help from the city*, I'd find a way to help them. It wasn't about me. It was about what was happening in me and what God was doing through me. I kept my focus. I was always helping people.

And then, when Dave Armstrong was elected to be county judge executive in 1989, he liked what I was doing and he kept me. I worked for him for nine years. That was splendid. I expanded my work from west Louisville to the rest of the county too. I was still working in the schools, still helping families as an intermediary, and still working on the dilemmas that came with busing.

Armstrong became mayor in 1999, and I continued to work for him. During his mayoral term, they were trying to figure out how to merge the city and county governments into one. They kept trying to get this merger, but the Black community didn't go along with it. So Dave Armstrong sent me and a couple of staff people to study this for a year to see if it could work. We were the Task Force on Merged Government out of the county judge executive's office. We worked out of Greater Louisville Inc. We spent our days researching the ways services would be merged or not: police department, public works, fire department, all of that.

We found out the problems with the merger. We were going to have problems merging the police. They were not going to want to do that. Cops in the county police differently than the cops in the city. Police in the city ran into crime where they had to get involved; police in the county rode around in cars and didn't have a lot of problems in the street. We knew that the philosophies were going to clash. And they were going to bring the fire departments together also. The city had the biggest fire department with all the equipment. The people in the county were going to want that. If they

With Mayor Jerry Abramson, ca. 1990

With County Judge Executive Sloane
and some department heads

were going to merge, they were going to want some fire protection like the city has, which was going to cost money. We studied it, wrote a report, and turned it in. We told them, "It's not going to work." They didn't pay any attention to us. They kept fighting politically. They got a few Black politicians behind it, and they merged governments anyway. That's all I can say. They did it. They merged the city and county governments.

When they merged, it was Louisville Metro Government, and Jerry Abramson was mayor. He said, "I really like what you've been doing. I'm going to keep you. But we don't have the budget for your salary."

Clockwise from left: Geoff, Tia,
Terria, Akia, Dierdre, and Kishya

I said, "Well, you can't keep me for free!" He raised the money and gave me a position at the city's Human Relations Commission as community police advocate, a position which changed my whole thinking about police reform.

I worked there for two years helping people who had run-ins with the police. When people would get abused, they'd come to me and I'd work it through the police complaint system, and internal affairs would hear the case and then do whatever they had to do; discipline the officer if they had to do that. I'd take them to the Internal Affairs Division, and they'd admit that they were wrong. But they didn't fire nobody. They'd admit, "Well, the officer shouldn't have done that, and we're going to spank his hands." And I just kept telling myself, *This ain't working. They ain't changing their behavior.*

And then one time, I took this lady down there. The police had roughed her up real bad for no reason.

We made a complaint with the police and afterwards, I went back to the office to get something I had left there, and I heard those Internal Affairs guys laughing about the case I had just brought in. They said, "That Black guy brings them people in, and we ain't going to do shit about it. We ain't paying any attention to him." I didn't say anything. They didn't know I was there. I told Mayor Abramson, "I can't do this no more. The people are coming to me and telling me these stories and I'm saying, 'Okay, let's go over to Internal Affairs and get this formally documented.' Then the police laugh about it after I leave." I said, "I'm not going to treat the people like this. They think something is happening, but nothing happened." I quit. I retired. I'd been in it nineteen years. I was ready to go. I saw too much. I saw too many things that people didn't know were happening, people that really have serious problems—especially in the West End—and nobody cared about it. I realized I wasn't changing anything. I was just watching the same thing reoccurring. I was rehashing the same fights: poverty, systemic racism, inadequate education system, and the like.

While I had been doing all this work in government, the Lord had called me to preach. All these years, I was doing all this other stuff, and in the back of my mind, I felt like there was something I wasn't doing, something I should be doing. I had always been in church, and I had felt the call when I was twelve, but I hadn't understood it. In 1990, when I turned fifty, I got the second call. I was always a jogger. I ran in a couple of mini marathons. I was in Shawnee Park running one day when I got this voice that said, "Go pastor my people." Usually, people get called to *preach.* But the Lord told me to *pastor* my people, which is a different level of engagement. Again, I wasn't *thinking* it; I could *hear* it in my head. It wasn't a big voice in the sky, it was in my head. I said, *Oh,* and I started running faster. The faster I ran, the louder this voice would get: "Go pastor my people." I found myself in a dead-out run. Shawnee Park's big. Man, I ran so fast out of Shawnee Park and over to the parkway where my pastor's house was. Ran into his house and fell on the floor. I'll never forget. I told him, "I give up." I said.

"You give up what?" he said.

"God's calling me to pastor, and I got to do it."

"Good." He said, "I've been watching you, you know. You've been getting more and more involved in church. I've been watching you. I understand." He took me in. He started training me. Then I got more formal training, and then finally I got licensed to preach.

I adopted that style of ministry that works outside the walls of the church called community ministry. Church is a building where you go on Sunday to worship, sing, clap, get happy, stomp your feet, and then go home. Come back next Sunday. That ain't the way I see ministry. Ministry is getting out there and feeding the people, dealing with people who don't have homes, and dealing with people with unsuccessful relationships. That's ministry. And I was always a leader in ministry outside the church, even for the AME Church, which is radical in its conception.

The AME Church was the first church for Black folk by Black folk. A Black man, Richard Allen, was the originator of the whole Black theology. In 1794, he was going to a white Methodist church, and he and his friends were sitting in the balcony worshiping. All of a sudden, he got an idea. He came down and said he wanted to pray at the altar alongside the white people. They said, "No, no. You can't do that. You got to get up." So he got up, took his people, walked out, and started the African Methodist Episcopal Church. Broke off from the Methodist Church. From that point on, Black folk started expanding to the CME Church, the AME Zion Church, and the Baptist Church.

The AME Church was a natural fit for me because it was so civil rights minded. The church is ingrained in Black life because we didn't own any institutions *except* the church. We didn't own the schools or businesses. We owned nothing. But the church was *ours*. We could think, express, conceive, and strategize whatever we wanted to do in the church. From our slave days, I think Black folks related to how God chose Israel as a special nation, even though they weren't the biggest and the strongest. Slaves felt like, *God has chosen us. He is going to take care of us.*

In the AME Church, you get four years of training before you're able to preach or pastor. I was fifty years old, so they saw I was mature and gave me a church after three years of training instead of four. I got St. John AME Church, located in the South End of Louisville on the corner of Colorado and Euclid Avenue in what is known as the Bingham neighborhood. The church was about to fall down. Somebody had built it with their own hands, but it was not a strong building. We needed to move.

One day, I walked down the street about four blocks, and I saw this other church up on a hill. Beautiful building. I went in there, and there weren't but two white ladies and a white pastor. I sat in the back for the service, and after church I asked one of the ladies, "Why are there only two people here?" She said that after the neighborhood was integrated, the whites moved out. They never came back. I asked if St. John's could have our anniversary there, and they said sure. Later they sold us the building. That was my first real church with a nice building.

That began my new life. Things happened in my ministry that brought me to where I am now and fulfilled me in my concern for people. We stayed there for twelve years in two different buildings. I developed some relationships that were out of this world.

Preaching from the pulpit at St. John's AME

Chief of Corrections honored at St. John's AME

Ones that I still have now. The kids from that congregation are now grown and got their own kids. They didn't want me to move from that church. They cried and cried. I cried. Everybody cried. It was one of my most successful churches. The AME church sold the building after I left.

In 2002, they transferred me from Louisville to another assignment in Elizabethtown. The pastor had built this brand new church building, but then he had back trouble and had to retire. I pastored there for four years. I was driving from Louisville to E-town all the time. I was able to keep the people interested and engaged. I worked the ministry, got the church property straight, and kept everything going. You have churches where you always need to fix the sink, fix this and that, renovate everything. But that church was brand new. I was very blessed to be there. Loved the people, still do. There were about three hundred people in that congregation. Some of them still call me. You really become a family. We were getting ready to build a family life center, and then the bishop moved me again. People were really devastated. My wife and I were too.

The bishop wanted me back in Louisville to a church that needed to be rehabbed. Greater St. James on 21st and Oak had about thirty-five people in the congregation, and they couldn't financially take care of a church that big. I didn't understand why they transferred me, and I didn't really like it. But my wife always told me I was a good AME. I was used to the military. I was used to the government. So, I did what was called of me whether I liked it or not. I'm a duty-oriented kind of person. That church needed a pastor, and I was able to get in love with them. I stayed there for seven years. I negotiated the sale of St. James, and the congregation moved to a church called St. Mark's.

Then my bishop re-assigned me again, to pastor Asbury Chapel AME. When I was born, my mother

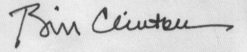

THE WHITE HOUSE
WASHINGTON

April 23, 1996

The Reverend Geoffrey Ellis
3803 Garfield Avenue
Louisville, Kentucky   40212

Dear Reverend Ellis:

    Thank you so much for your help during my recent trip. Your efforts meant a great deal to me.

    I hope to visit Kentucky again soon.

Sincerely,

Bill Clinton

A letter that Rev. Ellis received from President Bill Clinton

took me to the altar at Asbury Chapel and dedicated me to the Lord there. That's where I learned about God, Jesus, David, the Bible, theology, and Sunday school. I knew all the members there. I grew up with them. Now I was there pastoring them. That was God's intervention. He did that full circle. I loved it. I pastored there for two years before I retired from the ministry at age seventy-five. My retirement celebration was at the fellowship hall at the Church of the Living God on Seventh and Algonquin. All of my friends and colleagues were there. A bishop came, which was a high honor, and all my kids and grandkids.

I was at the head table, and I remember looking out there at all those people that were there because of me. People giving tribute, saying I was a community-involved guy, and that you couldn't find a guy as involved in the community and politics in his ministry as me. A couple of my daughters gave a tribute.

Rev. Ellis and Deirdre, 2022

I cried and couldn't get through it. It was just a glorious day to be alive; to have all those people think that you were extraordinary. I didn't think so, but they did. I'd not done anything that I thought was so special. It's just the way I lived my life: caring about other people in the community and my ministry and, ultimately, my family.

It's an oxymoron a little bit: being a person who spent his life trying to bring other people together, but I hadn't stopped to bring *me* together. Deirdre made me realize, "You have a whole family out there that you haven't given the kind of attention that you should." I give credit to her for bringing them up and over to me. It gave me tremendous realization of myself and my family: my girls, my son Mark who I mourn continuously, and Zina who I mourn continuously. It means a

lot, this realization, and Deirdre has been the glue that has bound all those relationships together. Without her I wouldn't have dealt deeply with these relationships. As I hit eighty-two and knowing that my time is shorter than it is long, it's enormously satisfying to have my family. It's overpowering and humbling. That's a godly thing and has given me an enormous amount of emotional satisfaction.

Deirdre and I moved back to Russell in 2017. We got a lot of publicity about moving and building a house here at 19th and Cedar. This is what Operation Rebound wanted to see: African Americans building houses in this area. And they have. People will come through this block and say, "Ooh, I didn't know these houses were here." They got this area developed and now it's moving west. Rebound's got a big spot over here on 21st and Jefferson where they're going to build more of these kinds of houses. Brand new two-story brick family homes. They're built to look like the homes we knew growing up in west Louisville.

If we want to keep attracting young African Americans to invest in west Louisville, we need the kind of stores and amenities that will bring them back. We are in a food desert. We got a shopping mall deficit. We have doctor, dentist, and medical deficits. If you go shopping, you have to go over to Indiana, or you go way up east. That doesn't make sense. There are enough people to warrant having those things. It's a continuous problem, but it's being addressed by developers and government and residents.

I see more financial investment in the west. Some Black folk are coming back and renovating houses down here. I see signs of progress. The big problem people hear about all the time is crime. I'm not sure there's more crime here than there is elsewhere in Louisville. But the media publicizes and sensationalizes it, so every night, we hear something about crime in west Louisville. Well, if I'm a young attorney, and I want to build me a home, I might have second thoughts about building it in west Louisville.

I believe there's a lack of political will and forward thinking among the political people. Politics decide who gets what, when, where, and how. But when politicians get in and start thinking about themselves, they don't think enough about the people and how they are living and the opportunities that people desire. Political will comes from us who live here. That's why I try to get young people involved in politics if I can. We have to demand more of our politicians. A whole different group of young people are coming up who are more aggressive about their advocacy and about what should happen and which parts of Louisville should be included economically. Systemic racism has really

Asbury Chapel AME

been recognized by young people, and they run right over it like it's something in the middle of the street. They don't get stymied by it like my era did. They just run right over it.

There are a lot of plans for economic development in west Louisville, and if those plans continue in the next political administration we're going to be getting somewhere. It's simple. It's about improving the housing stock. It's gonna take people continuing to advocate, and politics will change. The businesses will begin to locate in west Louisville. I think we're on our way. I see the promise. I think the West End will become as popular and developed as the far eastern parts of Louisville. I'm hopeful about that. That's why we built here, because this is where it's going to be happening: in Russell. It's exciting to be a part of it. ✦

Wherever We Are, We Should Make a Difference

Russell's Houses of Worship

REV. DAVID SNARDON

JOSHUA TABERNACLE

Over forty houses of worship hold regular meetings within the 1.5 square mile footprint of Russell, a higher concentration than any other area in the city of Louisville. Many of these churches have served the neighborhood for generations, even as families moved elsewhere in the city through the intervening years. But people return to their congregations every week, and the population of Russell is at its highest on Sunday mornings during worship.

No organization is as Black as the Black church. It serves Black people with Black leadership, Black economics, and Black vision. The faith community understands Black people. The need of a Black church comes out of the plight and struggle of slavery, to have a safe place to call our own where we can worship God freely without being ostracized, criticized, and made to feel like we were less than.

Other organizations may be for Black people and minorities, but they have to take money where they can get it to survive. The land that Black churches sit on is bought with Black money. Many of our churches own their own property. So we own what we have, which is why many churches were able to survive Urban Renewal. What this meant back in the day was that Black ministers were protected and in some ways immune from white involvement. They could speak their piece without fear of reprisal. This was instrumental during the struggle for civil rights.

We're able to do things with nothing. We're still able to keep producing on a shoestring budget, or no budget. We're still able to get things done. We're still here, time and time again. The numbers dwindle, but the bills get paid. That's the Black church and Black economics: under-resourced people helping other under-resourced people by bringing a little bit to the table. Stretching in order to serve a broader community.

There was a time when the Black church was central to the lives of Black people. We had freedom in church to excel and use our gifts in ways that were

not readily accessible to use in other parts of society: you could be chairperson of the board, the superintendent of Sunday school, you could preside over one of the many auxiliaries of the church. While we may not have had opportunities for such excellence in other parts of society, the level of quality we produced in the Black church was high. Many of our secretaries were so professional they could have worked at any Fortune 500 company. We printed our own material to contextualize our ministries, and every Sunday was a professional musical concert.

Like many churches in west Louisville, the majority of our congregation at Joshua Tabernacle once lived in the West End. But as people grew older, and children moved away, people began to commute to church more. However, we still have a strong connection with the community through family and friends who still live in Russell or are connected to Central High School where many of our members graduated from. People still have ties here. The new development at Beecher Terrace is challenging, though, because many people who once were connected with us have been displaced, and may not come back.

Time will tell if promises given will be promises kept when it comes to all of the development in Russell, specifically in Beecher Terrace. At the beginning of the development, there was a lot of skepticism. Many older people who remember how Urban Renewal hurt our communities wondered if we hadn't been down this road before. Rev. Dr. Geoffrey Ellis of Asbury Chapel AME Church came by my church in 2016 and asked me if I had been paying attention to what was being proposed for Russell. I told him I had been receiving mail, but I hadn't been paying much attention. He said to me, "Rev. Snardon, if we don't pay attention,

we'll wake up one day and won't even recognize our neighborhood."

So we made a list of churches in Russell—came up with forty-three—and we contacted as many of those pastors as we could and asked if they wanted to work together to keep people from being hurt by the developments in Russell like we have seen with past projects.

A group of eleven church leaders started the Concerned Pastors of Russell: Rev. Ellis, myself, Rev. Barbara Haigler of Broadway Temple AME, Rev. Gregory Wright of Plymouth Congregational, Rev. Kennedy Luckett of Magazine Street Seventh Day Adventist, Rev. Lois Caldwell of Philippian Baptist, Rev. Reginald Barnes Sr. of Brown Memorial CME, Rev. Troy Duncan of Christ Center Ministries, Rev. Gerald Joiner of Zion Missionary Baptist, Rev. Angus Dickerson of Spillman Memorial Missionary Baptist, Rev. Dr. Valerie Washington of Hughlett Temple Missionary Baptist, and Bishop Walter Jones of Baptized Pentecostal.

We wanted to ensure that *this* time part of the development money would be funneled Black people's way. We wanted to avoid repeating in Beecher Terrace what happened in Southwick, what happened in Nulu, where people were displaced and could not benefit from the commercial and economic development. These developments just benefited these big developers from out of town. We wanted some of this life-changing money to flow through our community. People don't want to wait for it to trickle down, they want it to come directly.

So, along with Louisville Central Community Center, the Concerned Pastors of Russell tried to engage the Mayor's Office, the Housing Authority, and McCormack Baron Salazar, who was in charge of the redevelopment in Beecher Terrace. We sought control to develop the blocks on Muhammad Ali Boulevard from Ninth to 13th Streets as mixed commercial and residential spaces—places to work, live, and play—for economic development for Black people in the neighborhood. We wanted to build nice housing and income-generating retail instead of just letting developers come in, build something for Black folk, but take all the resources out of it. We were trying to ensure that the millions of dollars coming in on the backs of poor Black people actually benefited poor Black people. This is Black economic development, an opportunity to do for ourselves. That's a different paradigm than wanting others to do for us.

After two years of working with other agencies, our goals for the project looked favorable. After being told that we would be able to be part of that development, Louisville Central Community Center and the Concerned Pastors of Russell were not named when it came time to vote in the master plan for the development. The plan fell through, and that came as a shock. But LCCC, which has always had a good relationship with the city and the Housing Authority, was able to reach some of the other institutional goals and maintain those relationships.

I was taught that faith and politics go hand in hand. Overwhelmingly, back in the day, you had to go through the church to get certain things done. When I was growing up, strong pastoral leaders were out in the community leading. Many of them were bi-vocational. They had jobs down at City Hall, or in the circuit court, so you could call them for information and they would help and guide you. You'd call Rev. So-and-So and he knew somebody down there. He'd say, "Give me a minute. Call you back." We'd call the pastor to

Rev. Garland Offutt baptizes a church member at West Chestnut Street Baptist Church, ca. 1950s

raise money for somebody that needed some help. "This person got into some trouble. They got locked up and they need to get out." The church was the first bail reform.

Today, we don't necessarily have those same types of people in key places that you could call on to be a bridge for some of these conversations. We used to have a lot more say about what happened in the city than we have right now. There are not as many people in those hallways that can speak for those of us who are lower to the ground.

Rev. Charles Elliott of King Solomon Missionary Baptist Church leading a protest, 1997

The church used to be out in the streets marching. We were leading it, we were organizing it, and we were calling people together. In the 1960s, there were strong voices in the church. The church was organized and had etched out its part against injustice. When the unrest happened in west Louisville in 1968, the pastors were out in the fray. They were trying to calm things down—it was just a powder keg—but also led the charge. People like Rev. Charles Elliott, Rev. Charles Kirby, Rev. C. Mackey Daniels. You had Zion Baptist Church on 22nd and Muhammad Ali, where A.D. King—Dr. Martin Luther King Jr.'s brother—pastored. Quinn Chapel was known for its social activism.

You had some prominent churches that had the courage to stand out and to lead the charge and to call people and churches together. At that time, the majority of people went to church. So when a pastor got up and called people together, there was some common understanding of how we were going to act. If your pastor went along with something, you would probably believe he was right. We're not there anymore. There's not that trust in institutions.

The protests in Louisville in 2020 around Breonna Taylor were possibly the first time a major protest like that did *not* come from the church. That came directly from a street-level frustration about police brutality, and overwhelmingly, those who were crying out did not identify themselves as church goers. These were community activists who believed in the advancement of Black liberation and who were building organizations outside of the church. It was not a '60s era movement where the church was at the lead and established its place at the head of the movement with a strong voice organized for its principles against injustice.

At times, it was frustrating and challenging for faith leaders because, on the one hand, we would hear, "Where is the church at?" and then on the other hand, when we would show up, they didn't want us to be churchy. They wanted you to be there, but they made it known, *This is not your movement, this is ours.* Some of the methods and some of the things that were going on made it very hard for the mothers of the church, the grannies and aunties, to show up. I don't see myself as a pacifist—and I'm not saying that there aren't some militant churches and some militant pastors—but the church's way is not "by any means necessary." Even those who I perceive as my enemy, I cannot destroy their humanity.

I have pastor friends who were very much a part of that movement. In my opinion, they served more of a priestly role for the protesters rather than a prophetic role. They weren't necessarily engaged in the protest; they were there as spiritual support for the protesters that were going through it. They weren't necessarily crying out, but were tending to people, making sure needs were met, building relationships. And their presence might have curbed some things because they were respected enough. But there are culture clashes and some amount of disdain for the faith community. Many people don't view the church as being central to their life as their parents and grandparents once did.

As the congregants of many churches have aged, our influence in society has been strained. The church is now challenged with revamping our methodologies to reach a new generation with our message. We are dealing with topics and issues that for many years have been settled for us. We are being asked to reimagine our place in the world and challenge our old assumptions about who we serve and how we serve. That is not bad, but it is unsettling for many of us, and yet can be an opportunity for us to find our place as a moral voice in society. These questions force us to be creative and speak to this present generation. It forces us to deal with topics that we struggle with in our own homes but somehow find taboo to talk about in the church.

If we believe in a God that's able to do all things, the churches should make a difference to the communities that surround them. The church really should be concerned about what's going on *outside* of the walls and *outside* of Sundays and Wednesdays when we worship and pray. We were told that our mission is to go help people. All that other stuff doesn't matter. Because regardless if you're gay or straight, regardless if you're Christian or Muslim, regardless if you're guilty as charged or not, everybody needs somewhere to sleep. Everybody needs something to eat. You need some clothes to wear. We are to introduce people to Christ and let Christ conform them to his image. It's not for us to conform people to *our* image.

That is a key point that sometimes I think even Black people forget: this is a reciprocal relationship. If the church is doing well and the community is suffering, something is wrong with that paradigm.

Wherever we are, we should make a difference in our community. People don't have to believe like we believe, think how we think, act how we want them to act, feel like we want them to feel. But blessings should fall on other people just because we show up. Black churches have always worked that way. ✦

And the Canaries Would Sing!

One family's life at Quinn Chapel

JOANNA NETTLES SMITH AND CARMINA NETTLES-HURST

SIXTH-GENERATION PARISHIONERS OF QUINN CHAPEL

We grew up in Quinn Chapel African Methodist Church, and our family has been at Quinn without any interruption for six generations. Quinn Chapel started off at Second and Main streets, upstairs over a blacksmith shop and overlooking the slave block. They say that if you were in church having services, you could look down on slaves being sold. We always grew up with that history.

The church has had six locations over the years, but it is best known for its location at Ninth and Chestnut, where it was for almost one hundred years until 2002. Our mother was a walking historian, and she always told us that that church building had previously been a white church that had been part of the Underground Railroad. People say that's not true, but we know it was.

When we were growing up, our Girl Scout leader and Sunday school superintendent was Evangelist Etta Graham. She was such a loving and giving person. We had the best time under her leadership. The old Quinn Chapel had apartments all the way down the side of the building and she lived in one of those apartments. She had a big potbelly stove, and I was fascinated by that. She made the best chili on that potbelly stove. I spent many hours sitting in her living room or her kitchen listening to her tell stories about growing up. She taught us a lot of life lessons. At that time women could not be ordained, so she was an evangelist. She would always tell us stories in such a way that you would get a lesson out of it. You would remember those lessons in life.

When we were little girls, we couldn't just go down to Fourth Street and sit in any restaurant. We couldn't try on clothes in the department stores. There were schools we couldn't attend. By the time I was grown, Quinn Chapel was the hub of the civil rights movement in Louisville. Quinn was the largest church close to the downtown stores, so that's where they would have most of the civil rights meetings. It was important that they had a safe place to meet. The meetings started with prayer and singing. You would have to get your mind ready so that you could listen to the directions. Lyman T. Johnson would bring his high school civics students to Quinn, and he would tell them, "Whatever happens, don't fight back." Which is a very difficult thing. So he would have prayer and singing and get ready for the march.

I was in my early twenties. My first child Pam was two years old at that time, and I would have to turn off

Carmina Nettles-Hurst and Joanna Nettles Smith

the news when she was around because one day she asked me, "Mama, why do all the Black people get beat up and the white people don't?" She was picking it up. We went to all of the protests and rallies. We marched. We were marching and singing with Dr. King.

When Dr. King—and later, Jesse Jackson—came to town, their lives were in danger, so they always had to have a big presence of security guards. Every time Dr. King would come, we'd go through the same thing. Those of us who were members of the church would volunteer to help out at the event. We would go in early, knowing we were expecting a crowd. We would set up extra chairs in the aisles. Sometimes my job was to sit in the hall, and if you didn't have the right badge, you just couldn't come into the back hallway. They

always said they had to give our names to security so we could be cleared. Only approved church members and those that were with Dr. King were allowed to go in the back of the church. Dr. King's people would come in and introduce themselves, then most of them would go upstairs to wait with Dr. King until it was time for him to speak. They had two or three men that would stand in the hall.

When Dr. King spoke, you could just hear a pin drop. Everybody was so attentive. When you walked into the sanctuary, there was a certain tone there, a feeling that one day we're not going to have this discrimination problem that we had. One day people are going to truly, truly be free. Black people would have the same privileges. It wouldn't be a glass ceiling over

Church members in front of the old Quinn Chapel on 9th and Chestnut, ca. 1984

our heads. It was a sense of hopefulness, and we knew that one day things would change. Our children would not go through what we went through. And after the meeting, there was a calm and a peace. And when we would stand up, hold hands, and sing "We Shall Overcome," you could be standing next to your worst enemy and they would become your best friend. He was so powerful.

The whole movement was important to me, and it was important to me that my church had a major role in solving a lot of those problems that were in the community. I felt proud that I belonged to something that was trying to straighten out this whole mess where everybody's not equal just because of the melanin in their body.

Quinn Chapel was a beautiful church. You would think you were walking into a European church. Oh, it was the most beautiful place. We would have more than a thousand people in the church sometimes.

On Easter, we had canaries in little cages up and down the aisle. Actual canaries! At Beecher Terrace, people couldn't keep dogs or anything like that. They could have fish and birds, and everybody who had birds took their birds to the Easter service. The canaries were an Easter tradition with our church. And the canaries would sing! The more the preacher preached, the louder the canaries would sing.

In 2002, Quinn Chapel moved from our historic location on Ninth and Chestnut to our current location at 1901 W. Muhammad Ali Blvd. On the day we moved, we had a motorcade from the old church to the new church for those who were too old to walk. And

Members of St. Thomas Lodge #3 laying the cornerstone for the new Quinn Chapel AME Church, 2002

those of us who wanted to walk sang church music the whole way. Someone would start singing one song and everyone would join in, then someone would start another song. My husband's lodge, St. Thomas Lodge #3, laid the cornerstone, and then we had a service.

Quinn Chapel is still involved in the community. We work mainly through the various organizations in the church. We keep a library filled with books that you can just take for free, mostly children's books. The library is located by the driveway on the Muhammad Ali Boulevard entrance. We give away food baskets to people in need, but since COVID, we've been buying gift certificates to Kroger and donating them to the Salvation Army and residents in the community. We give away backpacks to students with everything the kids need to start school. We have a mentoring program now that's reaching out to help keep young boys on the right path. Like all traditional churches, we have Bible school during the summer, and we average about two hundred kids. Most of them don't go to Quinn. We're an old church, so we're not still having babies. Most of the people around in the neighborhood have a church home, so their children don't come here except for when we're having Bible school and things like that.

When we were building the new facility, as they put the floors in, they asked all of the members to write scripture on pieces of paper. You could write as many passages as you wanted, and I wrote a lot of them. They mixed those pieces of scripture into the concrete and mortar. So scripture is buried under the floor all around the new church. The scripture is in the foundation of the church. ✦

You Can't Keep a Person from Working

MANFRED G. REID SR.

I was born in Lothair, Kentucky, down by Hazard, in 1936. We lived in Lothair until 1944, when my parents migrated to Louisville. My father died nine months after we relocated to Louisville, and my mother died eighteen months after his death. Both were tubercular. My mother planted seeds in my mind before she died. She told me from her bedside, "Stay in school. If you can't go to school, study anyway." There is so much that she related to me as to the ability to make it on your own. Those were long conversations. She said, "I won't be here with you, but you gotta do this."

My childhood training taught me submission. But when my parents died, I thought I had to become a man. And I began to develop my own perspective as to the kind of man I wanted to be as opposed to what I saw around me, which was my uncles. They were broken men. Good men—decent, respectful, religious—but broken. The men that raised me were former coal miners, born in the late nineteenth century, who migrated from the South at the end of the Civil War. They came to eastern Kentucky and the coal mines there, which was another form of slavery. Then they escaped and migrated into the cities and into low-income jobs. And so their perspective was submissive. Mine wasn't. Their philosophy was that the only way a Black man could make it was to find a good white man. I rejected that and began to adopt Booker T. Washington's theory and later on, in the late '40s and early '50s, the Honorable Elijah Muhammad's: do for self.

I attended Virginia Avenue School, Madison Junior High School, and Central High School, where I graduated in 1955. I attended Kentucky State College for one full term and a summer semester but returned to Louisville, where I was hired by the Louisville Fire Department. The Louisville Fire Department

Manfred Reid at six years old

Manfred Reid during his time at the
Louisville Fire Department

Manfred Reid in the 1960s,
before events changed his life forever

had integrated the year before. I think I was the first African American to be hired under the merit system and the first to be placed into a white firehouse. That wasn't a very pleasant experience. My tenure at the fire department lasted for one year.

I had married in June of 1957, and I was trying to feed my little wife. She was pregnant at that time, and we had a little apartment over on 29th Street. I worked at American Standard for a time and did some horticulture work. Then I got a job as a night watchman at Bellarmine College, and through that, I got a scholarship, and I went to Bellarmine for two years. But Bellarmine didn't pay much money. I think I was making about fifty-eight dollars a week. I just simply had to have more money, so I started selling

Fuller products. Then I got my real estate broker's license. Eventually, Luther Wilson and I went out on our own, and we started Reid-Wilson Realty Company. I also bought Novotex Industries in 1970 and managed it with my business partners Walter T. "Pete" Cosby, Charles Thomas, and Luther. We had a pillow factory, a whiskey barrel furniture business, and a greeting card business.

When I started selling real estate, I could finally afford to buy a house. I bought a house on 32nd Street in 1965. God, we had some good times in that house. We had never lived on that level before. With me being upper-income, I could take my family on vacations. We traveled every summer. That was a good time in our lives personally, but you're moving in the '60s toward the assassination of John Kennedy, Malcolm X, Martin Luther King, and then Bobby Kennedy. The temperament in Louisville was based on the national movement. I think this led up to those conflicts that included me. I guess you could say I was a victim of circumstance, place, and time. I was living a relatively middle-class life, a notch above the average-income citizen in the neighborhood. I had a good life. Later on, as we moved into the crisis, I started losing things. I lost it all.

On May 8, 1968, Pete Cosby, Luther Wilson, and I were going somewhere, and we saw that the police had stopped our friend and business partner Charles Thomas, who's since changed his name to Rev. Charles Todd. We stopped to see what was wrong with him. We walked over and asked what was wrong, and one officer told us, "Niggers, get out of the street."

We said, "Come on, man." Then he pushed me, and I said, "Okay, cool, I'll get out of the street." I started backing up to get out of the street, and he brings out this rubber club and hits me. He had no reason to do that. He was way out of line. So I just hit him.

That drew three hundred people out there in the street that night. The police officers, to their credit, did everything they could to keep it down. We did too. They arrested me and Rev. Todd. I was charged with assault and battery of a police officer and disorderly conduct, and he was charged with a bank robbery because they thought he was the person who had just robbed a bank. He hadn't robbed no bank.

Organizations and groups protested against our arrest. The emotions in the Black community all across America were at a high pitch. Martin Luther King was killed on April 4, so this was just after his death. Everybody wanted to know, *What do we do?* Everybody was looking for an issue or some reason by which they could express their discontent. So there was a rally on May 27 at 28th and Greenwood to protest the police brutality that Rev. Todd and I had experienced. Stokely Carmichael was invited to come to Louisville to support the effort against police brutality.

I was out on bail and honestly was not paying close attention to the protests that were happening on my behalf. I was just trying to get on with my life. When I heard about the rally, I went down there, stood at a distance, and watched for a few minutes. They were just speaking, so I went home. I've never really been in a protest. I really don't believe in it. I think what precipitates conflict is attention, and if you've got to fight, I don't see no sense in protesting; you've got to fight. And as much as I'm aggressive and militant in a sense, I don't think my militancy is manifested through demonstrations. I was in the Marine Corps. We were taught to fight. I think that protest may open the doors for some discussions, but you don't resolve issues. You got to fight. We're drastically unprepared to fight, especially against the government. It usually comes down to open conflict if groups want a stake at the table. Otherwise, you're pleading to your master for help. I believe in acting against the issue, being effective, and forcing the issue to the table, with you having some equity there by which you can re-establish some degree of order and a basis by which you can build.

Sometime after I left the rally, somebody threw a rock or something and the riots started. When the police got there, I wasn't there. I was home. The riots went on for three or four days. They called in the National Guard, and eventually, it ran its course.

This was a major event for our city, and what had happened to me was at the root of it. In the aftermath, I was mostly focused on my family because there were conflicts among us that preoccupied me. Over time, everyone became aware that I was going to be indicted.

On October 17 of that same year, six of us were indicted for criminal conspiracy. The official indictment was "Conspiracy to Destroy Private Property." The media and the public interpretation of the indictment was a conspiracy to overthrow the government. That's what probably led to federal intervention in terms of investigations. We were indicted and arraigned. In the process, I was brought to trial for assault and battery against a police officer. I was found guilty, but due to the public sentiment for our cause, Judge Nicholson probated the sentences, and I served no time.

We became known as The Black Six. There were six people: myself, Ruth Bryant, Walter T. Cosby, Kuyu Sims, Sam Hawkins, and James Cortez. We were all indicted. Cortez was a person that was supposed to have been a substitute speaker for Stokely Carmichael at that rally. In July 1970, more than two years after the uprising and almost two years after our indictment, the case was finally dismissed. They didn't have any evidence, and there was nothing to support the conspiracy theory. There never was a conspiracy that I knew about.

Sam Hawkins and Manfred Reid with attorneys Dan Taylor, Bill Delahanty, and Bill Allison
at a press conference upon their acquittal on one of the charges in the Black Six indictment

They said we were trying to blow up all the oil and gas storage tanks in the western part of Louisville, down Southwestern Parkway. If what they were saying was true, we would have blown up where we lived. One of the defendants, Ruth Bryant, lived across the street from there. She had a master's degree and was an English teacher. Her husband was a doctor. And she lived down there with four children. Why they believed that she would blow up her own home, I don't know.

There was no conspiracy. The whole concept of it was totally irrational. These were intelligent people across the board; weren't none of us fools, none of us drunkards, drug addicts, uneducated felons. You've got to try to figure out why there was the charge of conspiracy to destroy private property and the rumor of overthrow of the government. Was that a means by which officials on some level of government decided to attack a problem with investigations and undermining rather than dealing with the truth? I strongly believe that based on research that I've done over the years. I don't see any reason why the government should have been in this, but they were: the FBI, state police, and the National Security Agency. I think the indictment really was a means of capping the resistance that they felt was going on in the West End of Louisville and bringing in the powers of law enforcement to relate to it. That's my analysis of what happened.

Now what this does to the individual is that you lose everything. You lose it all. You have to struggle to stay alive. Some of our people died from it. They just got sick and died. A lot of us didn't make it, and a lot of us went to the penitentiary for nothing. Of course, in that period of time, you had to become outspoken because your life was on the line. Over a period of twenty-four months, I went from being a normal, upright citizen to being a "criminal" and a "fanatic." That transition has a tremendous impact on your personality.

I was running my real estate firm, and at the time of the indictment, I owned quite a bit of real estate: my own residence, a twenty-four-plex at 45th and Broadway, and three single-family homes that I rented out. Then I had my regular volume of real estate sales every year. The first thing I lost was that apartment building. I lost my house, and then I lost the other pieces of property. The stress on my family was huge, it was awesome, and it led to divorce. That's the hardest thing that can ever happen to a person.

I'd bought a little shack over on 20th Street, and me and the kids moved there. That was the best I could do for my children at that time. I stayed in that house for ten years. I had to settle down and figure out how I was going to live. During that period of time, I tried to rehab the building, but I didn't have any money. I started trying to rebuild my life, and that took thirty years. It took a long time. I used my instincts to stay alive: spot the police before they spotted me, move out of the way, and stay away from people. If I associated with people who were fearful either of me or of the law, they were going to call the law. So I just had to leave people alone. Everybody.

I don't know how many times I've been arrested. Most of the time I was locked up, there were no charges, and I've never been convicted of a crime. They could say I failed to make child support payments, but that's about all. I've never been a felon. I've had felony charges brought against me, but I've never been convicted of none of that. Most of the times that I've been arrested, I don't know why I was arrested. The police didn't know. Sometimes the police have told me, "We were told to come and get you." And I'd say, "Okay, let's go." They gave no reasons why I was arrested.

This didn't just last for a few months. This went on for ten years. But this is why I know that the involvement extended more than a normal law enforcement investigation. There was probably some form of involvement which went beyond the capacity of the Louisville Police Department.

During the court proceedings on the conspiracy trial, we had a whole battery of lawyers. We had a highly renowned and respected lawyer, Ben Shobe, who later went on to become a judge. We had Dan Taylor, Neville Tucker, Judge Charlie Anderson, Bill Allison, and William Kunstler. We had a battery of lawyers. But I didn't have money. So I had to appeal to them for pro bono services. Well, they wanted money, so I didn't get it there.

I eventually spent my time reviewing and studying my documents and trying to figure out what the hell really happened. Most of the analysis led me to the conclusion that there was more involved in this than just the local police. There was federal involvement. There were some documents where they had blotted the name, but you could read what was said. At the top of the page, they would have all the interested government agencies that were involved in the investigation. The interchange of information between the agencies is in there, and there are coded forms, but you can tell what it is. You know that if you got the NSA and the FBI and the state police in it, this is way above me.

In my study of law about this, I learned about restoration, which is based on the legal principle of

ELMER N. CARRELL, CLERK

JEFFERSON CIRCUIT COURT

404 COURTHOUSE
LOUISVILLE, KENTUCKY 40202

DATE _____ 196_

Received From, _____

Address _____

Judgment Date _____

CASE No. _____

CLERK'S COST

SHERIFF FEES

FINE

OFFICER FEES

WITNESS FEES

MISCL. FEES

Total

By _____ D.C.

Receipt for bail bond for Manfred Reid, 1969

reconsideration. I sat down, wrote a plea for reconsideration, and filed it in the U.S. District Court. I filed it pro se, of course, because I didn't have any money. I got a hearing under Federal Judge Allen. He was nice enough to give me a hearing in his chambers. He said he had read my filing, and he told me, "You got a problem. It's real. You're not imagining this. I don't know how you're going to get one, but you need a lawyer to help you deal with this." That was the greatest satisfaction, to confirm that this was not in my imagination. *This is real.* Because it's hard to believe that the government or somebody is that deeply involved in trying to destroy you. I requested Judge Allen to do whatever he could.

After that, all of that pressure lifted, and I haven't been arrested since. So that further confirmed to me, without any official sanctioning by the government, that the government was involved in this in a big way.

There were about twenty years when I didn't have the capacity socially in the community to support myself. It started in 1968, and I lived almost as a pauper until 1988. For a while there, about seven years, I didn't see anybody because everybody was trying to stay out of the way. Everybody was afraid of me. They were thinking, *You're on the indictments. You were supposed to blow up the whole city. You're dangerous. Plus, you're crazy.* I was really isolated away from the community, away from everybody. That went on for a long time, but I did re-establish support among comrades. Re-establishing those contacts with people that I'd been associated with in the past gave me somebody I could talk to.

I was mostly supported by my friends at that time. They would come around and give me the moral support that I needed. If it was a matter of sustenance, there were usually one or two people, my children or cousin or something, that provided me with money and food. People knew me. And they knew my condition.

The kids naturally went on with their lives. By 1980, I was pretty much by myself: wife gone, children gone. When you're in the streets every day, you can pick up things. You've got friends and people that you know. My main source of income was services that I rendered for minority contractors who would let me work for them. I used my talents as a paralegal, I wrote papers for people, and I'd type for people, and that brought in a little income.

I was rehabbing my house on 20th and Magazine, but I didn't have any money. I was doing it with whatever I could get my hands on and whatever help my friends would give me. It was uninhabitable by code standards because they'd cut off all the water and cut off the electricity. Then you have to do things that you wouldn't normally do, which increases your risk, but you've got to do it anyway. For example, when a man comes down and cuts off your water, as soon as he leaves, you cut it back on. They cut off your lights. As soon as they leave, you cut your lights back on. But these are things you have to do when you're trying to get back. You have to be able to weather the elements because a lot of times you don't have any utilities, and sometimes it takes two or three days to get your services back connected.

I was determined to keep working on that building. My objective was, *whatever you do, stay busy. Don't become an idle mind* because that's where your fears and suspicions multiply. You become paralyzed with that. You've got to get up and do something about your condition and move on with your life. My philosophy is that you cannot keep a person from working. You can deny him a job. You can deny him wages. But a person who really intends to keep themselves busy, you cannot stop him from working. So I went to work on my building. I started trying to gather material, whatever I could get for free, and started working on the building. But it reached a point where the city said, "No. No longer. This building is not going to be rebuilt. We're going to tear it down." They put a stop-work order on the house, and then the court ordered me to leave the house. That was in 1988.

I didn't have a telephone, but somehow someone got the word to me to go to the Legal Arts Building at Seventh and Market. I went over there. They said, "Are you Manfred Reid? We got an apartment for you." Within three or four days, I moved into public housing, Beecher Terrace.

When you go through what I went through, you will have a certain amount of withdrawal within yourself. So it took me a little time before I interacted

Manfred Reid with his daughter, her husband, and his grandchild in the 1980s, during the difficult period in his life before he moved into Beecher Terrace

with my neighbors at Beecher Terrace. There was a lady by the name of Irene James that was president of the resident council. She had seen me in and around the neighborhood. After I'd been living there about three months, she came to me and said, "What in the world's wrong with you? You done moved up here with us and you don't say nothing to nobody. We want you to come to a resident council meeting." She said they wanted to improve the community and that they knew me prior to my moving into Beecher Terrace.

I said, "Okay, I'll come to the meeting." That's how I got involved with the Housing Authority. Right after that, they asked me to be president of the resident council. I started working with Dare to Care and other residents that wanted to set up a food nutrition program. They would bring the food to our office here at Beecher Terrace and we created a food pantry. There was quite a bit of resident activity at that time.

Compared to now, it was more social. Social in the sense that they had a strong outreach to residents to participate in those affairs.

Moving into that neighborhood, what caught my eye was the overwhelming number of diverse activities going on. You had the little league football team. You had plenty of activity in Baxter Park. That tradition has continued down through the years. Most people refer to this neighborhood as being one that's plagued by violence, but you can come to Baxter Park any day. That's a crowded park. They bring food and they cook in the park, and then they have their own cleanup groups. That is something that has continued throughout the decades that Beecher Terrace has been in existence. That park has been a vital social factor as it relates to personal interchange between residents. It's right in the midst of the area, and it acts as a congregation place. It's an excellent facility. We're proud of the fact that it's going to remain in the new Beecher Terrace development.

I've related to the neighbors, the residents that live here. I find them open, welcoming, encouraging, and persuasive in terms of getting me to participate in resident activities. Beecher Terrace has always been open. People came and socialized and participated with residents. It wasn't until crime increased and began to filter into this neighborhood that people began to have concerns about it.

It started back in the '60s. There's a link between the suppression of the civil rights movement and drug proliferation. We could observe changes in the behavior of our youth, the relationship with the police, and the number of killings and arrests. The social order was deteriorating at that time within public housing: open peddling of hard drugs on the street, police picking up homicide victims all the time. The mothers were out protesting against the drug pushers. This was the temperament at that time. A lot of the resistance against the government was based on what they experienced during those times.

And when you put it all together, it just didn't make sense that *we* were the cause of this. Though the media made it appear that way, the causes of this change did not start within the neighborhood. *We* don't import or bring drugs into the neighborhood. *We* don't manufacture or produce drugs. So, when it comes to production and distribution, we always raised the question, *Where is it coming from*? That always baffled us. Nobody could tell us the truth about that. The police department couldn't tell you the truth. The city couldn't tell you the truth.

Why couldn't anybody tell us where it came from or who was distributing it? We always refer to the Iran-Contra scandal during the Reagan administration. Most people in our community believed that the CIA was involved in the proliferation of drugs in America's urban centers. And it appeared to us that the method of control was not economic opportunities but simply being killed by the police. It forced us to take a defensive position in regards to the health and safety of our neighborhoods, and people began to sort of withdraw. You didn't have a right to act on it. You didn't really trust the police. You didn't see any different changes in law enforcement or policing.

So we look to the future. It's a question of the federal government being willing to change its method of financial accountability and structure. Can it generate economic growth for all segments of the American population? That is the risk that we face right now as it relates to change. And if you're not going to fight now, you got to accept what the government offers you. I believe that all people in the world had to fight for whatever they achieved. America didn't get this country by "We Shall Overcome." They fought

From left: Manfred G. Reid, his brother Roy Kenneth Reid,
his cousin Sanford Mullins, his aunt Ida Mae Reid, and his uncle Phillip Reid

for it, killed for it, and died for it. That's the way it is. If you don't fight, you will be subjugated until you die. That's the truth about it.

I believe there can be a peaceful coexistence among people as long as there's open opportunity for everybody. We have to create that. Now we are at a stage where the American people are looking at how violence has played a role in the growth of America, and we want another way. We don't have to go through all this. When you see a child get killed, it does something to you. I've seen that during the riots. Police shot a kid in the back. Killed him. You don't want to see that anymore. It's terrible.

Beecher Terrace is a traditional housing project. It's been here since 1941. If you go back far enough, Beecher Terrace was a neighborhood of high expectations by the residents. The people who grew up here went on to higher academic, professional, and social achievements and involvement in neighborhood and city affairs. It wasn't that easy to get into Beecher Terrace because the quality of housing throughout the area was not very good, and Beecher Terrace was a shining light in terms of decent, affordable housing. So getting in there as a resident was more political. And therefore, they had a more professional and social-ly-connected resident population. As time went on and

To my good friend Manfred! Congrats on a great new development! Thanks for your help & leadership! Best Wish, Jerry 8-2-07

Breaking ground on the new development replacing
the Sheppard Square Housing Project, August 2007

About ten years after I moved to Beecher, the Housing Authority made it known that they wanted a Beecher Terrace resident to be a commissioner, and the residents recommended me. I was appointed Commissioner in 1999. It was the greatest uplift I'd had in twenty years, an opportunity to rebuild my character and reputation. It keeps my spirit up and keeps me going forward.

My years in real estate led me to consider various principles of fair housing in terms of encouraging homeownership in the West End. I was a young real estate broker when we began to see everything from Sixth Street to 13th Street being destroyed during Urban Renewal. At that time, all of the property that was being destroyed was not owned by Black people. The government came with eminent domain and paid the white owners huge amounts of money. It was the tenants who were running the businesses who were harmed. When you began to put the dots together, you saw the elimination of the initiative for growth, which is business.

The Russell neighborhood consists of four thousand housing units, almost all of them over one hundred years old. We're living in hundred-year-old houses that were built to last no longer than fifty years. So you've got to replace the homes. You go from city to city, and what you see is the existing housing stock going back a hundred and fifty years being sold to a lower economic group or minorities, and the sellers have the capital to go buy a house in the suburbs and a new car at the same time. But the low-income families bought the house, and they've got to carry this mortgage now. It's peculiar in the sense that you've got a portion of the population in Russell that do have homeownership, but the quality and value of the housing is poor because there were no economic initiatives in the neighborhood to actually impact poverty.

there was growth and expansion in the economy, a lot of those people moved out and became homeowners. That probably led to the changing status of the resident population, in addition to changes to HUD policies regarding who was eligible to live there. Initially, only married couples were eligible to live in Beecher Terrace, but they changed that requirement later.

Beecher Terrace played this role as a stepping stone to homeownership more efficiently at that time. Now it's more like people move in, and they're pretty much here until they die. People become stuck here because they don't have incomes that allow them to buy a house. So you end up with two generations living in public housing at the same time. We need to change that back to it being an opportunity for people to get a start in life.

Blacks have bought homes in the West End, but it didn't really bring success.

In the last twenty years, we have replaced four of the five major public housing complexes with new developments, and this was supposed to have been an economic opportunity there. But even with all of those dollars expended and a growing economy, poverty is up because there was no improvement in the economic conditions within those neighborhoods where the investments were made.

Housing is more economics than anything. The Beecher Terrace redevelopment project provides decent, affordable housing, but the economic gain from it is void. Homeownership gives you equity. That's wealth. Home construction gives you compensation. That's wealth. Land development gives you wealth. We residents don't get to participate in any of these methods of generating wealth.

The elimination of shop classes and vocational programs from schools has cost us two generations of skilled workers, such as masons, carpenters, and electricians. They're all gone. You can't have economic growth in a neighborhood or a community unless those skills are part of the living environment. And when they re-enhanced these skills through the technical colleges, minorities were not inclusive in that population due to racism. For example, sometime in the 1970s, when new technology came up to insulate homes, Louisville Technical College had a program to teach that. Ahrens High School is where the technical college first got started. I went up there and tried to get into that program to re-train myself so I could rejoin the workforce, but they wouldn't let me in the program. All of this has left us devoid of that skill in our neighborhoods. We need to develop the initiative through government to encourage students to take up these work skills as means to achieve even higher education.

The initiative has to come from the neighborhoods. Growth does not start somewhere in a high-rise building. Growth starts within the neighborhood, from the initiative of the people to create a better life, to build houses for themselves, learn from that, then build housing for others. That's achievable within a generation or two, but you've got to make those investments.

This investment in the new Beecher Terrace is over eighty million dollars. Louisville Metro Housing Authority is an agency of the city designated by HUD to carry out its programs. I serve at the pleasure of the mayor, who really runs public housing as determined by HUD. When residents are told certain things—relating to the health and safety of our children or financial matters affecting housing security, for example—and they prove to be untrue, they lose faith and they begin to attack the Housing Authority. Well, there are times when I have to relate to that. You have to call it what it is.

One of the problems we've had over the years is the changing administrations. Every administration would use public housing as a means to show that they are doing something new. Everybody's nice, they listen, and they agree. But you don't get any action to initiate changes or to continue an existing program that's working. It's frustrating to residents when they work like the devil to organize people based on what they were told, but when they come back for the resources, there's nothing there. Eventually, the residents get tired of being conned.

I can't come out here and tell them that it's something that it's not. I have to be honest with them. If it's something that the city government said, or directed by HUD, or policy changed by the administration and the Housing Authority, I have to call it what it is and say, *No, that's not what happened. Here's what happened.*

The issue that we've got to face now is the elimination of poverty. We're in this first phase of transition. The economic planning for this community should include economic incentives to replace homes and training residents to benefit from the skills that come out of that. And that's what we look forward to.

When the city tore down the original Beecher Terrace, the relocation of all residents was paid for by the Housing Authority, and they were compensated for their inconvenience, so all of that went very well. Relocation of the residents included disbursements of residents throughout the county. There were a sufficient number of people that moved into other areas of the neighborhoods, and they requested to stay where they were. They liked suburban life, so they wanted to maintain the new residence that they had obtained. There were a large portion of us that traditionally were part of the neighborhood and wanted to maintain our residency here. The new Beecher Terrace is a step up.

My apartment in the original Beecher Terrace was a place where people gathered for conversations, discussions, and planning the future of Beecher Terrace and how to get other residents involved. People congregated there for years. They're just so many people that had a basic anchor here. We depended on one another. We supported one another. I don't believe I would be alive if I didn't have that camaraderie with them over the years.

Individuals who have a reputation and character in the community in terms of being involved would stop by my place. Rev. Ellis, Rev. Snardon, Henry Owens, Rev. Walter Cosby: these people are part of the community itself. We talked about history. American politics was of great interest. Four or five people came at a time, though it used to be more. But there was and still is a fundamental spirit in the neighborhood that doesn't die. It may get weakened, or it may fall off

in participants, but it's still there, and it's always been there. In spite of the reputation, there are a lot of good people here. I've been here for over thirty years, and I've never had any trouble with anybody.

After thirty-two years, I was the last person to move out of Beecher Terrace before they tore it down. I wanted to show my determination. I wanted to be an example and stick around so people had somebody to talk to during the transition. I've been the chairman of Metro Housing for twenty years. I really believe that leadership is important, and the residents depend on people like myself to be there for them in times like this. They should be able to come to somebody, walk in the door, sit down, have some coffee, and talk. And that happened all the time. A lot of information the administration told them was just not clear to them. People would go to a meeting about the redevelopment of Beecher Terrace and wonder, *What's gonna happen to me? Where am I going?* They picked up their apprehension at the meeting. But they'd come to me and others for an explanation to eliminate that apprehension. So they came to me and we talked. It's a lot of trust. It's just a sense of making a person feel comfortable in that plight.

When you're relocated, your whole life is disrupted. I was informed by the administrator that managed the relocations that I would probably have to get rid of my books. I had a fully-developed library which I treasured. Every place I moved, I carried my library with me. I'm a history buff, and there were certain books I wouldn't get rid of, like *Two Centuries of Black Louisville* and *The Kentucky African American Encyclopedia*. I had a law library that was hard to let go. This was not just part of American jurisprudence; it was a full library. All the sets and volumes that were part of my life for a long time. That's how I learned to use the law as a way of understanding what was happening to me during a time of crisis in my life, a

Manfred G. Reid Sr. receiving the 2016 Dorothy Richardson Award for Resident Leadership from NeighborWorks America, flanked by his grandson Manfred G. Reid III and his son Manfred G. Reid Jr.

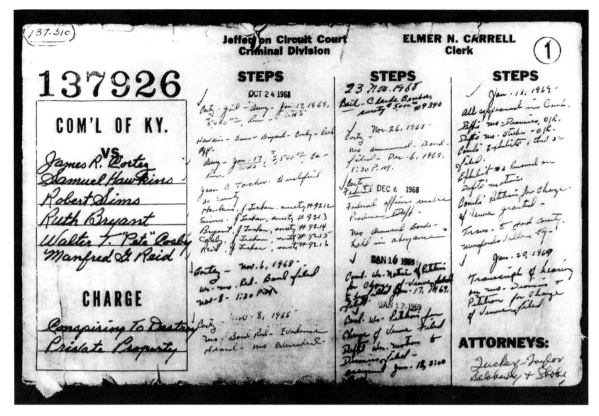

Court document outlining the indictment of The Black Six

time that cost me my marriage, loss of my business, my real estate broker's license, and loss of my reputation. It reduced me to homelessness and destitution.

The initial reason I started developing my law library was to study legal actions and conspiracy charges brought against me and five others in the wake of the 1968 riots. I had to devote a lot of time to finding records and requesting documentation from the government via the Freedom of Information Act. I didn't have anybody to provide any counseling. I didn't have anyone to help me learn law. I was always trying to improve my library by looking for books I needed. I used to go to flea markets, auctions, the Salvation Army, and the Goodwill store. That was a part of my

life for a long time. It was my law school, and it was a rewarding education. I ran into concepts and cases that encouraged me to go further and try to understand what American law is all about.

I got into the *Federalist Papers* and foundational writings of Jefferson, Madison, and Hamilton. When you read this material, you begin to see that both the slave master and the slave were uncomfortable with the system that they had to live with. You had men that dreamed of what society should be and then converted that into the ideology and philosophy of American democracy. I began to understand the basis of the laws that govern us today. You've got to work toward change. You get in the fight and change it. That's the character of America. I took notes. All my notes stayed on my desk. I could always go through my notes.

They brought me over to see my new apartment before they got it completed. I liked the ceilings. I liked the spaciousness. It's a one-bedroom apartment, but it's pretty spacious. I love it. It is in proximity to the downtown. All of my business is down here, so I really don't see the need to go anywhere. It's a modern one-bedroom apartment, which is all I need as a single person. I have my office there and do my work there. It's just as convenient as if I owned a five-hundred-thousand-dollar condominium right downtown.

Since the transition has gotten into this particular phase of this development, I do see people beginning to congregate more and communicate more. Resident councils are beginning to organize. I'm on the fringes of that because, as chairman of the Housing Authority, I can't get involved in that. I ran the resident council as president for about ten years, but now I can't do that because of a conflict of interest, though I do work with them and their relationship with the agency. We have another company that's the developer of the new Beecher Terrace and has the management responsibilities, so I work with them.

My place is still a meeting place for everybody. It hasn't changed. My new apartment is still an open-door kind of place. Making time and space for reception of guests is part of my basic milieu. Most of my meetings now are on Zoom. We make sure that we are able to congregate, so I still have people coming. I do appreciate the fact that at my age I don't have to go out as much. This open-door policy is my preferred way of living and socializing. It's a way to ensure that social ties will not be weakened or diminished because of the transition. My relationship with the residents is very, very good, but I work, read, and study all the time. The environment here is very good.

So when you look at the development of Beecher Terrace over the seventy years of its existence, it has played a great role in the growth and the development of residents in this neighborhood. It's taken quite a bit of time for us to get where we are today, but it's played a great role in the social development of the neighborhood. ✦

I Expect Better. I Expect Different. I Expect Change.

LAMIKA JORDAN

From birth to about six years old, we lived on Austin Avenue off Dixie Highway. My mother, father, and my three sisters. I'm second to the oldest. That little street instilled a sense of community. Everybody took care of everybody. It was nice. I don't remember being afraid of anything. Outside all hours of the day playing, making mud pies with my mother's 45s, or teaching myself how to ride a bike. My father was a welder by trade. I don't remember my mother working. Mostly she was a housewife, taking care of the house and the kids. What they went through as a married couple was none of my business. As far as we were concerned, it was a good life.

Some time after they got divorced, my mother got a three-bedroom on 38th Street right off of Von Spiegel, which was nice because my daddy lived right around the corner. I still had access to both parents even though they weren't together. My dad was fortunate enough to have a really decent girlfriend. It was just like having a second mother. She did everything for us, and he was a good dad. We never felt like we disappointed him. He never ever made us feel less than. He was always supportive. He was always asking, "What do you need?" One time I broke the TV in our bedroom. I didn't tell my momma, and when she found out, she put me on punishment for a whole summer. When my mom told him, he went out and bought two TVs and two Atari sets that same day. He told my mom, "Get her off punishment." He was a good father. Real good.

When I was about twelve years old, my mother married my stepfather and we moved to Germany. I lived there until I was eighteen, so basically, that's where I grew up. My mother, my stepfather, and us four girls left for Germany and moved into an apartment minutes away from the military base on the outskirts of

Lamika in Germany

Askern Manor

Schweinfurt, Germany

Schweinfurt. We lived in a place called Unter Terrasse, and I thought it was the best living ever. It was so picturesque. Reminded me of Bardstown, Kentucky. You'd walk up these cobblestone roads and there were vines of grapes hanging down. Everything was so fresh and organic: big sweet potatoes, yams, mustard greens. It's picked today, killed today, and you're eating it today. Wurzburg just looked just like a picture, but it was so real! You ever want to see a really white Christmas? Germany's where you want to be.

Later we got an apartment in military housing in a place called Askren Manor, and that's where we lived for the rest of the time. If you lived on the German economy, the military paid your rent. Whereas if you lived on post, there is no rent. You don't pay for anything. It's kind of like the Section 8 program. If you really want to know the truth, military housing looked just like the projects. It's not a whole lot different, other than the strict living; you just can't be dirty. They find out you're keeping a dirty house? You're in trouble. There is a consequence to everything you do. The military came to inspect the house at least once a year. And when I say inspect, I mean they come in and the place has to be *clean*. Everything has to be in its home. Nothing can be broken. That's why you find people in the military are a little more strict about things like, "My shoes go right here. Fold your clothes this way." So you got to make sure everything is clean, everything is tucked, everything is how it's supposed to be.

The first three years there I was homesick. *I want to go home. I want my daddy!* The next three years, I was like, *We can't stay? There's nothing we can do to stay?* If you ever have a chance, get out of Louisville and experience life. Because when you grow up in the projects, everything's so hard. It's hard to get, hard to do, hard to keep: just hard. We were fortunate and we know that we were fortunate.

Lamika in Germany

In America, everybody's in a rush. Over in Europe, things are more relaxed. They take lunch breaks and come back a couple hours later. The city just shuts down, hardly any stores open, hardly anybody on the streets. I had a good time in those days.

My first experience going out with my friends to go clubbing, I got caught. I told my mother I was babysitting at a friend's house, then went to the NCO club on base. I wasn't old enough to be there, but I got in anyway and saw my friends. "Hey! We gonna dance!" Techno was big over there at the time. I had on one of those spandex dresses with the sides cut out and I just knew I was too cute. Soon as I made my way to the dance floor, it was tunnel vision and the first person I saw was my mom. I thought, *Well, I'm in here now.* And I walked up to her, "Hey, Mom! I'm in here."

She's like, "How did you get in here?" So I had to sit down at the table where she and my stepfather were sitting. Everybody's dancing, drinking, and having a good time. I'm just sitting there watching my momma go up to dance. If people asked me to dance she was like, "No, she can't dance. She ain't supposed to be in here." I ended up meeting a friend of mine for the first time who would later become my brother-in-law. He asked me to dance. My mother was like, "Well, she's already here. Let her dance. Let her have fun." A month later he and my sister met and he ended up marrying her.

I dropped out of school in the second semester of the eleventh grade when I got pregnant. When I was sixteen I had a daughter named Asia. Her father was a G.I., but because we weren't in a relationship, there

Lamika and Asia in Germany

Asia as a baby in Germany, 1990

was no child support order enforced. He did what he wanted to do when he wanted to do it, and if he didn't want to, then he just didn't. I wasn't willing to stay in a relationship like that.

Everything changed when I went from just having to worry about myself or my siblings to actually worrying about a child of mine. I didn't have anybody to watch her, and I didn't have money to pay for anything. I couldn't afford formula. So, I had to compensate by putting my daughter on German milk. What we would call Pet Milk.

I loved school, so it was devastating to me when I couldn't finish. I never imagined not being able to finish school and not graduating with all of my friends. They all went to prom and all of that kind of stuff, and I was busy being a parent. And I was not mentally ready for it. I thought that I was grown and could handle it, but I wouldn't wish that on any kid.

My daughter's father was about to finish his tour in Germany. My mother was like, "Well, he's not gonna leave me high and dry with a kid." So, she came up with this idea to give him custody of my daughter. Since I was a minor and still a military dependent, my name's not even on any of the paperwork; it's just my mother and my stepfather, and Asia's father. We had an agreement that he was only supposed to have her for a year. I was supposed to get her back when I turned eighteen. He was supposed to return her to me in September of '92, but he didn't. I found out that he'd been kicked out of the service for being an alcoholic, and that he and Asia had come back to the U.S.

She was there, and then she wasn't. It was very painful. It was like somebody dying. It was a nightmare. We didn't reconnect until she was eighteen. She didn't understand the truth of what happened. The only thing she knew was that her father raised her and that I wasn't in her life. It was hard.

I came back to the States in 1992 when I was eighteen. Initially, I lived in Fort Bragg with my sister and her husband. I stayed in South Carolina for a year and was making $4.25 at McDonald's. I thought, *How in the hell do I survive on this wage?* My sister helped out tremendously. In August of '94, I came back to Louisville and I found out that I was pregnant with my son. What my family did for each other was to say, *You goin' to school? I got your kids. You going to work? I got your kids.* So I always had support. I could work as many hours as I wanted to.

My son John Thomas was born in 1995. I named him after my daddy. He was only the second boy in my family and we were crazy about him. I got an apartment in Cotter Homes in July of '96. That was my very first place of my own. We moved to Beecher Terrace for the first time in '97. Then I had Mekhi in '99 and DeeDee in 2001.

At that time I was struggling mentally and financially, not knowing how to manage money. Try managing $262 for a month. You're buying diapers, clothes, shoes, and everything else. Try having enough for recreational expenses. During those years, I was going through something. I didn't know it was called depression. I didn't know what depression was. For me, it was fear and feeling defeated, confused, and scared. All of it grew until it felt like I couldn't breathe. I felt like I couldn't trust the people around me. It was weird. I was drinking a lot. I spent quite a bit of time under the influence because that's the way I was taught that you handle stuff. *Just drink you a beer, get you a blunt, you be alright.* But stuff never was alright again. When you sober up, those problems are still there. And sometimes they get worse because you don't handle them. So what do you do?

One day I just left my apartment. My kids and I were technically homeless for a while. We had places

From left: DeeDee, Edna Mae, Cousin D'maya, Stevie Lynn

Makai

John Thomas

Steve with Edna Mae

Lamika and Edna Mae

to stay, but I didn't have my own place. We lived with DeeDee's daddy for a little while in Park Hill. He was hustling and these kids came to his house to rob him one day, and that was all it took for me. I was out of there.

I moved into my own apartment in Clarksdale where I met my future husband Steve. That was about twenty years ago. We've come a long way through the struggles, and have seen the benefit of the struggle. He was the one who initially brought it to my awareness that what I was doing was harming not only myself but also my kids. He made me seek out help. I learned about depression, having a chemical imbalance, and things that you can do to help it. I hadn't realized I suffered from depression. I just knew I wasn't feeling right.

So I checked myself into the hospital at University of Louisville. They had an NA meeting one day, and I told my story and everything. They were selling "The Big Book," but the guy who ran the meeting gave me mine. He was like, "You need this." I used to read it to Steve out loud just so I could have somebody going through it with me. You have to form a relationship with God, then you can work through it. But you have to be honest and you have to trust. This was really important. It's possible I wouldn't even be here today without N.A., so I'm thankful. I'm very thankful.

Sometimes when you want to seek help for yourself people will say, "Oh, you think you better than everybody." I got a lot of pushback—even from family members—and it was kind of hurtful. My brother-in-law used to say, "'Mika, you were so much fun when we used to drink." I'm like, "Was I really? Was I so much fun?" Because I don't remember it being fun. It didn't work for me. The best thing is to just leave it alone. It takes a lot of self-awareness and acceptance. I know I'm not perfect, but I don't want that life.

Steve and I met out on the sidewalk in front of my apartment in Clarksdale. He walked through without a shirt on, and he had a nipple ring. I saw him and he wasn't paying attention. I was like, "Hey. How're you doing?" I was in my late twenties, and he was in his forties, but his skin was way tighter, and he looked younger than he was. I would not have even thought that the girl who lived across the walk from us was his daughter. He looked like an uncle or older brother.

We started out as just friends. He'd give me rides when I was taking some computer classes at Wesley House. Sometimes he'd ask me to go riding with him, and we would just ride and talk. Eventually, it just turned into something. I thought he was interesting. I would see him spending time with his grandson. They would be out there playing football, basketball, and wrestling.

At the time, I wanted to find somebody to settle down with, but I didn't know how. Just seeing Steve interact with kids, I thought, *Okay, well, he's good with kids.* And he's always been good with my kids.

John was eight when Steve and I met. They didn't get along at first. Now they the best of friends, and Steve couldn't be more proud. He showed him how to make his own money washing cars, cutting grass, doing anything legitimate to make some decent money without doing anything illegal. Steve helped set that foundation and John Thomas is a success story. He can't do no wrong in my eyes. Steve's motivation is his kids. I've always been a family-oriented person too. I knew I wanted a family and I wanted my kids to have a father. That was important to me because my daddy was important to me. I'm one hundred percent an advocate for daddies.

I love my daddy to death. I was born on his birthday. You can't beat that. My daddy was nearly always there. We moved back to Beecher in 2004 to be close to my father when he had cancer. He died in October 2004. He was only fifty-four. He's been gone seventeen years, but he's still there. I can't walk in the grass without hearing Daddy say, "Get off the grass and walk on the sidewalk." There's still all those little things. Me and a friend of mine went to Cherokee Park and just the smell of the water brought back memories of going fishing with my daddy. We would get guppies and tadpoles and take them home, try to put them in the fishbowl, and see how long they'd live before you had to flush them. I had forgotten the way that lake smelled. It was comforting. So many good memories. Real good memories. He was a good father. Me and my husband were there to the last. Steve carried him into the house the day he died, got him settled in his favorite chair, and that was it. I'm glad I was there. You'd rather be there than think, *What could I have done?* I knew he

Lamika and her sister, Bookie, in Southwick

Homegoing Services for

Mr. John "Harlan" Jordan

1950 - 2004

Saturday, October 23, 2004
2:00 P.M.

G. C. Williams Funeral Home Chapel
1935 West Broadway Street
Louisville, Kentucky

Rev. John T. Porter
Officiating

Lamika's father, John Jordan

COURTESY OF LAMIKA JORDAN

From left: Rodney, Lamika and Stevie Lynn, Makai, Edna Mae

was going. It was just a matter of time. And so when he did pass, the grief wasn't so bad.

Everything has its ups and downs, but there was always a sense in Beecher Terrace that you didn't have to feel alone, because you're not up here by yourself. There's people in the struggle with you. If you ever were just talking to somebody and you asked, "Well, which project would you rather live in?" out of all of them—Southwick, Park Hill, Iroquois—Beecher always had the best reputation. And for the negatives that come with it, there were far more positives. It definitely felt like a step up at that time. Beecher had an atmosphere where you took care of everybody. If I cooked dinner and you didn't have a lot of food, then it was nothing for me to make sure that you got a plate. If somebody's kids needed food, clothes, shoes, whatever, you was receiving, or you were giving. Somehow or another, we would work it out to where everybody got what they needed.

There was always somebody around. There were two ladies named Irene, we called them "The Irenes," who were like surrogate mothers to many of us. They were the people that helped lift you up, helped you with raising kids, in your relationships, or finding resources, they were the people that you could go to to get information.

That was a great feeling to know that sense of community, to know that somebody had your back. If you knew that Mrs. Such-and-Such was always home, she would be the one you would give your key to or send your kids over. "If I'm not home, y'all go over to Such-and-Such's house." Back in the day, that was what you did. If I saw a kid and I knew their parent wasn't home, I'd be like, "Come over here till your parent gets home." Or I'd come over and say, "Is my kid over here?" Yes, your kid was over there, and they were safe, had been fed, watched some TV, and probably got their hair done.

When we moved to Beecher, Steve started fixing up bikes for the neighborhood kids. One kid needed a tire changed, an inner tube or a kickstand put on, somebody needed their handlebars tightened, and the next thing you know, he was collecting bike parts, taking a frame apart, adding tires, and putting another bike together. Just parts in every single place. Everywhere you look, you got a compressor, you got screwdrivers, kickstands, and bike chains, most of it in the living room. It was just like living in an auto body shop or something. It was a nightmare! We weren't supposed to have that kind of setup in front of our house. Bike parts for days out there. And he used to get onto people's nerves, but the neighborhood kids would just start coming, "Mr. Steve! Can you fix my bike?" He never charged the kids. The thing that you loved about him was the fact that he was doing it primarily for the kids, or if somebody needed to get to work and they needed a bike, he'd loan you a bike.

There were good times back then, but there were some real challenges too. Just living in the projects is hard in and of itself. Once you're in the system, it's a catch-22. You're damned if you do, you're damned if you don't. Trying to better yourself is not easy. You go to work, you try to get on your feet, then your rent gets raised sky high. There have been times when we had no food in the house, absolutely nothing. The kids ate

Lamika and Steve

Lamika and Edna Mae

Private John Thomas with his daughter Brooklyn

COURTESY OF LAMIKA JORDAN

every day, but we didn't have any food in the house. That does something to your psyche when you can't feed your kids. I was working as assistant manager at Family Dollar from 2:00 to 10:00 p.m. with no lunch break. Only thing I could do was run outside every few hours to puff a cigarette. To think that I'm making fourteen dollars an hour, working fifty-five hours a week, and we didn't have any food? This is the stuff people have to think about. It messes with your way of thinking as far as how to be a more productive citizen, have a better job, and live in a better community.

Back when John Thomas was younger, I wanted to provide a better situation for him. He was always getting whooped on by older boys when he'd walk up to the store because he had good hair and tucked his shirt into his pants. He never wore saggy jeans. We just don't do that. He was cute. He was a class clown. So he was different. I just couldn't see my son growing up in the projects. I just couldn't see it. My ultimate fear was seeing my son on the corner selling dope. I mean, when I looked out my kitchen or bedroom window, all I saw was groups of guys and hot girls selling dope. That's all you saw. So a child grows up thinking that is cool. If they don't have a lot of support, sometimes it's where they end up. What can I do to prevent this? What can I do to ensure that my son knows better? Not just hearing about people living better, I need you to *know* better. It's not easy. It's not. It's so much harder now to try to teach your child to stand up for themselves, but at the same time, what is it gonna cost them?

My sister went to Louisiana and later to San Antonio, Texas. So between fifth grade to graduation, my son would periodically go back and forth to live with my sister and her kids. He left when he was ten, and that was right at the moment. He was comfortable there. He's gone on to do great things. He has a family in Texas and is in the Army now.

Steve

I'm trying to make sure my daughters respect themselves and others. That's the main thing. Stevie Lynn is fifteen. Edna Mae will be sixteen in November. When there's drama, Steve has taught them to get away. If people are doing something you know is not right, you need to get away, you need to remove yourself from this situation. If that means you got to come home, they know that. Be cautious and aware of what's going on, and know when to remove yourself.

They're good kids. Edna Mae is very, very talented. She cooks, makes bread and homemade butter. It's so good! She makes her own versions of different things that I cook that she wants to tweak, like chicken pot pie, where she'll put peas in it. She'll add something that makes it her way of doing it. If there's something she's interested in, she'll put all her focus into it.

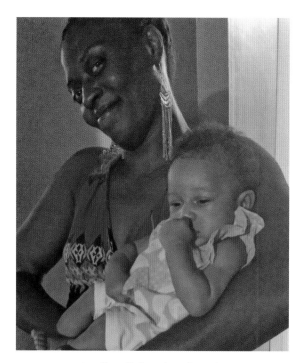

Lamika with her niece, Augusta

Asia

If she gets into it, she's all in. She'll research and figure it out. And then Stevie Lynn just gets to reap the benefits. Because whatever Edna Mae learns, she'll try to share. Edna Mae started learning how to braid on YouTube. It's just something for her to pass time, but she'll save about a hundred and sixty dollars a month by doing it herself. Stevie Lynn is the sweetest kid. She loves giving hugs all day long. She's pretty emotional, and a fighter. She's an advocate and won't tolerate being mistreated. She's an independent thinker.

The way those two girls talk to each other all day long, it's like they haven't seen each other in ten years. They never run out of things to talk about. They talk all of the time. *You all were just at school together all day. That much happened in a day?* They talk a lot.

I have to let them be kids, but I have to educate them too. If they're educated, then that's their armor. The only thing that I can do is educate them and pray that they will make the best decisions. They know that, *If I do this, these are the consequences. Period.* The main thing is to respect yourselves, and respect others, but don't allow people to disrespect you. You have to say, "You don't get to do that. You can't treat me like that." Or vice versa.

We moved out of Beecher when they started the redevelopment at the end of 2019 and moved back in April of 2021. And I was glad to move back.

I like living in Beecher Terrace. When I got here I was just so excited to be back in an environment where I know what is going on. The sense of community means something, and that's why I came back. They said it was supposed to be mixed incomes up here in the new Beecher. But how do you get over that project mentality? Because it can't be both. There's this whole feeling that it doesn't matter that you tore the buildings down, this is still the projects. When you say, "I'm up in Beecher," people say, "Oh y'all up in the projects?"

Why are we bringing back that stigma of "Beecher where they eat'cha"? What's the purpose of coming back with that mentality? So I can still keep doing the same things I was doing before they tore it down? If you don't want better, then why?

Sometimes people say I'm bougie-ghetto: that's someone who lives in the projects who thinks they're better than everybody just because they're not doing the same things as everybody else. Could be just because you read a lot. I'm not better than anybody and I'm not bougie-ghetto. I'm a regular old person with pretty much the same aspirations as the next person. I've had my own triumphs and troubles. I'm not trying to put on airs about anything, but I am honest. Don't ask me if you don't really want to know. People will say, "This is Beecher. It's the projects. What do you expect?"

I expect better. I expect different. I expect change. I do.

I asked my kids how they feel when they hear someone say, "They live in the projects." And to them, they were just blind to it. They don't get it. They haven't gone without decent clothes or shoes and stuff like that. Their idea of somebody living in the projects is someone who is struggling with a dirty house, or they don't have food, or their parents are addicts or stuff like that. But my kids think they've had the best. When I tell them, "We could've had better," they're like, "Well yeah, we could've, but for what it's worth…" And that makes me feel good, even if it's hard when your kids know there are better environments where they could live.

But as far as them feeling safe and knowing where they are, they're totally comfortable walking to Family Dollar, or just hanging out at Baxter Park, and moving back up here with some of the people that lived here before who they knew well. It's still familiar, and at first, I was happy about the location. It's not the worst it could ever be, but it could still stand to be better.

There's some people that are against each other and some kids have been fighting. I just wish that part of the atmosphere would be different. I was looking forward to that sense of community like we used to have when a village raised the child. The only thing I've ever really wanted was to be someplace where we're just at peace and safe. ◆

100 Pipers

DONNIE BURTON

There was an ice house called Arctic Ice at 19th and Walnut with a lot behind it for the trucks to come in to pick up the ice. That was our playground. We played basketball, football, and baseball, all in that same little lot. Until televisions really got popular, we'd just listen to the radio. The radio station I liked to listen to was WINN. It was a local station that played pop music. Then WAKY started to play The Platters, Chuck Berry, and all the rest of the rock and rollers at that time. We'd get up, dance, and just party in the house, and by nine or ten o'clock, everybody's in the bed.

I grew up at 19th and Madison Street. We went to Third Christian Church on 16th and Chestnut every Sunday. There was a Holiness church called Beulah Temple across the street from my house at 19th and Madison. They had guitars, drummers, horns, and everything, and man, they used to *rock*. They'd be praising the Lord, and we'd be outside patting our feet.

The whole neighborhood was one great big happy family with about thirty children. There were the Crawfords, the Stevensons, and the Saunders. We had to give all the parents the utmost respect. There was no talking back. Whatever they said you do, you did it. It was a hood that you were proud of. We didn't have anything, but we had each other.

Boy, we had a ball. That's all we did was have fun, because there wasn't much else that you could do. We would go to dances, skate up and down the street, and ride bicycles—we didn't have new ones, but we'd put on a front wheel and a back wheel and take off. One time they made a play street between 18th and 19th on Madison. They put little humps across the street and had a little circle at each end for the children to skate or ride their bicycles or do whatever they wanted to do in that area. If cars wanted to come through, we'd charge them a nickel. Then it was, *Hey, let's go to the candy store.*

Everything was in walking distance because nobody had a car. We could go over to Sheppard Park Pool in the summertime and swim. They had lifeguards and a diving board, all that. We had what they called "the chain," where everybody would hold hands and run around the pool. We'd start jumping in at three feet, five feet, six feet, and if you were on the end of the chain and couldn't swim, you were in trouble because you were gonna end up in eight feet of water. That was summertime fun.

The businesses on Walnut Street at that time, from Fifth Street all the way down to 28th Street, were primarily Black-owned businesses. They had a club between 12th and 13th on Walnut called the Top Hat. Anybody that came to Louisville, that's the first place they wanted to go. Big-name people, Cab Calloway and all them, used to perform there. There never will be another Top Hat. The Little Palace hamburger stand was across the alley from the Top Hat. The Lyric and the Grand were two theaters across the street from each other. They had all the good movies that were coming out at the time. Right next door to the Little Palace hamburger stand was another theater called the Palace Theatre. We could do a lot in this neighborhood at that time.

Then Urban Renewal tore it all down. It was heartbreaking to see it just disappear. They got rid of the Sheppard Park pool and the theaters. Urban Renewal was nothing because it didn't bring back nothing. It didn't progress anything. When you come down Walnut Street—now it's called Muhammad Ali Boulevard—you see what replaced Urban Renewal: nothing.

My older brother was a musician. His name was William Burton, but he later changed his name to Rahn Burton when he joined the Muslim faith. He was a very good piano player. My sister taught him how to play when they were kids. He played jazz.

Donnie working at Seagram's

He played with Roland Kirk, who played three or four horns at once. Kirk was totally blind, but he had ways of getting around. Friends or band members would take him anywhere he wanted to go. Rahn played with Roland for about ten years. They toured everywhere, even overseas.

One time back in the 1960s, Rahn and Roland Kirk came to the house to practice. At that time, I was working at Seagram's Distillery out on Seventh Street. We had some barrel whiskey from Seagram's around the house—perk of the job. If a barrel of something was leaking, we would find some kind of way to catch that leak. It wasn't what you may call thievery; it was just trying to keep the liquor from building up on the floor. So, we had our little container, then when it leaked into the container, we would take it home. It was much different from the liquor you got in the bottle that was proofed with distilled water. What came out of that barrel was straight liquor, so you can imagine the kick it had.

So we was sitting in there with Rahn and Roland. My brother was playing the piano, and Roland had out his horns, and they was sipping on that barrel whiskey. Man, they got to whoopin' and hollerin', laughing and joking. I could tell they was intoxicated. That barrel whiskey kicked their butt. That was one of the fun times. Old Roland Kirk, he was something else.

One Saturday morning in the early 1960s, me and my friend Leon Britt were sitting out at 12th Street watching guys shoot dice. I ain't gonna never forget it. He said, "We sitting here out with these mother-fuckers. They shooting dice and shit. Let's just form our own club." And I said, "Well, okay, Leon." At that particular time, we were hanging at a place called Jesse's at 18th and Magazine. When we got off work, all the guys from the neighborhood would sit there, drink beer, laugh, joke, and tell lies. Leon and I got some more guys together and said, "Hey, we was talking about forming our own club."

We decided we was going to name our club the 100 Pipers Club. The name 100 Pipers came from a bottle of scotch out there at Seagram's, where I worked. We all drank 100 Pipers scotch at the time. We started meeting at each other's houses. Then we started meeting in Samuel Terrance's little apartment on the corner of the alley that ran behind 18th and Magazine. We paid our little dues and got started. We used to have what they called quarter parties. At a quarter party, you get a little card for a dollar, and each corner on that card is worth a quarter. You buy what you want for a quarter and then tear out the edge of that card. You could buy beer, sandwiches, everything.

We built up our funds, then said, "We going to try and see if we can get our own building." It was about twenty-five of us at that time. There used to be a club at 1940 Walnut St. that was real popular, but they moved because the building was about ready to fall down. This

The original members of the 100 Pipers Club

guy who lived next door to me owned that building, and we asked him if we could purchase it. That's how we got into the bar business.

The bar was in there, but we had to do all the rest of the work: floors, carpet, and everything. This one member Chuck was a carpenter, you might say. He did all the work, but we all helped. When we got off of work, that's where we'd go, and we'd remodel the interior till it got dark. One day we decided we were gonna paint it white, and when we got through, we had more paint on us than we did on the building. But we got it done.

There was a guy named Ruel Stephens who was older than most of the rest of us. He had owned clubs around the city, and he got us to think about getting a lawyer and getting it set up as a private club. Bobby Haddad was the lawyer who dealt with the paperwork to get a private club liquor license.

We partied every day over at the club. Everybody was just dancing, partying, cussing, and having a good time. People would come through because it was on Walnut Street, which was the main drag at that time, and they'd see all the cars parked out there. They'd stop to see what was going on, come inside, sit down, drink beer, and party with us. A lot of the time, that's how we'd get new members. They'd see what was going on and want to be part of it. At the time, dues were only ten dollars a month. I'd leave there at one or two o'clock in the morning and have to be at work at seven o'clock. I had one eye open at work.

One night, I had been at the club partying. When I got home, I said, *I'm just gonna heat up this pot of chitlins, take a bite, and then go to sleep.* I put the pot on the stove, then sat down to watch television and fell asleep. I set that whole pot of chitlins on fire. My next door neighbor, Flora, came over and said, "Hey, Donnie! Wake up, motherfucker. Man, you going try to set the house on fire!" Man, that house was full of smoke. I quit drinking for a long while, then. I didn't drink at the club. I'd just sit up in there and act a fool.

Donnie at the original 100 Pipers Club

On a typical day, when I left work, the first place I'd stop at would be the club. We'd sit there till we got tired, around about eight or nine o'clock. Then we'd go home. I'd eat dinner when I got home. This retired guy named Henry Johnson—we called him Skinny—would open the club up for us. He'd stay there until the last person left, and we didn't have to worry about hardly anything. He did that because that's what he wanted to do. He was just about one of the best persons you would ever want to meet. He liked it. At ten o'clock in the morning, he'd be there. The earliest member who would come in would be the mailman, Ruben Rucker. He'd stop by when he got through his route, and him and Skinny would sit down there and talk. Ruben would drink some beer. Skinny would drink liquor. Sometimes Skinny would stay there all night long. He would go upstairs and sleep on the couch. He didn't have anything else to do, per se, so he said, "Well, I'll just make this my home away from home." It was great.

Each member had a turn to work the bar. When your turn came to work the bar, if you wanted to drink a beer, you could drink a beer, there wasn't no problem. But if you weren't working at the club, then beer cost around about twenty cents a bottle. That went back to the club.

The jukebox didn't cost nothing but a quarter. Back then, if you put fifty to seventy-five cents in there, you could play music half a day. Then in the late 1970s or 1980s, when LPs were still pretty popular, I got a little set together and I would play music. That knocked out the jukebox a little. They used to call me Disco Don. People would dance so much there'd be sweat pouring off of them. We had one carpeted side where the bar was, and the other side had the jukebox, tables, and tile floors where a lot of people would dance.

We all had families with young children then. We would throw egg hunts every Easter in the graveyard at 15th and Jefferson. Each member or his girlfriend or wife would dye two dozen eggs, so you had fifty dozen eggs or better. We'd bring the kids to the club and let them stay there eating potato chips and drinking pop while we'd go hide the eggs. After we got all the eggs hid, we would come back to the club and tell them, "Come on, y'all. Let's go." And we'd spend half a day over there. There might still be some eggs over there to this day. Some of the graves were caving in, but we didn't have no kids fall in. They got what they could, and we'd give five dollars to the ones who found the most eggs. It was an annual tradition until the kids got older, then it kind of died off.

For Thanksgiving, we used to get boxes of turkeys and have all the members and their friends bring canned goods to the club. A club member who worked at Dann C. Byck School would get us a list of names of people who might be in need of a Thanksgiving dinner. We would box up the turkeys, canned goods, macaroni and cheese, dressing, and cranberry sauce. We had a couple of trucks and would go around the neighborhood, knock on doors, give it to them, and say, "Happy Thanksgiving." We'd deliver anywhere between twenty-five and thirty, maybe more. If people didn't want it, we would scratch them off the list and give it to

somebody else—people that come to the club, mainly. Wasn't nobody rich at that time. To this day, still ain't rich. It was just to help.

The club had a little baseball team. We'd go out there and play ball, and after we got through, we'd come back to the club and drink beer, win or lose. We played everywhere. We played over at Victory Park. We went to Bloomfield, Kentucky. We used to go up to Massillon, Ohio. I was still playing ball in my forties. I mainly played left field, but I played any position that nobody showed up to play. I would pitch. I would catch. I played third base. I just like to play ball. We'd play other clubs and bars. One team we played was Jabali's. I don't know where their club was, but they said it was up in the East End. And we used to play up there in the East End, and down at 34th and Southern.

The new crew at 100 Pipers. From left: Smokey, Vivian, Mary, Maurice, Donnie, Nita, and Doc. Not pictured: Candice.

Some of the most active members of the 100 Pipers Club today. Back row from left: Nita, Ocky and her boyfriend, Maurice, Tonya. Front row: Boobie, Mary, and Vivian.

A bunch of guys used to hang over at 28th Street Park, and we'd play them, too. We had a game going on three times a week after work and sometimes on Saturdays. We were pretty good, but there were a lot of teams that were better than we were.

We were like a big family because there were no problems. If you worked, you worked. If you didn't, you didn't. You still was fine as long as you had your heart and your mind together. Most of the members were from the neighborhood. The whole time we were over there on Walnut, we had fun. I mean, *fun*. We had a little barbecue pit next door to the club, and we'd give out food. Just a neighborhood thing.

Then in 1976 or 1978, the city sent out letters saying they were thinking about renovating the neighborhood and giving us a heads-up on what was coming. I didn't like the agreement they offered, so I didn't go anywhere. I stayed right there. It wasn't until years later that they started telling us we had to move. There was a club across the street from us called the Green Turtle, and they also had to move. We had just put a roof on the building. For the negotiation with the city, I had to get an attorney, and it came up fairly good. We came to an agreement that was decent for me. I would rather have stayed there because it was the main drag where all the traffic comes through, but it is what it is.

The city bought the old club in 1998. They tore down the addition we had built and left the original one-hundred-year-old building and made an apartment out of it. If you ride past it now, it's boarded up. They said the people who moved in there heard water running, people talking, and ghosts. They couldn't stand that because wasn't nobody in there but them. At least, that is what they say.

We took the money we got from the city for the sale of the building and purchased a new building at 2801 Chestnut St. This club had been vacant for about five years. It had shag carpet all over the walls. It was terrible. They used to call it Club Shag. Roscoe Tobin and I took two years to fix it up. Roscoe could do anything: plumbing, woodwork, welding—you name it, he could do it. He built the bar and did all the ceiling work. Roscoe did practically all of it except for the electrical. We had another guy do the electricity. Roscoe did three-fourths of the plumbing, but we had to have a licensed plumber put in the vents in order to pass the city inspection.

We opened the doors at the new location in 2000. People came in because they still remembered it from up on Walnut Street. During the time Roscoe and I was down there doing the remodeling, they were going elsewhere. But they always said, "When are y'all gonna open up down there?" And as soon as we told them we was open, here they came. And they ain't left yet.

Most of the customers came from the other club, the ones that was still living. Everybody in this neighborhood knows somebody, and when they brought their friends, they would come back and stay. The sign on the door says "private," but it don't take much for us to welcome you.

We don't have as many people as we did back then. The club started dwindling because we were getting older and people were passing on. Hell, I'm eighty, and all the younger people close to my age have passed on or just don't come out anymore. Things have changed.

When we first started out, it was tons of clubs. I can't even count how many. Now, most of them are gone. Costs went up, and they couldn't afford to keep going. Being in a club, there's no profit. None. Every dollar you make, LG&E wants some, and Louisville Water Company wants some. I have a beer man coming today, and he wants his piece. You gotta sell a whole lot of beer and liquor to pay a five or six hundred dollar light and gas bill. If you don't own your building,

you gotta pay rent too, and you're not gonna make it. There's a whole lot of difference when you own your own property. If I didn't own this, I wouldn't be here right now.

Over the last twenty years, we've been doing pretty good down here on 28th and Chestnut. We don't stay here all day long anymore. We get here at four o'clock and leave around twelve o'clock at night. On the weekend, we might stay till one or two o'clock. It all depends upon who's all out, the participants in the club.

The club is for everybody to have a place to come to, enjoy themselves, and go home. This is not my club. This belongs to all the people that come here. All that's different is that it's in my name.

Roscoe (right) with friends

I've always been a person that was easy to get along with. I say to everybody that might come through here, "Hey, you're alright. You're a nice person." I don't have no grudges, and that's the way I've been for fifty years in this business. Sometimes you might have to tell a person, "Look, you need to go home and come back tomorrow." But you always stay as pleasant as you can possibly be.

Everybody that comes through the club is special to me. And I mean *special*. We watch basketball games and football games. We sit around, laugh, joke, and tell lies. Tuesdays, we have movie night. They'll bring up hot dogs or hamburgers. We got a lot of stuff that we do around here. It's nothing extraordinary, just something to do to pass the time. You'd be surprised how fast time passes when you're just joking and being yourself. Nobody's trying to be nobody other than who they actually are. You just walk in, sit down, and be yourself. They call it Cheers: where everybody knows your name.

Before the pandemic, we'd have a free food day every September. We called it the Pig Roast. It was like a neighborhood picnic. We'd have grills in the backyard of the club and give out meals to anyone who came by. We barbecued chicken, hamburgers, and hot dogs, and made potato salad, deviled eggs, the whole deal. We had juices for the kids. We'd start at seven in the morning. We'd cook it all at the club. There were a lot of guys who did the cooking: Roscoe, Norvell "Papa" Easton, Jeff Warner, and Caswell Deberry. It was our way of giving back, just something for the neighborhood. People would be lined up all around the building. We'd feed two or three hundred people. The people really enjoyed it.

What the club means to me is I'm helping somebody else. You'd be surprised what people will tell you that they don't tell nobody else. It means a lot to me. I'm around the people. They come to me, and I enjoy every day I can be here. Most of the people that come through here, members and non-members, tell me they enjoy it.

Fun is what it's all about. Until COVID hit, we used to have dances every year, primarily around Valentine's Day. We'd go out there on Millers Lane, where they converted some of the old Philip Morris warehouses into dance halls. We'd have dances down at the Catholic Enrichment Center at St. Martin De Porres at 32nd and Broadway. We used to take a cruise on the *Belle of Louisville* every year on Father's Day.

Then not long before the pandemic, Roscoe died. I really miss him. I don't know if anybody else could have done what he did to the club. It ain't nothing like it was when we first came in here. Roscoe ain't never really left because every day, his name pops up. Everybody loved him. He was the bartender here most of the time. I can't describe him. He was just that type of person. The whole club misses him. Roscoe was comical at times, but he would cuss you out if you did something.

While the bar was closed due to COVID, my cell phone was how we kept in touch. If I hadn't seen you for a while, *bam*, I called you. "Hey, what's up? How you doing?" I'd have a short conversation just to make sure that you alright. "Catch you later." Click.

I had a brother-in-law die from COVID. He got it and didn't live three weeks. I got COVID in the fall of 2020. It was terrible. I got a continuous cough that was just aggravating more than anything else. My lady friend and my niece said, "You need to go to the doctor." So I went to Norton's out there off of Poplar Level Road. They gave me a chest X-ray, and the doctor said, "Your lungs have all these little black spots in them. That's COVID." They said, "You going upstairs." Nobody could see me but the nurses and the doctors. I stayed in there for a whole week.

When the lady came in saying, "Mr. Burton, get your clothes on, you going home," I wasn't really feeling all that good, but I was ready to get out of there. My girlfriend and my nephew came and got me. They had an oxygen machine I had to put on my nose, and I slept in it for about two weeks. I also had the portable tanks that you can carry on your shoulder. It was pretty tough.

I've always believed that if you keep the faith, you can get through a whole lot of stuff. I don't mean you have to get down on your knees and pray and slobber and stuff like that. Just keep the faith. Just believe there is a higher being. You will get through this.

I never thought that I would live to be eighty years old and still running a bar and being around people almost 24/7. It never even entered my mind. I just take things day to day. I wake up and just keep going through the same old ritual. When I go to sleep, I'm me. When I wake up, I'm me. I ain't never been no more than me. ✦

◇◇◇◇◇◇◇

Donnie Burton passed away in November 2022 after he completed this chapter. He was beloved by many, and he will be greatly missed.

Hope Grown and Hope Harvested

STEVEN EDWARDS

For my forty-first birthday I said, "I want to buy a piece of land," so I went and started looking. I found a piece of property that was $3,000, took money out of my mutual fund and bought a vacant lot at 513 South 26th St. It had been abandoned for as long as I can remember. When I was a kid, it was on my granddaddy's paper route which covered Madison and Muhammad Ali. When I bought it, there was nothing but a little shack and a lot of tall grass we had to take down with a weed eater. There were three empty lots next to one another. I purchased the first lot from another individual and bought the other two from the city later on.

When I first got the property and was thinking of building a community garden, I was there talking to one of my friends when a guy stopped by and said, "Oh, you just bought this? You gonna build some apartments or something like that?" But we don't need any more houses. We need communities. Everybody's plan is just to build a whole lot of houses, but they don't build an economic structure. They don't build anyplace where we can heal, where people can come together as a community. When there's just a lot of houses, your neighborhood is just a hood, not a neighborhood, because you don't even know your neighbors. At Hope Garden, I'm trying to create an atmosphere where people get to meet their neighbors.

I didn't know anything about planting or harvesting when I started. I bought a tiller and figured I'd learn how to garden because I want my kids to be healthier and to understand the importance of food, that food is our medicine. I'm not a big vegetable eater, but I'm working on it. It's new to me. I have my good days and my bad days. So I mowed my lot and tilled up the land. I went to a garden center and got some cabbages, greens, squash, and tomatoes and just planted them. I had no idea what I was doing. It always seemed like I looked stuff up on YouTube a week after I really needed to know the information. *If I'd have done this in April, I wouldn't be having this problem right now.* Thank God for YouTube.

My broccoli never did turn out right because I didn't know anything. My cabbage got eaten up by butterfly larvae. But my greens, tomatoes, and peppers were beautiful. Unfortunately, the people in the community didn't know how to harvest greens either. They were completely cutting down the whole stalk instead of cutting off leaves and allowing it to grow back. So it was a learning process for everybody. You know, everybody learns a little bit more that first year.

I teach gardening classes now. We learn about how to garden, the difference between fruits and vegetables, different soil acidities, and how that affects what you're growing. I don't have the capacity to do a garden to feed everybody, and my goal isn't to have a lot of people working in the garden. It's more to bring awareness to gardens, because I prefer for you to keep a garden in *your* backyard. I give you the resources to create your own garden at your own spot. We do seedling giveaways to encourage people to start their own gardens in their backyards. The first year I gave out like 250 seedlings. My goal is to fence the garden in but to keep grow beds on the outside if somebody needs something.

When I started out, before I knew that I was going to turn it into what it is now, I just wanted to garden because I thought it could help me through some stuff. It was me healing *me.* Helping me deal with the depression and anxiety that goes with life, with grief, with separation, trying to figure out where I fit in this world. I found that gardening relaxes and frees your mind and gives you a time to be by yourself but not *feel* by yourself. Everybody's biggest fear is being alone. When you're scared of the dark, what you're really scared of is being alone, right? The way you fix that

feeling is to have something else with you; at nighttime when your baby's scared, you give her a teddy bear and she doesn't feel alone. Gardening provides that too. You're still alone, but you can deal with these things that you need to deal with because you have something else there comforting you. You can work through your thoughts.

But there's the communal part too. You have somebody come up and say, "Hey, what are you planting?" and you have a conversation about planting tomatoes. They say, "I used to have fried green tomatoes over at my grandma's house all the time," and that conversation turns into this healing thing, because you're talking about something good, something natural. That little bitty interaction just triggered a happy memory and both of us feel satisfied because we just made a connection on something. That might be all that was said, it might be the whole conversation, but that helped heal everybody in that environment.

People in the community come up and talk to me all the time when I'm gardening. They've told me their stories, and the stories are amazing. They're humans. They've got real lives. They've got families. I've met people over there who are struggling with addiction who come from rich families. Their families have begged for them to come back, but they say, "No, this is my thing. This is my struggle. I'm working through it. I don't want nobody. I need to do this on my own." I'm like, *You live in a tent at night. In the back of somebody's shed. What happened? How did you get here? Man, you're smart. What happened?*

I've been a teacher and a mental health counselor for twelve years. I've never ever heard anybody say, "When I grow up, I want to be on drugs and not be able to take care of my family." I've never heard anybody say that. Society has let these people down at some point for whatever reasons. They're doing what they're doing

mostly because of trauma. I've listened to their stories. They're deep.

One day, I came over to the garden because a tree fell down on my property. I bought a little electric chainsaw, thinking I knew what I was gonna do with it like I was Paul Bunyan. When I got there, this guy was sitting in the shade right by the tree that had fallen. I came to him and said, "Hey, can I help you?" and he was like, "Well, after I get off work, I like to go and get me a drink and find a nice little shady area to read and drink a beer." I told him I was about to tear down his tree, and he says, "Do you mind if I help you?" He knew what he was doing and went at the tree. It turned into a big project. We ended up cutting down all the trees and removing a gate, and since then he's been a tremendous help.

As we talked that day, he told me he's ex-military, U.S. Ranger. And that's something we bonded over, because we're both veterans. I joined the Army in 1999 and did two years as a military police officer at Fort Knox and four years in the Army Reserves. When I enlisted, I wanted to get as far away from Louisville as possible, but I guess God wanted me here for a reason, and the Army is where I really learned what it means to do service for your community.

As I talked with the Ranger about our time in the service, I learned that he'd done twenty-five years in prison for murdering somebody. While he was in prison, he converted to Buddhism. He's an ordained Buddhist priest. He lives in the community and helps people out. He comes over and helps us in the garden. He has experienced so much in life—the all-the-way-ups and the all-the-way-downs—and what he's taken away from it is, "I took twenty-five years away from society while I was in prison and society paid for me to live. So I feel I owe at least twenty-five more years giving back."

He's still going through his troubles, and the troubles that you have as a felon. Talking to him, and getting to know who he is and what's going on with him, I've seen how we can sometimes let our mistakes define us, or forget who we really are instead of realizing how much we're capable of. He called me a couple days ago and said, "I'm an alcoholic," and I stopped him and said, "No, you're not an alcoholic. You're a Ranger and a Buddhist who happens to have an alcohol problem. We have to change how we define ourselves." There's a lot of people I've met who are in horrible situations. They're not bad people at all. Not at all. They were just in the wrong place at the wrong time.

The community around the garden reminds me a lot of Hemlock Street, where I grew up in the '80s and '90s during the crack era. I did paper routes all my life with my family. We were a paper route family, so we were up at four o'clock in the morning, and we saw what people were doing to get their money for the next high. I had an uncle who was my role model—everybody has that cool uncle—who I loved to death. He got addicted to crack. They flooded the West End and inner cities areas across the world with crack. He had a great job, he was doing everything right, but he got addicted. I saw him go from the top to the bottom. And then, even when he built himself back up, he never was what he used to be. At that time, it wasn't considered a sickness. Drug addiction didn't become a sickness until it became a white problem. But when it was a Black and brown problem, it was criminal. So I had to sit there and watch the community that I grew up in just go down.

The community around the garden reminded me a lot of the trauma I had seen growing up. I saw all the same stuff over by the garden: drugs, prostitution, a lot of pay-today-stay-today type houses. So I thought, *Be who you needed when you were younger.* This garden is

When I first got there, all day there were prostitutes jumping in cars. It's a high traffic street. Prostitution and drugs have been such a permanent part of the community that everybody has been numbed to seeing it. They just ride by. One of my friends was like, "Why would you build a garden here when they prostituting and all of this?" Well, the garden is something new and positive, and positive energy always trumps negative energy. What ended up happening is even better than I would have imagined. The prostitution and all that stuff has pretty much disappeared during the daytime when we're out at the garden. It's been a very positive thing.

We started thinking about the healing part of the garden, and somebody asked about doing yoga, so we started it right there. I cut the grass on the two lots next to mine so they could have enough room, and now we have tai chi over there every Wednesday. We do health fairs. We have people giving out Narcan for drug addictions. We have people doing blood pressure testing. We have Humana there updating people on some of the policies that can help. We have a free clothes table for people who just want clothes. We give away food at Thanksgiving. We have resource fairs and do the seedling giveaway. There's a lady named Deanna who works in HIV with the University of Kentucky, and she set up an HIV testing and needle exchange every Friday at the garden now. So not only have people had direct benefit from the gardening part of it, but also from the health services and mental health services. I have been in other organizations where we have a whole lot of meetings about what we want to do, then we come up with a thousand reasons why we can't start right now. I was so tired of that. I was like, *Let's just do it*, and it's just been a really beautiful thing.

In 2020, we were all working through a lot of current trauma of Breonna Taylor, and protesting, and COVID. All that was happening when I just happened

what I wish that people would have done for my neighborhood. And that is what it turned into. On B96.5 they used to always say, "If you can't change the people around you, *change the people around you.*" It always kind of made me think, *Who am I? What am I about?*

I like serving. That's what I like about me, that I serve. That's my "pay it forward," and it looks different than your pay it forward. When I see you doing something, I think, *Wow, how's he doing it?* But it's simple to you because it's just what you do. When people think Hope Garden is radical, it's because it's not how they would do it. For a long time there were people who could not get it. They'd be like, "I don't see why anybody would want to just buy a lot and start doing stuff for people. Why would you do this?" Well, why *wouldn't* I? This is the real question. This is my gift and my passion. It almost costs me more when I *don't* do it. I'm frustrated with the status quo.

to buy this plot of land. 2020 was rough. It really affected west Louisville in ways that I wouldn't have ever imagined. Not only were folks from Russell and Portland already financially strapped—they've *been* check to check—but a lot of them lost their jobs. They didn't have savings to fall back on. They didn't have relatives who could come help, because their family was in the same boat that they were in. Libraries were closed, so a lot of people who didn't have the internet or computers couldn't even apply for jobs.

You didn't have much at all to begin with, and now you don't really even know if you've got that. You didn't have enough money to feed your kids Monday through Friday, and now your kids are at home with you every day, all day. You're frustrated because you are trying to be a teacher and a parent. I had a parent tell me, "I didn't do good in school. How am I going to teach him?" All this on top of the fact that you're being told that your people are dying at a higher rate than anybody else from COVID. You're seeing these numbers go up. You keep hearing that people in your community are dying. But how do you know? You're in a house. You can't go anywhere.

Last year during the pandemic and the protests, we only had one major grocery store in the West End: Kroger on 28th Street. The next closest Kroger is in Portland. Everybody was buying all the food off the shelves. When they said they got looted, it was shut down for about a week. Where are we getting food? I have a car, so I could drive to another Kroger. What about people in the community who couldn't do that? People didn't feel secure that our food was even going to be there. After David McAtee got shot, there were days when Kroger was completely not open. The police put barricades around the whole parking lot. Taco Bell was shut down. There isn't a Burger King over there anymore. We just had the McDonald's, and you

From left: Steven, Kaniece, Stephanie, Steve, and Morgan in Las Vegas, 2021

Feeding the community at a resource fair, 2020

couldn't get into it because it was in that barricaded Kroger parking lot. So we couldn't even get the *bad* food. That's when Hope Garden turned into a food justice thing. People needed food.

Louisville has more Black urban farmers and homesteaders than there's been since my grandparents' days when everybody had a backyard garden, but there still aren't that many of us. We need more gardens to take care of our communities. I can think of a handful of people who have started gardens like Steve Lewis, Mike Jackson, LeTicia Marshall, and Mariel Gardener. Everybody has their own way of gardening, but all of it goes back to social empowerment: understanding the social implications and human rights that come with access to food and access to land. We communicate. Everybody gets in touch with each other and everybody knows something. We're pretty close knit but loosely affiliated.

What we all agree on is that everybody should have a right to provide nutritious food options for the community. But the city, for whatever reasons, has put up barriers. There are a lot of barriers to us being able to have access to and create a space to grow food. Mariel Gardner runs Fifth Element Farms in Parkland. She has a greenhouse on her property where she grows food to give away on her block. She just gives it away. She has other spots where she wants to do that exact same thing, but the people from zoning have told her, "No, you can't do it. Because if you buy a piece of land from the city, we want you to build a house." But they don't even live down here, and these lots already have abandoned houses on them. Let her do what she wants.

People mean different things when they say "urban agriculture." When I say urban agriculture, I think of creating greater self-sufficiency in impoverished communities. There are too many people trying to dictate what we do without giving us resources to do it. As an urban agricultural community, the biggest thing is to have more say on what happens to these vacant lots which have been vacant forever. Wouldn't it be great if you didn't need to have food stamps because your backyard is already set up for you to grow your own food?

There was a heightened sense of anxiety in 2020 in the West End. There were fireworks all summer long that went off until like midnight. We knew it had to be something else, because who's got money for that if they don't have money for rent? Every day we heard about somebody new getting shot. So there was a lot of anxiety. It was a heightened sense of, *I need to learn to protect myself.* People didn't feel comfortable with the police, the people who were supposed to be protecting them.

We had a lot more participation in our Wednesday tai chi as a result. DeAndre Dawson comes down and teaches it. He's a community activist and a martial artist who teaches self-defense with the Revolutionary Black Panther Party. He's really good at tai chi. While it is

Seedling giveaway, 2020

a martial art, we learn a lot about breath and breathing and going with the flow. There are other health benefits to tai chi. It's multifaceted. It allows you to really learn about yourself. We learn about our bodies. We talk about how to eat, when to eat what, and how to breathe. There's a breath for the winter and a breath for the summer. We do it out in the open on the lot. We do it so people will ask questions about the garden as they walk by.

I say that my first year at Hope Garden was my first year ever gardening, but it wasn't. I went to the Cabbage Patch Settlement House when I was a kid, and there was this amazing guy there named Roosevelt Chin. They named an alley after him over by the Cabbage Patch. I used to always hear about Mr. Chin

and all the cool things he did and I was like, *I need to go somewhere with Mr. Chin*. One day, they were loading the kids up to go to the Seed to Table program. I had never heard of it, but I jumped in the van, and next thing you know, I'm in a program where we're working on a couple of plots at a community garden. We grew our food, then after the harvest we made a big dinner out of it. At the time, it was just something to do. But then as you're growing older, you think about it and you say, *I can produce what I eat, in my backyard?* That changes how you budget food expenses.

I started at the Patch in middle school. My brother and my cousins went there too. We were just one big family, so what one kid did, all the kids did together. The Cabbage Patch was just a babysitter thing at first.

On a Cabbage Patch trip to the Current River in Missouri, 1996

My mom knew them, they could drop us off, pick us up at nine, and we were safe there. But as we were there, we started getting into different clubs. They could kind of pick out who needed what. Mr. Thompson and Ms. Shay would go and grab us and say, "Hey, you should join this program." We had a club called "adventuring" where we learned how to canoe and stuff like that. Most of the stuff I saw at the Patch are things that I wouldn't have ever seen just being in the West End. We didn't have the money to go out and see *The Phantom of the Opera*, but the Patch took us. Even though I didn't understand anything that was said in *The Phantom of the Opera*, I still remember going to see it. They took us and got us suits. We went to Kunz's and ate. It was a whole experience.

So many people who have never experienced stuff don't know how to work through the nervousness of getting started doing something new. I learned a lot of that from the Cabbage Patch. They showed me that when you teach somebody something new, it actually opens them up to want to know more new things. I've got two master's degrees. I know I wouldn't have gone to college without the Patch.

The garden was the place that reminded me of the lessons I learned when I was younger, the lessons I had forgotten. We were all taught to be mindful, but we forget that being mindful means listening, paying attention, being mindful of the next person. That's what true mindfulness is. Thinking about how everything that you do affects the bigger picture. Those were some

of the lessons that I was reminded of as I was gardening. I remembered them while I was outside weeding.

From a counselor's perspective, I always try to see how things translate back to us as humans, and how we interact. Every time I do something with the garden it teaches me so many other things in life. In my first year in the garden, I learned that you get in what you put in. I learned about patience. I learned about listening to nature. A plant's going to let you know when it got too much water. It's going to let you know when it doesn't have enough water. It's going to let you know when it's not feeling good. You have to take the time to be mindful of the plant, and you will learn a lot about what's going on.

This is an experiment over at the garden. Sometimes when I know that I'm talking to somebody who doesn't understand I say, "I'm an artist. This is a social art experiment." The summer of 2020 was beautiful. Especially with yoga and tai chi. It was all just tied in together. Most of the time while they are doing the class, I'll be weeding the garden or something. There's simplicity in just getting back to the basics, working with our hands: go weed the garden. It's a moment. Everything else is not important. What's important is that I get these weeds out. I know there's about a thousand emails; everybody wants something from me. Get out there and weed the garden. Just focus on that. You can yank weeds as hard as you want, and at the end of the day you feel better. It's a really nice experience. Gardening is simple. It doesn't matter what everybody else wants from me. This is what I'm focused on right now. This is what I'm doing. ✦

A Separate Flame
Western Branch Library

NATALIE WOODS
BRANCH MANAGER

Louisville's Western Branch Library was the first library in the nation to serve and be fully operated by African Americans. When the city began to establish a municipal library system, Albert Meyzeek led strident lobbying efforts for access to library resources denied to African Americans during the Jim Crow era. By the time the Louisville Free Public Library began constructing branches in 1905, Andrew Carnegie had donated money for nine buildings, including one to be run by and for the Black community. The Western Branch has been a fixture in the intellectual history of Russell and west Louisville.

When I was a kid, my family had a premonition about what I was going to be later in life. I always loved books—my parents bought me boatloads of them—and I would sit and read all the time. Everybody would tease and say, "She's gonna grow up to be a librarian." Well, I've been in the library system for over thirty years now. I started as a page at the Shawnee Library and then I worked myself up to be a part-time clerk. Eventually I got a full-time clerical position and was the order clerk for the entire system down at the main library in the basement. I did that for over twenty years. Harry Potter is still a sore word in my mouth; I ordered every single copy in the public library system, and there were never enough.

One day maybe ten years ago, the manager of my department said, "I'm gonna give you this project. We're in the process of digitizing some documents. Would you transcribe them when you have time?" She gave me this folder of the papers of Rev. Thomas Fountain Blue, the first African American in the U.S. to head a library, *this* library. Some of them were typed, but many of the pages were correspondences or pages from a tablet that were handwritten in this beautiful cursive. It took me a while to get the hang of reading his penmanship—*is that an S or a P?*—but as I sat there reading these pages, I realized this man was ahead of his time. He was writing about the same approaches to library services that we think about today: the processes for

Natalie Woods, Manager, Western Branch Library

circulating books, keeping tabs on the different types of books in circulation, collecting information for the patrons, and tracking that information. How many days should somebody be permitted to check out? He was so meticulous and detail-focused.

He wasn't a trained librarian when he was hired for the job. You can only imagine trying to start the first Black library in America and figuring out how to run it as smoothly as possible on your own. His vision for the Western Library was that it would be a center for the community. At that time, if you were Black you had no place to go. You couldn't even go to the library to read. That's why Western was created. If you look at some of the pictures, you see the kids dressed to the nines in hats and everything just clamoring for books on the table. The tables were packed with kids reading books. This was where everybody went. This was the community center. They had a stage set up in the meeting room for performances. You name it, it was here.

The Western Branch was so successful that Rev. Blue also instituted a library training program here.

Western Branch Library upon its completion, 1908

If you were Black, at that time you couldn't go to library school, so he created one here at the Western Branch and people from all over the South came to be trained in providing library services.

I don't know why I was chosen to transcribe Rev. Blue's papers, but I feel like things happen for a reason. God puts you in the right spot. I spent a lot of time with Rev. Blue's papers, and reading them rekindled my interest in going back to school. I said, *You know what? I wanna go to library school*. I got a master's in library science and eventually, I applied to be a branch manager at Western, and it's been the greatest blessing since I've been here.

I'm still working on Rev. Blue's papers, which are now housed in our archive in the basement. It's a wonderful archive housing the majority of Louisville's Black history in the library system. My aim for the African American Archives at Western Branch Library is to preserve the history in the archive before it crumbles on me, and make it available to the public. Everything in the archive is relevant to the community because it is our history. It's the city's history.

We have a document in the archive about the creation of the Ninth Street divide. It's called "The Negro Housing Problem in Louisville," and it was written in 1932 by a gentleman named Harland

Bartholomew who went around the United States writing plans instructing cities on how to institute redlining. It's not an easy read at all. It's a hard pill to swallow, and we're still dealing with the repercussions of that today. But it lets you know the mindset of that time. For years, that document has sat in our basement but has not been available online. It's online now. Anybody can read it.

When I went to interview for this job, I walked in with a report in my hand and told them my vision for Western: "This library needs to get back to its roots as a center for our community. That's what Rev. Blue's vision was for this branch. Our website says that Western Library is 'a separate flame,' but we haven't been separate from the rest of the library system for a while. What about the importance of Western's history? We used to have a block party but haven't had it for years and years. Maybe we need to bring that back. How come nobody's brought back the Cotter Cup, the storytelling competition that Rev. Blue set up in the early 1900s? What are we doing with the archive that's sitting down here?" I knew that it needed to get back to its roots and really be a community leader, to listen to the community and try to provide some things for them. We needed to do more diverse programming.

A lot of people get caught up in thinking about libraries as just a place for books, but in some ways, the library functions as a community center going all the way back to Western's roots. So if we're returning Western back to what it was, it needs to continue to be here for the community. Rev. Blue wanted to "provide services for the betterment of our people." And every single day that's what the library as a whole should be striving to do. I train my staff to pay attention. To listen to the community. I have a note on my computer that

Rev. Thomas Fountain Blue and Western Branch staff, 1908

says, "Programming with a Purpose." Any programming that I do here will have a purpose.

We put on public programs like the Russell Block Party and the Cotter Cup. We had over 750 people show up to the block party this year. We also held a series of events called the Visions of Beecher Terrace which we did at multiple phases of consideration, demolition, and new construction in Beecher Terrace. We had panel discussions with people who were directly involved in making the decisions, as well as current and former residents. They talked about their experiences and what they hoped to see in the redevelopment. It was important to me that we were removing the barriers to access information. We can put things up on websites and hand out pamphlets, but residents need a place where they can sit and actually talk to the people making those decisions. I wanted to make sure that if they had a question about anything, they could flat out ask it.

The very first panel we had Renee Murphy from WHAS 11 as our emcee. Lavel White, Sen. Gerald

Children's Room, Western Branch, ca. 1915

Neal, and Metro Housing's Lisa Osanka were on the panel. We had some current and former residents who took part in the panel. It was a very open, no-holds-barred kind of conversation about what they were actually doing with the buildings. I was happy to see that healthy dialogue where people could actually get their questions answered. And there was no sugar coating. Those were some of the most successful programs we have had.

But "programming with a purpose" is not always what you think it'll be. When I thought of programming for kids, I knew that the kids were not just statistics, little numbers that come in and use the computer.

What is it that they need? What are they lacking? The only way to really know was to spend time with them, to sit down and have conversations. But of course, kids will not readily open up to you if they don't know you. So I started things like game time. Kids really let down their guards if they can beat you in a game of Connect Four. They come for you cutthroat style, but they let down their guard and you can get in there and talk to them. They talk to you a bit more when they understand that you are really being sincere, that you're not just blowing smoke. I learn all about their grades in school, what girls they like, what teachers they don't like. I hear about their school days and they say things

Rev. Thomas Fountain Blue and Western Branch staff, ca. 1930

like, "Ms. Natalie, I'm having trouble with my writing."

When I got here, we reorganized our programming to make sure we could be beneficial not just to the kids, but to all patrons coming in. It's not just kids, it's also adults. An older lady called to make an appointment to come in for some help. She was struggling to keep up in a computer class. She was starting a new career path and needed to know this stuff for her job. I had my staff work with her doing one-on-one computer appointments. She was happy because she was getting help, but she said, "I'm just so frustrated with myself because I feel like I should already know these things. I'm too old to be doing this." I said, "No, no, baby. We're

never too old to learn. I've got you. The important thing to know is that you're not by yourself." She just burst into tears and cried so hard on my shoulder that it went straight through my jacket to my skin. She bawled and said, "You do not know how much this means to me. I've never had anybody to help me like this before." Moments like that remind me why we do what we do.

I used to think, *Wouldn't it be funny if I ended up at Western?* And now I'm walking in Rev. Blue's shoes. I'm in the exact same position that he was. He just paved the way for me, and I make sure he's honored daily. I'm making sure Western goes back to the roots of what he envisioned here. ✦

My Part in the Arrangement

MCDANIEL BLUITT

I was born in Jasper County, Texas, in a little town called Magnolia Springs. This is East Texas, like you're heading towards Louisiana. It was a very rural area: country town, farming, cattle, logging. We had several hundred acres with cattle and a dairy. We milked cows in the morning before we went to school and then again in the evenings. It didn't seem like hard work because that's the way we lived. We had Holstein cattle and Jersey cattle. Holstein don't give the high butterfat content, whereas with those Jersey cattle, half of each gallon is butterfat. You set it aside to make butter later. When you go to a sale, that's what they're going to be looking at. That's what you get paid for. So, it was really a good thing to have Jersey cattle in your dairy.

I was about seven when Dad sold some of our property in Magnolia Springs and decided to move to a little township near Houston. Barrett Station is a suburb of Crosby, Texas, and was mostly Blacks and Creoles. When we'd drive back the 120 miles to see about the cattle, we'd drive through areas reeking with oil wells pumping on the side of the road. Plenty of money floating around up there. There's a couple of townships you go through, and where you'd normally see a sign saying "Welcome to Saratoga" or "Welcome to Kountze," you'd see a sign that said, "Run, Nigger. Run. If you can't read, run anyhow."

One time we were driving back to Magnolia Springs and Dad turned off into Kountze. My brother and I looked at each other like, *I know he ain't gonna go through Kountze.* Dad said, "We're going through Kountze to get some lunch. I'm gonna go ahead inside. Y'all can just wait in the truck."

I was a little fellow, six or seven years old, and I had to use the bathroom. I headed to the building and went in the door I thought he went through. When I went into that diner, I didn't see Daddy in there, and one

McDaniel's father, Clifton Bluitt, in front of the Bluitt home, Barrett Station / Crosby, TX, ca. 1958

Clifton Bluitt with cattle in Magnolia Springs, TX

Harvey Bluitt's house in Magnolia Springs, TX

Emma Lee Bluitt, 1958

man got up and said, "Somebody better get this nigger out of here." By that time, this huge Black lady had come from behind the double doors in the back. She scooped me up with one arm, and while she was taking me out, she's apologizing, "I'm so sorry. We're so sorry."

The lady says, "You Clifton Bluitt's boy, aren't you?" She took me through the kitchen, all the way to the back, and all the Blacks were sitting there. I got back there and Dad said, "What are you doing in here, boy?"

I said, "Dad, I needed a bathroom."

He says, "You're not supposed to come in here. They don't care for Black people at all down here in Kountze."

There'd been countless lynchings right there in Kountze and Jasper. They've got a real gruesome history of treatment towards Black people. In the evenings by the courthouse, if there was some lynching to be done, people came out like they were going to see a football game. It was an attraction. As late as 1998, Jasper made

national news when a Black man, James Byrd Jr., was murdered by being dragged behind a pickup truck all through town, arms and legs fastened.

When you hear the stories it is one thing, but when you actually see it, you don't forget it: the ropes, the people standing, a man getting up and yelling out, "This is what happens to the niggers when they violate the law." I saw that with my own eyes when I was six or seven years old. At that age, you don't have the cognitive skills to understand something like that, but you know it isn't normal behavior. We hadn't seen that in our own community. You remember that. You take a snapshot of things. The document is written there. You don't forget it.

My dad had been in the military but wouldn't talk about it at all other than to say it was not a place for a Black man. He didn't encourage us to join the military. "Go to college. Take advantage of opportunities. The best you can do is be the best you can be." That's all we ever heard. My daddy wasn't really a religious person, but he stood firmly on religious principles. He believed that a family should go to church together. That's what families did. If you didn't go, you stood out in our little community. Everybody knew about it. The good part about it was we established strong camaraderie and family connections.

We had a pretty rich experience at True Vine Baptist Church in Barrett Station. Dad was the treasurer and Mom played the piano. My mom was a real people person and very bright. She went to college at fourteen years old at Texas College and got a certificate to become an elementary school teacher. She was a really beautiful woman, long red hair and freckles—her father was half white and half Indian—and she was a really artistic person. A real creative thinker. Very innovative. She painted, did sculpture, and could read music well. When she was younger, she'd played clubs as a pianist in Houston and elsewhere. She was also an accompanist for Sammy Davis when she was in college, and he'd come by the house sometimes for a visit. He'd play for us and dance and all of it.

My mama had an amazing record collection: The Mills Brothers, Nat King Cole, Mahalia Jackson, Sarah Vaughn. If you read the backs of those old album covers, they told a real storyline about the artists. You could almost get a picture of what it must have been like to live the life of a professional entertainer. We didn't get to travel, but the back covers of those records helped shape my dreams and where I wanted to go. That had an effect on how I pictured my future. What I should do and where I wanted to travel. Later in my life when I got a chance to see the world, I'd think, *That's the same thing I read about when I was a little boy.*

Music was natural for me. It's really all I wanted to do. When we went to church, the music was what I took with me when I walked away. There was plenty of music in the family. My musical education started right in the living room with Mom. I'd sit on the bench while she played, trying to learn to do what she was doing. I was probably about nine when I started playing, but I was picking it up before then. She never sat me down and told me, "This is middle C." She'd just say, "Start with the note you hear." My ear became really attuned to what I was hearing and playing. I took piano and trumpet lessons. I wanted to play trumpet like my brother. He was a fierce player.

When I got to high school in Barrett Station, the town mailman was the band director. Old Man Warner would come in, take off his mailbag and his cap, and do an hour and a half of band. When it was over, he'd put his bag and cap back on and go deliver the mail. Old Man Warner was pretty stale. He was not trained to be a teacher or a band leader, and his playing was not the sound we were growing up with.

1968

McDaniel and a classmate, 1966

Then they hired a guy named John Roberts, and it was a breath of fresh air for us. He was this smooth, sharp Black guy that played French horn with the Houston Symphony. When he wasn't doing the orchestra, he had a band called John Roberts and the Hurricanes. He was the band leader and trumpeter.

High School Graduation, 1967

They were something. He had the best musicians from around the country, and they traveled around the Gulf Coast from El Paso all the way down to Brownsville, Texas, all the way to Opelousas, Louisiana. You could hear him on the radio and see him on TV, and it was very exciting for us as kids. He would come in wearing these tailor-made sharkskin suits, and we were all mightily impressed by his demeanor and his presence.

He'd come to school on a helicopter some mornings. I'm serious. He'd fly in from San Antonio and get dropped off on the practice football field. We'd hear that helicopter and say, "John Roberts is here." When he'd get off the helicopter, he'd be dragging. He'd have his dark shades on and his trumpet under his arm, and the principal would be out there saying, "You're late, man. You're late." John would be wearing

a suit and shoes that cost more than the principal's wardrobe. John would take the shades off and say, "I'll do better next time." We coined that. "John said he's gonna do better next time." He'd burst out laughing. The principal fired John after the second year. He couldn't take it no more.

What John taught me was to play with guys that love what they're doing, like you do. That went a long way. I could already write a little bit, and I'd model our selections after whatever John was doing at the time. I did the same instrumentation he had because I liked the sound. My band was called The Continentals, and we did pretty good. We did all the proms and carnation balls in all the little towns around there. I graduated high school in 1967 and went immediately to college at Texas Southern which was only about twenty-five miles from where we lived in Houston.

In the spring of '69, I ended up going to North Texas State University for one semester and then I headed up to Interlochen, Michigan, for the summer. My trumpet teacher from Texas Southern was a good friend of mine. He said, "Why don't you go up to Interlochen?" It was a rich boys' music camp in Michigan, though my folks were not rich. I think there were maybe two African Americans in the entire camp out of about eight hundred kids. That's the summer I met Leon Rapier. He was the principal trumpeter in the Louisville Orchestra. I took lessons from him that summer.

When we left Interlochen, a few of us rode to Louisville in Mr. Rapier's station wagon along with his fifty trumpets. I'm not exaggerating: he had about fifty trumpets in there. I was to fly out of Louisville and back to Texas so I could go back to school. It seemed like all of Leon's connections were with the top echelon in Louisville. He was good church buddies with the President of UofL. Rapier said to him, "I've got a student who wants to come to the University of Louisville. I'd like to have him study with me. Can you work something out?" They worked out quite a package, and I didn't have to pay to come to UofL. University Louisville was still private, which meant very few minorities were there.

I started in the fall of 1970 at UofL and was studying with Leon Rapier. I loved that man. He became a real go-to guy for me. What made him a great teacher was that he was a friend. His enthusiasm and mastery were contagious. He taught me that you can't control the audience, but you can control the art. And he taught me how to treat playing the trumpet like an art form. But, I left UofL before the spring semester ended because of an opportunity that I couldn't pass up.

I was in touch with my friends from Houston. One of them had heard about a big audition down in New Orleans. Ernie Wheelwright, a running back who played with the New Orleans Saints, had a nightclub and was calling for bands to come audition for this two-week expenses-paid trip to the Montreal Expo. They were looking for raw talent to play a showcase and also back up other artists who didn't have a band. I went back down to Houston and reunited with The Continentals, and we rehearsed for this audition. We went down, and we won. I was twenty years old.

We got to Montreal, and it was fire, man. Musicians everywhere. Players coming from as far south as New Orleans and Florida. Guys coming from New York. I recognized a lot of names because of the songs that they'd produced.

We stayed at the McGill Conservatory, and they'd pick us up and take us to the Expo. The Continentals played a showcase and then we also backed up other artists. Somebody would come up and give you the charts or you'd go do your own charts. Sometimes they'd just tell you the key. We'd say, "Gimme the first

Mc DANIELS BLUITT

Danny is a Music Education major with a minor concentration in math. He enjoys checkers, chess, and the practice he does with his trumpet as hobbies.

After obtaining his goal seeking a doctorate degree in music, Danny plans to teach private lessons to aspirant pupils of music who specialize in mastering the trumpet. Al-

From the TSU student newspaper, ca. 1969

eight bars, man." They'd play "My Girl" on guitar and we'd say, "We got it. We got it." We had some very, very good ears. We'd learn five or six songs real quick.

We backed up five or six cats at the Expo. We backed up Joe Cocker. He said, "I'm a white man, but nobody knows it because I sound as Black as the Blackest man here." And he did. He opened that mouth and had that raspy sound. Very unique. Everyone was screaming. Old boy could sing. One of the girls we backed up was Sue Raney out of Atlanta. We'd heard about her but we'd never played behind her. It wasn't hard to play behind her because she had charts.

We were some of the hottest young cats up there at the time. Montreal is when we got connected to Motown by backing up Edwin Starr. That was the first time we met. He was still riding the waves of "25 Miles from Home" which was the last big hit he had. We'd been doing that number since it was on the radio years before, and Starr was really impressed with what we could do. He liked it and we backed him up at the Expo. Starr was very talented. When it was time for him to execute the higher notes, he didn't have a problem finding that upper register.

There's a guy there who dressed you before you went on stage. You didn't go on stage representing Motown unless Harvey Fuqua gave you your uniform and made sure you looked right. Everybody had to go through Harvey. Didn't matter if you were Marvin Gaye or the Temptations. Now when Starr came out, he was still doing that old "25 Miles from Home," but that was also the first time he played "War." Starr needed a band to tour and get "War" out there. In those days you didn't have all the technology we have now, so if you had a new recording out, and it was hot, you had to go on tour to sell the song. Edwin Starr says, "Take my card. See you in Detroit." We didn't have but two days to get there.

We did one week in Detroit and played at the Felt Lounge. In the evenings, we'd rehearse with Starr. He would come over and teach us eight or ten songs. We knew most of them and just changed the key on some. He had a good voice. He didn't strain to get to his notes; he was there. We went on tour with him, and that was really a high point for us. We were just kids traveling around, playing to big crowds of people, and the money was good. That was really a great time.

The launch for "War" was at the Cobo Arena in Detroit. Edwin Starr was the opening act for The Motown Revue, the top vocalists and ensemble players on the Motown label who all toured together as one big R&B musical revue. The whole show was backed up by Motown Sounds, a touring orchestra led by a guy named Bohannon who was the bandleader and director.

The whole entourage of Motown acts was there, man. Nobody missed it. The emcee would tap dance out between songs and call the next act. "And now we're gonna have…" Marvin Gaye, Martha and the Vandellas, The Supremes, The Four Tops, Stevie Wonder, The Chi-Lites, The Spinners, The Delfonics; you name it, they were all there. All the most famous Motown artists performing with a big-band grid of twenty-six musicians lighting the place up behind them from the very beginning. Something like that makes a big difference. People see and hear that and think, *We're going somewhere tonight. This is gonna be good.* And Edwin Starr was the opening act for all of it, with my band The Continentals backing him. Starr had changed our name to the Houston Outlaws. He said, "You need something that has some geography." I said, "Well, Houston has a lot of outlaws. That's what we'll call it." And that's how we ended up being the Houston Outlaws.

We did fourteen nights opening for the Motown Revue in arenas, coliseums, and huge auditoriums all the way from Syracuse, New York, down the Eastern Seaboard to Jacksonville, Florida. One-nighters are a lot of wear and tear on the body and the brain, but we were so young we didn't know the difference, and each band member was making around $250 a night. The tour ended in Houston at the Coliseum.

My parents came out to the show at the Coliseum. I said, "I can't believe Dad's coming to hear me commit the cardinal sin." Not that he would ever say anything like that. After the show Dad said, "That's a pretty fast lane out there, Danny. Pretty fast lane. Get back in school as soon as you can. If you need some help, just call me." Dad never would judge you, but I knew what he stood for and what I was doing certainly didn't reflect that.

My mom had played clubs with Sammy Davis and some other guys of that era when she was younger, and she talked about how great some of them were. She understood the nightlife and would tell me, "If you spend your time with people who are upward thinkers, they'll rub off on you. On the other hand, if you stay in the nightlife, some people don't recover from the nightlife. It's fast-paced and you don't last very long. I don't want you to be out there with people who are not looking forward and who don't have ambition. She asked me in Houston, "Are you staying healthy?" I said, "I think so, Mama."

When we left Jacksonville, Bohannon, Motown Sounds, and The Funk Brothers—all the rhythm guys—went back to Detroit. Gene Keys was Stevie Wonder's arranger, and he called the musicians union to send guys to fill in for Motown Sounds. A lot of them were older guys, and the chops just weren't there anymore. The music wasn't right. You're used to hearing guys like Maurice Cook, Louis Smith—fire blazing across the back of the stage—and all of a sudden, there's some guys up there that are just missing notes, punking around, laughing at each other, taking a little sip.

Stevie Wonder says, "Gene, you gotta do something, baby. The music ain't right. Your brass section is hurting me, man. I can't sing with this here going on." Stevie didn't want to do the rest of the shows. And if Stevie ain't happy, ain't none of them happy. Berry Gordy called and said, "Stevie ain't happy, Gene. You gotta do something."

Clifton Bluitt Jr. and McDaniel with unknown children, ca. 1974

Family gathering in Magnolia Springs, TX

Gene called some of his friends from Detroit to come back down and called some players he knew from Atlanta. I was one of the few in my group that could really read the charts, and I played two nights with Stevie. They told me I could stay with them, but I said, "Man, I can't keep up with you guys." Those guys open

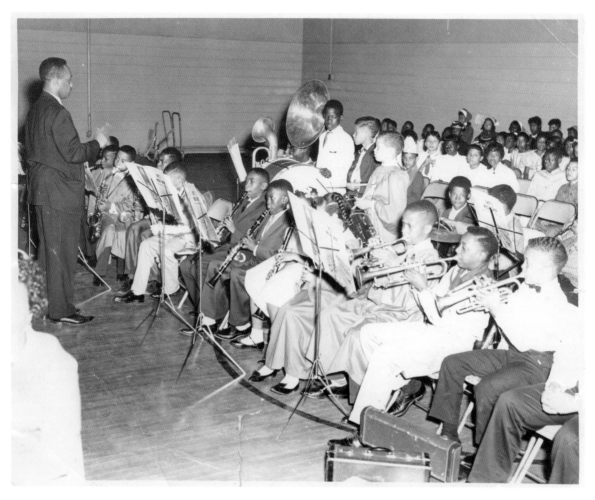

McDaniel, third from right, front row, led by Mr. Warner in junior high band, ca. 1962

up in high G and don't even flinch. I didn't think I had enough. I hadn't graduated yet—not that college will make you play any better—but I didn't think I had the experience to keep up. They separated the butter from the cream, as they say.

We toured with Edwin Starr on and off for about two and a half years. That was an eye-opening experience for me. "War" sold three million copies in just the first few months. Motown didn't have anything like that. *Marvin Gaye* didn't have anything out that

could do that. I had been plucked out of a country town in East Texas, and all of a sudden I was playing huge arenas with the biggest talent in the world. The real movers and shakers of soul music and R&B in America. I was just picked to do it. I guess God has a way of making our dreams come true.

I had what I'd call an inner conflict between what I was taught when as a kid and what you see when you get a little farther away from the walls of a church and its disciplines. I had a little boy's prayer once; the type of little secret prayers you pray, and you and God have a real clear vision. It's interesting how we make contracts; you give something, and then the other person gives something. I said to the Lord, "This gives me great joy. Playing music is all I've ever wanted to do." I said, "You know, Lord, I'm not really living right like the good book says out here on the road, but I didn't make myself like this. This is something I've gotta do. I don't know why I'm like this. I don't even know why I think this way. But it's in me. And I've gotta live out what's inside me. You made me." I said, "Tell you what, let's make a deal. You watch over my soul while I'm gone and let me live out what's in me. I'll give you the rest of my time when I come back."

God said, "You do what you got to do, and when you get through, I want you to come back in and help kids do what they do." I knew I was coming back. I had to come back. That was my part in the arrangement. It was kind of a winding road.

I was back in Montreal one night in 1973. Edwin Starr was opening up at the La Coque D'or. I was feeling withdrawn from the environment. My joy wasn't there anymore. And I got where I just didn't want to address that environment anymore. The joy of doing it was all of a sudden disappearing. I had a harmonica and was playing "Swing Low, Sweet Chariot," which gave me a lot of release inside. I want to say I had an epiphany. Somebody said, "We goin' to church tomorrow, Bluitt. Get ready." Some of them would go to church on Sundays when we were out on the road. We were brought up in church. If it's Sunday morning, you go to church.

I said, "No, I'm not going to church. We're not going to end up doing anything different than we did last night. We'll do the same thing we've been doing all along." We were running around with girls, living a life outside of what we'd been taught in church growing up.

The Houston Outlaws with Edwin Starr
on the "War" tour, 1970

How you gonna go to church? I said, "I don't think God wants us to be playing with Him like that." I felt strongly that God had given me a chance to do what I asked him to let me do. I mulled it over for a few days, and eventually told the guys, "I wish you well, man, but I've got something else I gotta do." I got up and said, "I'm going back to Louisville. I'm going on back to school."

I called Leon Rapier on the phone, it was about two o'clock in the morning, and I said, "Mr. Rapier, this is McDaniel."

"Hey, Dan. How're you?" I'd woken him up.

"I'm doing pretty good," I said.

"How's the band doing?"

"Well, we're doing pretty good. They're heading out to California tomorrow," I said.

"And what are you gonna be doing?"

"Well, that's why I called you," I said. "You told me to call you if I ever decide I wanna go back to school. I'd like to come back. Does that offer still stand? "

"Well, yes," he said. "When you gonna be here?"

I told him I'd be there in the morning, about 8:00 a.m. He laughed about that for a long time.

UofL was a private school back then and very white. So when you saw another face that looked like yours, you tended to raise your hand and wave real good. I met my wife Mamie at UofL through her sister, Laura, who was my tutor. She told me, "My baby sister is coming to the music school, and I don't want no stuff outta' y'all." So I met Mamie, and we got to talking. We'd play cards in the dormitory. She was a clarinetist studying music to become a music director. We'd go out together and go bowling. The summertime came around, and I asked her, "You wanna get married?" I meant like tomorrow. And she said, "No." When I asked her why, she said, "It's too hot!" That was July. I asked her again the next spring and she said, "Sure." So there I was. I was on my way. We got married in April 1973.

I got saved right around then too. My wife had church roots. Her family attended Guiding Star Baptist Church at 28th and Muhammad Ali, but she and I were looking for a church. We rode through the streets, and wherever there was a church with a sign that said, "Church inside, come on in," we went in. We really needed a church. We had one child on the way and needed a place to call home.

We were invited to attend the Church of God in Christ Convocation—a big picnic—and that's where I met Bishop A.T. Moore. The first time I heard him play his saxophone, I said, "Who is that?" Mamie and I grew up in Methodist and Baptist churches. We'd never been in a Holiness Church. They didn't do like we did. The place was on a slow beat, but when that man went to the pulpit and started playing the saxophone, the place got up to singing and dancing.

When you hear somebody play, you can usually tell who they listen to. Not Bishop Moore. You couldn't give it to Coltrane or Charlie Parker. The sound just had an emotional impact on whoever listened. Maybe that's why it was hard to figure out. His sound was

McDaniel with his mentee, Dawn Bosan, ca. 1976. Dawn studied at YPAS and later received a full scholarship to the Cincinnati Conservatory of Music where she earned a master's degree in trumpet performance.

something God made. I didn't grow up in a Sanctified church, but I joined one that day.

Moore came up in an era when there was a real surge in spirituality. There was a great emphasis on what God said and did. I didn't appreciate sitting in a pew listening to people talking about something I didn't understand. I took offense to it, actually. Thirty minutes after church let out I'd have my nose in a Bible trying to get the answers. The only man I didn't have major questions about was Bishop Moore. He was my pastor for thirty-eight years.

Before he purchased Moore Temple on 23rd and Broadway, Bishop Moore's church was located at 19th and Cedar Street in a tiny little concrete building. There was something about Bishop Moore. He attracted musicians, man. I remember one bishop in town saying, "Man, this just ain't right. Moore got all the good musicians locked up in his church over there. Here I am, I gotta pray for the people, take their offering, I gotta get up and preach *and* play the organ." He said, "Moore got all the best musicians." And he did.

Bishop Moore said, "Bluitt, what do you think about us getting a band in the church?" I say, "You want a band in the church?" I didn't come from COGIC. He says, "Well, yeah, make a joyful noise to the Lord." So my wife and I started a thirty-piece orchestra at that church in about 1974. We had sometimes seven or eight saxes, ten trumpets, three or four trombones, organ, keyboard, bass. It was the old big band style. On Sunday mornings, whenever the choir didn't sing, the band filled the choir box. I used ten clarinet players, and about six or seven flutes, that made up my soprano line. And those high trumpet and high sax players that can go into the upper register, that was the sound of the Moore Temple Band, and you almost wouldn't miss it in heaven.

I started teaching as a band director at DuValle Junior High School and would go on to teach in JCPS for thirty years. Mamie and I were also teaching private lessons at this time. She didn't have the volume of students that I had because we had a little one at home, but she taught woodwinds and I taught brass, rhythm, and guitar. I'd teach after school at DuValle, and at Moore Temple, and many times I'd go to the students' homes. There was one subdivision where I taught several kids in the neighborhood out of one house. I can remember one time looking up and it was 10:00 p.m. and I was still teaching. It was a lot of work, but it didn't seem like work.

One day, I was up in front of the church and the guys were having a car wash, and one of them said, "Where are you teaching at, Bluitt?"

"I'm teaching everywhere, man. All over the place. I just need to find a place to centralize my instruction."

He says, "How many kids you got?"

"I got about fifty."

"There's an old building right down on Muhammad Ali," he said. "The old Bourgard College of Music and Art. I think it's shut down, but there may be somebody in there."

I walked over there that same day and knocked on the door. I went in, and as you walk in, there's huge sliding doors on each side. An old Black lady with beautiful white hair opens the door and says, "Yes, young man? What can I do for you?" She had a very proper voice and way of speaking. She was taller than I was. Had to be in her late sixties. If I'd ever seen an expression of Black aristocracy, it was Elizabeth Anne Buford.

"My name is McDaniel," I said. "I teach school here in Jefferson County. I'm a music teacher. I hear you might have some space available so I can teach my students."

"Come here," she said and beckoned me over. She was sitting behind this beautiful mahogany desk with all these beautiful antiques, stuff you don't see in homes. You don't hardly see it anywhere. These little lattices with little beads going all the way across the doorway. I thought, *Woo-wee, this is a nice place here.*

She had a very noticeable china set, and she was sipping tea. She said, "Can I offer you some tea?"

"No, ma'am. I don't drink tea."

She says, "Well, we have rooms available," as though this was a full-blown operation, which it wasn't at the time. "And there is a fee."

I said, "How much do you charge?"

"We charge two dollars per student." Which wasn't nearly enough for the time. I was charging five dollars per half-hour lesson. She had been kind of trapped in a little bubble of time. If you saw that china set, you'd see she was pretty stuck in an earlier era and the aristocracy of that era. I took her up on the offer and that's how I started teaching at Bourgard.

When the doors were closed, and everybody was gone, Ms. Buford was just as wild and crazy as everybody else. I'd make her smile and laugh. If she wanted to go somewhere, I'd say, "Well, girl, I got the limo right outside. Come on, get in the car."

She'd look at me and point at my Volkswagen. "That is not a limo."

She was such a gentle person. She had a great sense of humor. I loved Ms. Buford. She was a prodigy. She'd graduated from Julliard and had been hand-picked by a woman named Ms. Caroline Bourgard to run the Bourgard School of Music in the 1950s. They were really good friends.

Ms. Bourgard was a white German lady. She was providing instruction for Black kids in the West End, and Bourgard College of Music and Art was the first art school for African Americans in Louisville. Ms. Bourgard also taught adults from UofL, Transylvania, and Centre College, who got college credit for her classes. She was not your everyday run-of-the-mill music teacher type. She had connections very high in the state. She had her own office in Frankfort. She was skilled and surrounded herself with an affluent crowd. The governor appointed her as the state supervisor of music, an office that hadn't existed before.

The Bourgard School had always held these garden parties. People looked forward to this beautiful display at Bourgard's. They'd come sit on the lawn and porch at tables with colorful tablecloths and little umbrellas. Students would sing as a part of that festive atmosphere

Caroline Bourgard

THE BOURGARD COLLEGE OF MUSIC AND ART. 2503 WEST WALNUT.

50 year anniversary of Bishop A.T. Moore's church.
Bishop Moore seated center

that they had created. There'd be an ongoing train of people who showed up. They'd come and sit and talk, and they'd drink tea. They would get up and they'd go inside the building and look around and say, *Now, this is something*. It was almost unbelievable. I showed up to an era that I didn't know much about. It was really special. The emphasis of the music in those days was more operatic and classically trained. There were spirituals, though. At one of these garden parties an old guy sang "Amazing Grace." There are so many verses to that song. So many that I believed this guy made some of them up himself. He was a student of one of the board members, Old Man Diggs, and had a beautiful voice.

After Ms. Buford's health got bad around 1975, the garden parties ceased. That was the end of that era. She had a stroke and couldn't go like she once did. She called me and said, "McDaniel, I will not be coming in for a period of time. I'm going to have to get my health together. But I'll call you when I come back." Her family lived in Indianapolis and she went to stay with them.

She told her board, "Find McDaniel Bluitt and ask him to take charge of the school until I get back on my feet." And that's what I did. Students were just rolling in through the doors. My wife started bringing her students; she had about twenty-five of them. We brought some other teachers in as time went by, such as Ron Jones from the Jazz Quartet. I served as director for six or seven years. We held memorable recitals at Zion Baptist Church where Rev. Cockerham was pastor at the time.

When I left, Joetta Perkins came in after me. She was quite a capable musician and was good at teaching music to kids. She taught at the Brown School for a long time and was at Bourgard for about three years. About two years after she left, there was a guy named Louis Lipscomb. When he left, the building was shut for I don't know how long.

I was still band director at Moore Temple. I told Bishop Moore one day, "A lot of kids running around here, and they don't seem to be doing anything."

"Got any ideas, Bluitt?" He said.

"Well, why don't we start a band program for the kids? That's what I've been trained to do all these years." And that's when we began to translate the energy we were using in private lessons into little recitals we would have at the church there. I had white kids, Black kids, and Latino families.

The West End Boys Choir started in 1989. I had been to see my good friend Dr. Walter Turnbull who founded the Harlem Boys Choir, which was a significant and highly regarded choral program. I mean, he had his own *school*. Had about 1500 kids on a waiting list to audition to get in. I went to the academy to see it with my own eyes. I didn't know anybody in the country doing that. There were boys choir directors that would come from all around the world to sit in his camps and hear his thoughts.

Turnball was from the Seventh-Day Adventist organization— they're very orthodox—and they basically put him out of the church when he started the community choir, almost like he'd committed sacrilege. They took him down from all the positions he held. He said, "They didn't want to hear any of my music. They didn't want to see my program because it became nationally recognized." If you went out into the world, you were taboo. You were gone. The Seventh-Day Adventists of that era were real big on this. Even the gospel musicians making gospel music. The church told him, "Give up the worldly association of the boys choir and come back home. You can repent and come back to the church."

Turnbull said, "I repent every day when I pray, but not for *that*. Jesus' ministry was to help people, not beat them up and push them in a corner somewhere." His story made me cry. It still baffles my mind today.

When I came back, I told Bishop Moore what I'd seen and how this boys choir program could be a real special touch for our community, our church included. "We have fifteen to twenty young boys who come to church with their families every Sunday, but they're not engaged in anything; they're just here. We have kids who come and play in the parking lot and have a great time playing ball out there, but they're not connected to any church. They could really benefit from being a part of what we've got going on, and they don't know what's going inside because they don't go to church here, and we don't advertise." The church was not reaching out of the four walls like I thought it should have. I told him about Turnball and the boys choir. "Well, we'd teach them how to be young men. We'd use music as a template for how it's done. I think we can get a lot of the young boys engaged around the church instead of going out and doing something they shouldn't do."

Bishop Moore was just waiting on somebody to

McDaniel and Arthur Patterson
with contestants in the Bible Bowl

bring an idea like that. I suggested a way to do it, and he said, "That's a good idea. I think we can do it."

I said, "Bishop, I got a question for you. I'm a little concerned. Dr. Turnbull, the guy that started that program up there in Harlem, his church put him out. If I bring this program here, I wonder if my church would put me out?" If you were a member of the Sanctified Church, you didn't go to the nightclub. Period. The biblical teachings say, "He came to deliver you from the ways of the world." Those stigmas were very well pronounced.

Bishop Moore busted out laughing. "Oh, no, no, no," he said. "You just do the program you feel like you know to do it." He got up and told the people in the church, "What Bluitt is doing is helping all the children and helping our community. You need to get your children in this choir." And man, my recruiting got simple after that. I had people coming from everywhere. That's been thirty-some years ago. Since that time, we've had thousands of kids participate.

McDaniel and Mamie Bluitt, his wife of fifty years

My real joy with the kids is not directing the choir or writing the songs or rehearsing them, it's seeing the compassion that develops within the group. You might get a little guy who comes in and wants to sing but maybe having problems. One of the older guys might say, "Come stand by me. I'll show you what to do. You're gonna get it, don't worry." Musicians can be unforgiving, but this group is really supportive. If they learn the choir, they learn that compassion side. They come out of it, and it's a joy.

We changed the name to West Louisville Performing Arts Academy in 1990. We've been housed at the Kentucky Center for African American Heritage, and now we're at the UofL School of Music. We hope to occupy Bourgard School of Music again someday.

I pass the old Bourgard School sometimes because I take kids home after rehearsals. I have lots of great memories there, and one day in 2021 I drove by and decided to check it out. I walked up the sidewalk and looked at the building and said, *The door is wide open.* I walked into the building, and it was just rubble. Walls had holes knocked in them where they had taken copper out of the walls. Antiques you can't find anywhere else were vandalized. There was an armoire sitting there with its legs broken. A mirror that had all kinds of etching work up and down the side was just destroyed. All of the decorative lattices, the pocket doors, the banisters: all wrecked. Those pieces were irreplaceable. They'd absolutely riddled the place. I said, *My God, what in the world happened here?*

It looked like complete rubble. It was so saddening the order of destruction that had taken place. That's one day I cried. So much of what I knew was no longer there anymore.

The property is now under the purview of the mayor's office. The National Parks Service donated $500,000 to redo the Bourgard School. They emphasized Lady Bourgard's mission and said the money had to be placed in the hands of someone working with children in west Louisville. Bourgard also had a trust fund that was set up in a very smart way like an endowment. It's an irrevocable investment which means you can't change the mission, you can't change the layout of how the money is being dispersed.

The building had ended up in the land bank, and the trust fund was overseen by PNC. Well, I got a call in 2019 asking if we'd be interested in assuming control of that trust. When the woman from the mayor's office called me, she said, *We have a trust fund here that they wanted your organization to take charge of because the mission of West Louisville Performing Arts Academy overlaps with what Bourgard intended years ago.* I said, "Who recommended that we be considered for this? I haven't filled out any paperwork for this."

She said, "McDaniel, all I can say is that there is somebody up there who really thinks a lot of what you're doing." I never found out who it was.

Fortunately for the West Louisville Performing Arts Academy, we got the money. We don't have the building yet, but I believe pretty strongly that the Bourgard School will one day end up in the hands of the West Louisville Performing Arts Academy. It would be a natural fit and a much-needed facility.

I've been gratified by this work. Kids gravitate to music, and I think the idea of them getting enough courage to take on an instrument or learn to sing and perform is monumental. These kids walk in and can't

McDaniel and the girls choir at
Juneteenth event at Fourth Street Live, 2017

sing a lick, and before long they're saying, *Look at me, man. Wait until my mama hears me. She's got no idea I can do this.* This is especially important for kids who don't have much of a family structure. We have always sought to provide a sense of belonging and to be engaged in what we teach.

When I have thought about the arrangement I made with the Lord—where I asked for his protection and said I'd come back someday—I know I was in the right place doing what I should, doing what I'm put here to do: working with children, taking the experiences and the music I've learned, and sharing them in a way where kids can pull up, do better, and make better lives for themselves. ✦

People College

JANE GRADY

My father had our home built at 3321 Dumesnil St., and he also purchased the lot next door. All my childhood life was in the West End. That's where I stayed from when I was born in 1937 until I got married and moved out at eighteen years old. It was a beautiful home. I can look back and see how nice it was as a child. He had it beautified with rose bushes all around the wooden fence. He was a carpenter and he made some furniture for the house. While Mother was doing dinner, he would go down to the basement workshop. He made my sister and me a playground with a swing and a seesaw, and he made most of the furniture for our playhouse. He built us a dinette set with a buffet, a wooden table, and two high-backed dining room chairs. He made my baby buggy for my dolls.

We had a big Victrola. Daddy had a whole bunch of them big 78s. I wanted to dance and do a little singing. He had Paul Whiteman. I loved Lena Horne and Marian Anderson. I saw them in *Life* magazine. I can remember how graceful Marian Anderson stood and how she sang. I could have been a dancer and a singer. I loved ballet and tap dancing. We used to see Bill Bailey, Pearl Bailey's brother, when we first got it on TV. And I really kept up with Sammy Davis so I could tap behind what I could see him doing. But my mother didn't know I had that talent. Then her play sister came to town from St. Louis and told me that Mother used to be a dancer, could jitterbug and do that other dancing that I could never learn to do. She said, "They used to throw money down at your mother's feet to see her dancing." I got my dancing genes from her, but Mother had no dream about me dancing. Instead, she had me take up music lessons from Emma L. Minis, a Seventh-Day Adventist lady that taught piano lessons. I had to go to her house at 32nd and Grand every weekend. Fifty cents per lesson.

Wedding photo of James and Pearl Johnson, 1927

Jane's mother, Pearl Senter Johnson Sadler, ca. 1920s or 30s

Jane Grady's parents Pearl and James Johnson (right)
with her Uncle Charley and Aunt Eugenia Johnson

Jane Grady's mother Pearl, baby sister Bertha,
father James (rear) and Uncle Maurice
in front of Johnson family home, ca. 1945

I went all the way to the twelfth book, but I didn't want to be no pianist.

I had no brothers, so I patternized myself from two of my uncles. My play uncle, John Lay, was a Red Cap porter for L&N Railroad. They wheeled the baggage on and off the train. I was fascinated with trains. The train tracks were up the street, six blocks from us. If the train caught us when we were going to the A&P, I would count the boxcars. I loved to see the trains come in. I begged my mother to go up there so I could hear the whistle. And I never missed a chance to go to the L&N station on Broadway to see the trains coming in with people. There was a passenger train called the *Hummingbird*. That was a pretty one. I got a chance to see the front of the engine once. I have postcards of trains now. That's how fascinated I was with them.

The railroad was one of the largest employers around for Black folk. Pullman porters and cooks were two things that Black men had for a job at that time. That's what brought most of the people in from rural

Jane Grady at eleven or twelve months old, 1938

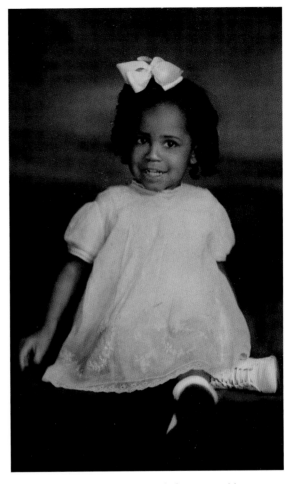

Jane Grady, approximately four years old

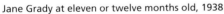

areas and from further south. There were also jobs at Jones-Dabney's paint factory. There was also Vultee Aircraft over at Standiford Field—my daddy worked there. Then, during the war, lots of them winded up working over in Indiana at the ammunition plant. The Reynolds Aluminum Company brought jobs in for Black men, too. Reynolds was close to my neighborhood. That's where my stepfather walked to work. Most of the Black men could walk because they were close. Then you had the Falls City brewery at 28th and Broadway, between where Promise Land Baptist Church and the Kroger is now. They could also get jobs as butlers and chauffeurs with wealthy families in Indian Hills.

People also moved further north because the money in Louisville was much lower than in northern cities. When the people came from the country, it still was low pay; it was nickel-dime. It was a struggle. Some crossed over to Cincinnati. Some migrated on to Boston, Detroit, and Cleveland.

The Johnson sisters, Martha, Bertha, and Jane, ca. 1950

From left: Martha, Jane, and Bertha Johnson
in their backyard, ca. 1950

James Johnson, Jane Grady's father

Wasn't a lot of Black people at the time in the neighborhood. Down the street was still white people, and the Jewish people had stores where we would shop. I loved going to the grocery at 34th and Virginia and getting candy. The food was good too. When you went and got lunch meat, it was always wrapped in wax paper in a paper bag. The grocery stores would extend credit if you needed help.

I loved going to Fourth Street. But my mother did not take us three kids there unless it was Easter, or maybe around Christmas. We didn't go uptown otherwise. My play auntie Bertha Lay would watch us while my mother took care of bills in town and on weekends,

and we got a chance to ride to Walnut Street with her. It was a busy neighborhood from Ninth Street down. I loved going to the chili parlor and the fish place. They had benches where you could go and sit and get a milkshake or have a club soda. That was enjoyable. We always got a chance to go to the fair or to the circus when Aunt Bertha came into town.

Don't let me leave out the picture show. By that time, the TV done eased in, and it kept some people housebound. I said, "Oh, c'mon! Let's get out from under the TV. Let's go out. Let's go out to the movie." Movie didn't cost that much. If there was something good, we went to the Palace. If it was something going

Pearl Johnson with daughters Jane and baby Bertha and
Aunt Jane Welch, 1940s

Jane Grady at Beecher Terrace with children Michael,
Rochell, and Darrell, Oct. 1962

on at the Grand, we went to the Grand. I looked at the pictures so hard I had a headache because my mother didn't allow us to be on Walnut Street.

There were some kids in the neighborhood whose families would take them to the YMCA on Friday nights when they had activities. I couldn't see why I couldn't go with them. But with my mother, it was always, "No, no. You don't want to impose." My play auntie and my real auntie would say, "Let 'em go!" they'd say. I would be so happy just to get away from the neighborhood. I was waiting to get grown and old enough so I could leave home.

I wanted to see things because I'm a people person. I was always around older people, asking questions, and watching. I even tried to act and walk like State Representative Mae Street Kidd. She was tall, and I was tall; everybody's shorter than me. I loved the way she wore her hair and everything. I got a chance to talk to her—bless her heart—before she passed. She was amazed for me to come to her, and we got into that conversation. When I have talked to kids about getting in the conversations, I say, "Don't feel ashamed. It's three words a person gonna say: yes, no, or I don't know." Then you let that go till you go to the next

Jane Grady (second from left) with her sister Martha, her sister Bertha, her mother, Sam, and Michael

Beecher Terrace, 1960

Donnie Hartman at Jane Grady's apartment
in Beecher Terrace, 1134 Cedar Ct. #34, 1960s

person, and if it's still on your mind, ask. You ask questions in order to learn. But in my home, it was: "Be quiet," "You don't know what you talking about," "Are you meddling?" That puts a damper on children. You closing them out.

My mother was a seamstress. She made all her clothes, and ours. She made the cover for my doll buggy. It was painted yellow with a touch of cream color. I played church and school with my dolls. I had a Mickey Mouse tin tea set because I always played house with my dolls. I took the dining room chairs, and I'd line them up. That was my trains, and my dolls was the people. It was just my imaginary mind, because wasn't nothing else going on. My mother thought something was wrong with me, though.

She was a housekeeper and taught me a lot of things. My mother worked for the Heyburns. While we were in school, she done the laundry that the chauffeurs brought to our house. Mainly shirts for the chauffeurs and the butlers, not the Heyburn family laundry. After

two or three days, they'd come back and pick them up. Later, she worked for the Dabneys that owned Jones-Dabney paint company, the Barnes McFerrans, and the Churchills: all of them was in that area of St. James Court in Old Louisville. They were big-time people. She later worked for the Swope family in Indian Hills for twenty-five years.

My daddy was a chauffeur for a judge who lived on St. James Court. He'd drive judges and attorneys out of town up to Michigan. Only time I got a chance to see him was when he came home. My father passed from hypoglycemia at Lakeland Sanitorium when I was seven years old. We had a den in the back, off from the dining room, and that's where they set up his body. They set up the background with drapery like you see in funeral homes now and put two floor lights on the side, then they brought him in. Back then, that's what they did. People would come and sit with the family, and they would bring food. That way, you was still bonded with the dead. I stayed upstairs, and

Bertha Louise Johnson, mother Pearl Johnson Sadler, and others at the park

Jane's children Rochelle and Darrell with two friends in their apartment in Beecher Terrace

that evening they told me to come down. I didn't want no part of it. Mother grabbed my hand and had me touch his chest. I thought that was so weird and scary. It might have been three days the body was held in our house. Then they went to Virginia Avenue Baptist Church for the funeral.

Mother was upset about losing my father from his sickness. She didn't talk much about him the rest of my life. I don't know why. She didn't tell us the story. I only had to play it from my memory. Older people didn't do much talking and telling the story about their lives. I always had flashbacks about my daddy. Years later, when I was living in Beecher Terrace with my kids, I had a spiritual dream. Out of the blue, my father appeared back to me. It was so weird, like he must be spiritually keeping up with me. I was out on my own and was a little scared, and the dream gave me the feeling that everything was going to be okay.

It was around my son's birthday—February '59— when I moved into Beecher Terrace from my family

house. I wanted to move out on my own. It was kind of hard to find an apartment. I wanted to move into Cotter Homes when the first phase was built because I thought they were such attractive apartments. But they was really trying to give the apartments to two-parent families with husbands that had been in the service. I wanted to be grown, on my own and raising my two sons, but their father and I were separated. That's when I moved in Beecher Terrace. Didn't have a clue who I was going to meet and know from there. It was just something new.

My first impression of Beecher Terrace was that it was a beautiful place. Mr. Pruitt was the manager back in the '40s and '50s, and he lived on the premises. There was eight maintenance men that took care of beautification in Beecher Terrace under Mr. Pruitt. He was proud that the government had built them for the colored people. He took time to walk the grounds of Beecher. No garbage cans were allowed to be hanging around, and garbage wasn't thrown around.

Little by little, I learned the whole circle of people. Some of the residents found out I could do hair, so I started as what we called a kitchen beautician. I'd started doing my own hair when I was younger because the beauticians were kind of rough, especially if you were tender-headed. My hair was so thick, and I never was satisfied how they styled my hair. I thought to myself, "I'm gonna start doing my own hair." And by the time I got to junior high, I learned my own way to curl my hair and style it. That was one gift I had.

On the weekend, my neighbors in Beecher would come to me and say, "Can you fix my hair?" They'd be getting ready to go to a party or a dance. I'd say, "Yeah, come on down." At the time, money was low, so after I'd gotten home from work and made sure the kids had eaten and did the washing and cleaning and stuff, my neighbors would rush by my house and I would do their hair. Wash it, dry it, and get them all prettied up. I was the kitchen beautician. That would be the weekend.

My first job was as a nurse assistant at Red Cross Hospital, the all-colored hospital. Then I left, and I wound up babysitting my friends' and cousins' children, which amounted to at least eight children, counting my two boys. I was the daycare. I love kids. I taught them different little things, like nursery rhymes, and would take them out for outings. When their parents veered off into daycare, one of my neighbors got me a job at a shirt factory at 18th and Oak. Then another friend of mine got me a job at Louisville Linen, but I didn't stay there long.

I started working at the Pendennis Club in the 1960s. The members were men who had organizations through their ancestors. They were company owners, bankers, doctors, and attorneys. It was a whites-only club, but I liked the work, and I felt good when I got to talking to the members. Looking back, I remember them as open-minded and open-hearted. I got familiar with them through the parties they would have.

Ms. Rankin—they called her "Mother Rankin"—was in charge of the debutante parties and the weddings. She taught me how to cut those big cakes and serve them. I loved the weddings. I knew how to do the work, and I did not have to ask too many questions. One of the ways I knew I was doing a good job is because the club members would tell the head waiter they wanted me to work when they had graduations or debutantes with their children at the club. They liked my service. I was a friendly person.

I was there about three years. And them three years, we worked, worked, worked. The members that I got acquainted with would introduce me to they wives and they daughters. I got acquainted with Ms. Heyburn, the Ballards, the Horners, and the Peabodys.

I had a neighbor at Beecher Terrace named Ramona. She was the cook for Charlie and Katty Middleton. Charlie was Senator Middleton's brother, and he was an attorney for an oil company. His office was right across the street from the Pendennis Club. He had developed polio, so he was in a wheelchair. Ramona told me she was leaving her job and she needed someone to replace her. So I left the Pendennis Club and started working at the Middletons' house, which was a nice place out in Indian Hills. I started going out there and doing their cooking five days a week. Then their laundress left, and I started doing their laundry instead of cooking.

My auntie did the cleaning for Mimi and Robert Horner, and she asked me, "Would you like a job?" That's how I came to do laundry for the Horners while I was doing the same thing for the Middletons. I didn't know what Mr. Horner was into until after his death. He worked for the cement company in Kosmosdale.

I went to work from nine o'clock until four o'clock. I had to find somebody that would be neighborly to look out after my kids. I had foster neighbors that took

Jane Grady at Pendennis Club, 1960s

care of my boys while I was at work. All the domestic workers took the Market Street bus to Indian Hills. It was lively all the way to Indian Hills. I called it the Joy Bus because everybody on there was always laughing and talking and joking. One bus driver I got acquainted with named Mary—she knew my mother because my mother rode that bus when she worked for the Swope family—said, "Y'all the loudest! Talking and laughing." I never rode a bus where everybody was so joyful. Wasn't a dull moment. We traveled on that Market Street bus to Indian Hills off of Brownsboro Road, where the bus would drop us off at Taylor's Drug Store. Then we'd wait for our rides. If Ms. Horner didn't come pick me up, I took a cab and they paid for it.

Ronald Hayes, Beecher Terrace

They made sure they came after you, and they brought you back. Everybody winded up back at the same drugstore. Five days a week.

Once they could trust you, the Horners would just leave the door unlocked if they were gone. You came in and you knew what your chores was. If I hadn't ate, I would fix me some breakfast, then I would check the clothes and start the washing. I didn't have to clean the bedrooms or make up the beds and the furniture. My thing was getting the dishes together. Most of them went in the dishwasher, except some gold-trimmed china that you couldn't put in the dishwasher.

The Horners had two girls and one boy, and the nanny was still there at the time. Mrs. Downing, from England. She was a nice person. She could crochet, and she made my daughter a hat and some mittens. I did the kitchen and the dishes, cleaned up, and then the rest of it was washing their clothes. After I was there for a while, Ms. Annabelle, the cleaning lady, left, so I started doing their cleaning too.

They trusted me. I was one of the family. I became part of the house and took care of everything. If I wanted to cook, fine. Whatever I wanted to do made them happy. That went also for the Middletons and their two boys. I winded up taking over the whole house and was able to alternate what I wanted to do. I was comfortable. There never was no comment other than I'd done well. That's the way that went. If I got through early, I'd call the cab. If it was a nice day, a summery day, I would walk because I like watching and seeing the scenery.

I worked in Indian Hills for about eight years through the '60s. My dream was to move out to California with my sister. My kids, my mother, and I had been to visit my sister Bertha, and I fell in love with it. We went to Disneyland, Sea World, and the largest shopping center. It was fascinating to see thousands of people that I didn't see here in Louisville. I said, *Oh, we are country* compared to what I saw. I called us the "country bumpkins."

I moved out to Los Angeles around January 1971. I got acquainted with quite a few people on Bertha's street. It was on Buckingham Row, where quite a few of the movie stars was living. They took me in just like I had been there my whole life. I took a bus tour to learn about Los Angeles. I would tell the drivers that I was new here living, and they welcomed me.

Lots of people said, "I'd love to go to Los Angeles, but it's too expensive." I said, "Well, I went there on a down-low of a few dollars, but I got a job." Many of my classmates from Louisville lived in Los Angeles at the time. They had a Louisville club, the Kentucky Derby Club. I met lots of them. I got jobs through word of mouth from different friends. I got experience through job after job. I took a one-week course of electronics. I caught on and got a job at a company called Electric Cord that made large power cords for washing machines and things like that. Then I got a job at Teledyne, where I soldered electrical parts for airplanes. Then I worked on an assembly line at Paper Mate pen company. They teased me because I talked Southern talk. I said, "That's okay. You all got a Southern-Northern talk," and they would laugh. Sometimes they called me "Kentuck."

Then in 1978, my niece called and told me that I needed to come home because my mother had taken ill. So I moved me and my two kids back from there to Louisville. When I moved back, I went back to the Horners five days a week after Ethel Mae, who had been cooking and taking care of the house for them, fell dead getting ready to come to work one day. Later on, Katty Middelton asked if I could give her some time, so I started back with her too. My mother hadn't passed yet, and she asked me if I could give my sister Martha a little job. So Martha fell in the slot with the Horners so I could split and go to Katty's.

When I got back to Louisville, I had no intentions of moving back into Beecher Terrace. I wanted a house.

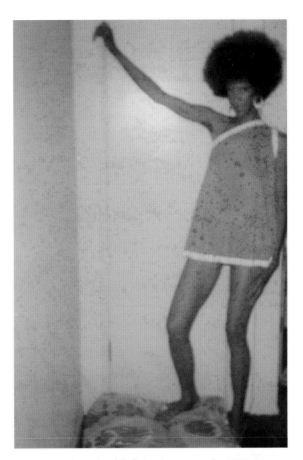

Jane Grady while living in Los Angeles, 1975

Ms. Georgia Braham, Beecher Terrace, 1960s

Downs, maintenance man at Beecher Terrace, 1960s

But in looking at houses that Martha took me to, all of them was drug houses and had been boarded up. I couldn't find what I wanted in a neighborhood. I was able to get an apartment in Beecher on 13th Street, across from Porter Paint.

When I moved there, they said they were apartments. But I believe the way we took care of ours back then was more like condos. We made sure our windows looked pretty, inside and out. We planted flowers and shrubs in our yards. We hosed down our porches to freshen them up. I encouraged others at that time to do likewise. We knew how to do things in our neighborhood. We were good neighbors. Sometimes they'd say, "You wanna have breakfast? Eggs and bacon? Got the coffee going." Other times we'd start out at a ball game. "We're all gonna hook up over at the baseball game at Ninth and Walnut Park." They had competitions, and different outside ball teams would come use that park. That was a good time.

We loved sitting out in the yard during the summertime, drinking our beer, and making sure our place was always clean. It never really was a dull moment in Beecher. Muhammad Ali Boulevard was busy, all day, seven days a week. Sunday was church time. Children had to go to Sunday school, but on the weekend, I would be the one to instigate to keep things active—Bingo, Pokeno. It wasn't boring.

We always had Saturday night parties and gatherings with our close friends. We'd play Patti LaBelle and Al Green, and we'd have our highballs. Whichever house or apartment we went to, we always had some food. I always put hors d'oeuvres on the bar. We would sit around. Sometimes, one of the guys would put up a card table and play cards. We'd put the children to bed upstairs—most of us had bedrooms upstairs—and sometimes the parties lasted till two in the morning, maybe three. It was clean fun.

Children knew each other and we knew the other parents. The children loved to come to my house. I always had something for them to sit down and do, like teaching them how to tell time. I'd have them look at the clock, and I'd say, "Tell me what time it is." I was a teacher in my apartment. That gave the kids a reason to come if they got bored playing outside. They felt welcomed. I always had a drink and something for them to eat. And they learned how to work. Right up to today, they remember. I had them cleaning the fingerprints off the wall, cleaning the steps. Never no complaint. When you gave them some cookies and some candy, they were gonna take care of that area. They did under my supervision.

I had been Beecher Terrace resident council president before I moved to California. When I came back, they asked me to join the board again. I said, "I did not come back to do the same thing that you all could have done," but I was soft-hearted, and they talked me into it. I told them, "I'm a business person. Business come before pleasure. So, we not gonna do lots of pleasure and fun because I'm a serious person." I also joined back with the Clients Council Tenant Union on Fifth Street and Muhammad Ali, which worked with people in different neighborhoods to help them find jobs, housing, health, and everything. I was in outreach, reaching out to people that was in poverty, giving them information, and inviting them to come so they could learn how the system worked. I was also PTA president of Coleridge Taylor School.

Ms. Johnson was the Beecher Terrace resident president before me, and I learned a lot about how things were run in Beecher Terrace. She told me the way she organized resident meetings with the tenants and how they organized little plays with the children at Baxter Community Center. The center had boxing and basketball. Anita Neil was a Beecher resident that

Jane Grady at party at Baxter Community Center, 1960s

Libby Mickens at New Year's party at Baxter Center

Jane Grady with daughter Rochelle (2nd from left)

taught ballet and dancing there. And there were lots of choir rehearsals with the young people. A man started the Boy Scouts in Beecher.

I was trying to figure out how to get some money from Metro Council to help to support the kids in Beecher Terrace. I said, "The kids could go camping. They could go to movies." Their parents maybe couldn't afford for the kids to go to places like YMCA camp.

They weren't doing very much at Baxter Center, which had a large auditorium with a stage. So, to raise money for the kids, I thought about holding a dance there like they used to have in the '40s when they dressed up in evening dresses. An old classmate of mine named Jackie Bradley came up to me and said, "I will start the first dance with my men's club, Family AC." When people heard that they could come back to where some of them were born and raised for a dance, it was like a joyful family reunion. These were people older than me. I think we counted up to three or four hundred people was at that dance. Tickets were no more than about ten or fifteen dollars.

When they found out that I was in charge, so many people who were in clubs started asking me could they book their club at Baxter Center. It was accessible and had the parking lot and everything. I said, "Wait a minute. I'm gonna have to get a notebook and a calendar. I'm business and run things accordingly." I ran it that way just about every weekend. The money we raised allowed us to have recreation activities for Beecher residents. We gave money for Parks and Recreation employees to take our children camping, take them to movies, take them to get pizza, and things like that during the summer when school was out. We made sure the seniors had things to do. We hosted Christmas parties and birthday parties. We sent Christmas and birthday cards to all the seniors in Beecher every year.

Jane Grady at event honoring cancer survivors

I was able to report back to Metro Parks and say, "The first dance we had, everything went fine. No fighting and no shooting. I will conduct each of the dances for these clubs." I think I chaired it for about four years. I enjoyed every one of them. My son and some of his friends helped set up the tables, break them down, and clean them up. When I started tiring out, another group of people decided they wanted to carry it on. So they tailgated me.

I've been living in the California neighborhood for more than twenty-five years now. But those were good days at Beecher Terrace. My Beecher people was my family. I'd like to thank all of them for being a neighbor to me. We really had a joyous time.

Some people can be content not being around too many people. But me, that's where I want to be because somewhere or another, it's gonna be a connection. I can always connect with people quickly. That's been my spirit going through life, whether growing up on Dumesnil, in school, at the Pendennis Club, in Los Angeles, in Beecher Terrace, or anywhere else. Some of them say, "What college did you go to?" I say, "People College." That's what I got my degree under. ✦

Light Up the Night

DEREK "HEAVY" PRESSLEY

I've been coming to Elliott Park since I was a little boy. When you come in, it's a tree right there on the 29th Street side of Elliott Park. It's what greets you. It's my spot. My spot in the world is right there. That's where me and my boys hang out, right under that tree. That's our area. The tree's like an umbrella for us. I feel safe under my tree.

If there's a breeze in Louisville, it's at 28th Street Park on the 29th Street side. When I pull up right there, I'm home. "What's up, everybody?" And it's just laid back. We've been there about thirty years. We got togetherness. We don't play on each other. We cook. We eat with each other. We break bread and have a few drinks. We look out for each other. There's Chester Murphy, my best friend from childhood. There's Mr. Bill Tolbert; we call him Commissioner. He's in his 70s, retired from Ford, an Army veteran, and respected. He's a guiding light, keeps us kind of level. He's been doing it so many years, and now he's kind of turning everything over to me. I'll train someone else to take it over after me. There's William Campbell, who we call Darnell, who grew up in the neighborhood and just come back. Like Mr. Bill, he's also retired from Ford and an Army veteran. There's Sam, who lives across from the park and works at the Yum! Center and the new track and field complex. He's my dominoes rival. There's John Goatley, who grew up with us, but he was different from us; we were thugs, but Goatley was always a good boy. He went to UK. They my boys. They're my people. I love them.

I'm the cook, mostly. Goatley cooks, too. I make sure the boys always eat. I'll take donations. A lot of time, guys will throw in five dollars or something, but you don't have to. I just enjoy seeing people eating and conversating and being happy. Maybe I get it from my mother or from being in a big family. I don't know why, but it just makes me happy. I just like cooking. I like

to be busy, and then I like to talk and visit. And when I've cooked something, and people say, "That's good," it gets me off. I learned by trial and error. Watching my stepfathers, my brothers, and my mother. Just watching and asking questions.

You got to know your grill. All you gotta do is control that heat, and it's just seasoning the meat and cooking it. It's so easy. It really is. Just don't cook too fast. Cook it slow. Let that seasoning get in there. Season a day ahead of time and let it get in there real good and just cook it slow. I also fry turkeys. I fried three of them this year. To fry a turkey, it's three minutes to a pound. If you got a twenty-pound turkey, it takes about sixty minutes at 325 degrees. Just something you learn. Trial and error.

We got big plastic storage containers with plates, napkins, sauces, salt, pepper, and ketchup—everything you need for a cookout. Goatley got one, and I got one. We can go on a minute's notice. Just take the whole box. All we got to do is find out what we're gonna cook and get it and prepare it. We go to Kroger or wherever and get our meats and just put it on. I like to season my meat the day before. It makes it better. You get a little more taste. But I can go ahead and season it on the squirt if I have to.

The last time I cooked, it was a fish fry. We went to the fish place on 14th and Chestnut. Goatley got a box of whiting and a box of cod. I brought my propane tank, my stand, and some grease, and Goatley had everything else. Everybody ate good.

When other people come up and they ready to start something, we say, "Oh no, man. You've got to go. We don't have that fighting down here. You're welcome when you're cool. Come back when you're cooled out and get a sandwich or whatever. Right now, you gotta go because we don't have that down here." And that's the way we keep it. We do this all the time.

From left: The Mayor, Oinky, and Heavy

We feed everybody. Everybody's full, we go on home, and it's a good day. We done it again.

On some Friday nights, you'll see us over at the park. At ten or eleven o'clock, it'll be pitch black out, and the only thing you'll see is that flat-screen TV. We'll be sitting in our little group with our grilled bologna sandwiches or whatever we fix for that night, and we sit there, and we watch movies together. Never have no problem. I know all the people see us, but they never mess with us. Sometimes I'm leery. I'll look around and I'll think somebody coming, but they leave us alone.

They got electricity at the park. They be coming and setting up computers and everything. We set up long cords and run TVs, run a DVD player. Sam has the DVD player and the TV. He lives across the park on the 29th Street side. So, he brings the stuff over and sets it up. A lot of times on Sunday, if the weather's right, we sitting in the park watching football. Somebody fires up a grill, or we get pizza or White Castle or whatever, and we sit in the park. It's just us together again. If it's cold, we'll sit in our trucks side by side and talk to each other. It's our spot.

I used to throw horseshoes a little bit. We had some bad boys over there throwing those horseshoes. Mr. Bill ain't no joke. He good. We got Lil' Fifty and Mr. Bill and Tommy. Those three are the best around. And they would go different places and play for trophies or for money. Our horseshoers go everywhere. Every place we go, we be winning, too. This summer, they didn't do as much. Hopefully, they'll build us some new pits in the park, and get us straight.

Mr. George inspects a bike

We got a couple people we've adopted. Like Mike. He's something else. Mike's from Alabama, and he likes it up here. He's just a guy in a wheelchair who just loves to drink. We got to look out for him because he drinks too much a lot of times. But he'll just say, "I don't care." It's his favorite words: "I don't care." And he probably don't. Maybe it's because he's in that wheelchair.

If you're cool, we adopt you right in. If you act right and peaceful, *Come on, man, we love you.* Just act yourself. Eat, drink, whatever. Just be cool. That's all we ask. Be cordial with each other. And we have a good time. And we treat everybody the same. As long as you're being reasonable, you can come on in and sit with us.

One day we was hanging in the park and someone just said, "Who got bikes? Let's take a ride together." We've been riding bikes for about fifteen years now.

First, we just rode one day a week. Then we said, "Let's ride two days a week. We having a good time." We ride and go have lunch or dinner somewhere. No telling where we'll be at. We ride the walking bridge, go across Indiana, eat over there, and come back. Ride all around town. When it gets colder, we'll ride at like one o'clock when it's warm. But during the summertime, we meet at like six o'clock in the park. Anything special comes up, we might ride to it. We ride to Jazz in Central Park; we do Hike, Bike, and Paddle every year; Bardstown Road has things going on every year. We wear bright colors so that you can see us riding at nighttime.

The other day, people at the park said, "You all are the ones who ride bikes?"

"Yeah, we're the ones who ride bikes."

Derek's bike lit up at night

They said, "You all the orange people or the green people?"

I cracked up. "We the same people. We ride orange on Thursday and green on Tuesday." We light our bikes up so you see us at night. We got lights on our wheels. We got lights around our frame. We light up the night. That's what we do. We show we ain't scared. We ride anywhere, any time. We light up everything like a Christmas tree. Everybody's always getting more lights. Everybody constantly buying and upgrading. Every time you get something, everybody gets it.

There are about fifteen of us in the club. On any given week, anywhere from seven to eleven of us

will ride. Some of us have electric bikes. My bike even got cruise control. I enjoy my bike. I have a good time. I have music on a Bluetooth speaker that hooks up to the back of the bike, and I got another one that lights up when I want to really be colorful. I bring it out, and it lights all across the back of my bike as the music plays.

Some men in the neighborhood used to have a little club, an apartment they all paid on. It was their club back then. I remember all those guys way back then. They was all cool. We had some cool old guys. We took care of them, too. Now only one of them is left. A 101-year-old man named Kool is the last one of that crew.

Kool lives right by the park. He's lived on the block between 27th and Broadway to 27th and Elliott for over fifty years. He's always been there in one house or another. A lot of times, I'd see Kool there sitting on his porch. He's been there on 27th Street all his life. That was a hangout. A lot of old men and cards and beer. For years, that was the meeting place.

After Kool retired, he'd go up to University Hospital and just stand around and meet and greet people. People thought he worked there, but he just liked going up there to hang out and speak with people in the lunchroom. He'd catch a bus over there just to have something to do. I don't know what started it. Next time I see him, I'mma ask Kool, "What makes you go to the hospital?"

Same at Dino's at 26th and Broadway. He'd hang at Dino's and greet everybody. And he done that for years. Dino's has changed. It was real nice back then. Now, I don't think he'd hang up there, the way the crowd has changed. Neighborhood changed, too. It was so safe back then because we looked out for each other. You couldn't grab Kool in that neighborhood; we'd come for you. But now, it's just not the same. I'm leery. A new breed up there.

Kool's porch is the hangout. There's people hanging there from morning to night on his porch. As long as I can remember, they hang on his porch. That's what they do. They do things for Kool. They go run his errands. Whatever he needs, somebody always there. I used to hang there. I been through many hours sitting on the porch. The man who owned the house come down there and said something, and people stayed away for a minute. But I'm seeing them coming right back now.

Every one of them sons of guns drinking, and boy, they have some bizarre conversations. Sometimes, I say, "Man, I should go get my phone. I ought to film this." Oh, man. I tell you what, I'm a bad man sometimes, I've got to admit. I come over there and feed them. The other day, I had a half a gallon of Maker's Mark, and I put out about twelve beers. They will get drunk, boy.

It's so many things that happened with those jokers. They comical. And the things they say, it's something else. This dude Albert was drinking with us, and he drank hard, guzzling it down. I looked over there, and Albert got in an argument, and then he started fighting and kicking, but there wasn't nobody there! He was just fighting nobody. Whoever he was fighting, Al went to hit him, but I guess dude stepped aside and hit Al, because Al went straight down to the ground. He ain't fighting nobody and he went down! We rolled. I was crying laughing. It was so funny. We had to carry Al to the house. Al got in a fight with nobody and lost.

On Kool's porch, you're gonna hear something from everywhere. You go there and they gonna talk about what happened in this neighborhood and that neighborhood. Lately it's shootout stuff. "That was my nephew that got killed." That was my such-and-such. Mostly it's things like that, bad news. Every once in a while, somebody say something good, but most of the time it's bad news. It seem like that's what you hear of more. But I don't care what goes on in this world, I'm

Mr. Bill

gonna try to do what I do. I'm gonna still ride my bike. I'm gonna light up the night. I'm gonna stay me forever.

I'm the fifth child out of nine by my mother. I have two big brothers, two big sisters, two little brothers, two little sisters. I had one big brother pass. I had a little sister pass. So, we're down to seven now. My mother worked two jobs to take care of us. My father wasn't around much. Although we was poor and we was hungry, she kept us out of projects. We was always in a house somewhere. It might be crap, but we was in a house. And she done what she had to do to get us through. I used to think my mother had it good when she was a child because they had a farm.

They always had plenty to eat. Her father run a farm down in Bowling Green. She's a country girl. God bless her soul, she's still here: eighty-eight years old, and her mind's just sharp. She gets around better than I can. My mother can go to bingo at two thirty in the afternoon and not come back until two or three o'clock at night. She don't play. She got that power.

I spent my really early days on Dearborn, which is a street that only has two blocks on it down in between 38th and 37th, and between Garland on one end and Broadway on the other end. Dearborn was our street. I think that's where I first got my togetherness, because on Dearborn we had so many kids in each house: ten kids in this house, six in this house, five in this house, ten in that house. We had so many kids on our street. We was like a gang. We were Dearborn kids. Any place we went, we went together. I still got a friend from Dearborn, Chester Murphy. We been best friends for fifty years. We went to elementary school together, and we started running together. Chester's family had air conditioning way back then when we was in elementary school. I didn't have no air conditioning until I was twenty or twenty-one. But I played at his house, so I enjoyed the air conditioning. That air would be having you cold when you go over there. Mr. Murphy and Mrs. Murphy's good people. They worked hard. Mr. Murphy was a construction worker. He drove heavy machinery. He was driving big tractor things and backhoes, and he made a nice buck with that.

When I was about eleven, my father became a bigger presence in my life, and I moved with him up on 27th and Madison. I would walk from Madison back to Dearborn. Then I started knowing everybody in my new neighborhood. I was meeting them and still going to Dearborn. It was like a split neighborhood thing. Then, I just started hanging more in my neighborhood, 28th Street Park, shooting marbles and stuff.

When it's ten kids, and your mother worked, our big sisters pretty much raised us. She had to sleep. She had to work. And she had to have some type of life. I did a lot of things a young guy probably shouldn't have done. I got put out there pretty early. I was walking from 38th and Broadway all the way to 27th and Madison at ten or eleven o'clock at night by myself. Me and my friend Tommy Briscoe would get on our bicycles. We'd go after girls together. We'd shoot basketball somewhere. We'd go to football practice. We played in little league football together. It was a lot of joking with the players. If we got in a fight, we'd be hugging each other later in the day. It wasn't as vicious as it is now. Nowadays, kids be hating or jealous of each other and start something over nothing. But we was more family back then. We really was.

There was this old drunk, Ernest Mayfield, who would hang at 27th and Broadway, got drunk every day. He was a drunk, but he was smart, college-educated, and proper. He always had something to tell you or talk to you about. He'd tell us things like, "No girl don't like no men with no stinky tennis shoes. Keep your tennis shoes clean, and you'll get along with her. Stay neat." Me and Tommy heard that, and we always had two pair of Chucks. One pair we'd wear and one pair we'd clean. We took that advice and kept our tennis shoes straight. Little things like that, we listened to Ernest. Ernest would talk so bizarre sometimes, and you'd just have to listen for the message.

Ernest stopped getting drunk about ten years ago. After that, he was just such a different guy. I couldn't believe it. He was a happy drunk anyway, but when he stopped drinking, he was quieter, a little fresher, and talked even more proper. He died about two months ago, God bless his name. I got to see him at the last 28th Street Day. I'm glad I did because I was so happy to see him.

Derek during the time when he was a lifeguard

I got in a little trouble when I was about eight or nine years old. I was real hyper back then, but my big brother Donny was always able to calm me down. So he took me under his wing. He was a lifeguard at Fontaine Ferry Swimming Pool, and he taught me to swim real good. And when he taught classes at work, I was his demonstrator. He didn't have to swim, he just walked back and forth saying, "Flip. Prone. Glide. Flip. Freestyle." All he'd have to do is say it, and I'd demonstrate. I'd show them exactly how it was done. He didn't have to get wet. I was his protégé.

When I was fifteen, the Red Cross sent me to camp to become a water safety instructor. They kept us

nine days and nights, and then I got a license. I come back down to Algonquin Pool to be a lifeguard and water safety instructor. I taught swimming classes and taught lifeguards to be lifeguards.

Every day at the pool, the kids looked for me. They called me Baby Jaws: B.J. I'd wrestle the whole kid network. I'd go in that pool and they'd charge me. I'd be walking through them, slamming them, throwing them. They got a kick out of it. I'd put baby oil all over me so I could slide away from them. I was like Jaws on them. We really had a good time at Algonquin. I hate that these days the city has such a hard time finding lifeguards for the public swimming pools. This summer, if they have a hard time finding people, I'm gonna go. I can still be a lifeguard. I'd like for them to open those pools up because these kids need to get off the street.

After I graduated from Male High School, I got me a girl, Fontaine, and got married. My son passed when he was eight days old. Didn't make it home from the hospital. I don't quite know what happened. He stopped breathing in bed. He didn't make it. People don't understand that just because that child didn't come home and you didn't have him but eight days, it don't matter. That was my baby. After that, I don't remember what happened. I just couldn't take it.

From left: Derek, Fontaine, Angelina, and Alicia

Angelina and Fontaine

I started smoking crack, and a year later, I was in jail. I still wonder what happened that year.

Fourteen months later, I got out. A friend of mine told me that Kentucky Trailer was hiring welders. Chester Murphy's father had an old welder in the garage, so I said, "Murph, I need to learn how to weld." He went out back and said, "Here's a helmet, here's your gloves, here's some sticks, there's your steel: start welding." So I got in the garage and practiced and practiced, and I got it pretty good. I went out to Kentucky Trailer and did the welding test, and they hired me. I worked as a welder at different places for twenty-five years.

Fontaine got pregnant again and our daughter Angelina was born. It was the most wonderful time of my life, but it was scary too, because we'd lost our son at birth. But when she got there, she had five fingers on each hand and five toes on each foot, and everything was cool. I was so happy.

But all this time, my addiction was still going strong. I was a working addict. I wanted to go to work because I wanted to get high. I lost my marriage behind it when Angelina was about five. My addiction was taking me away, but any time Angelina needed something, I made sure she had it. But I should have gave her more time. I should have been home more.

I kept praying, and after fifteen years of using, it finally let me go. I was so happy that I could take that yoke off of me. When you're in your addiction, it steers you. But I was free now. I was so much happier. I started enjoying life more. I could take trips when I felt like it. I fished more. I came back home to the park and started being there a lot more, and it became my anchor. I started setting up right there in the park with the guys. My relationship with Angelina and Fontaine got better. Fontaine became my best friend. When they turned me down for disability, she helped me with all

Derek and Fontaine at a party

the paperwork—it was a whole book of paperwork—and I got approved. She was such a good person. When my grandson was born, that was another happy thing. A grandchild is a whole new different love. It's more powerful. When I seen him, that was something. Angelina went to school to help kids with behavioral problems. She had a big heart. Angelina loved the park, and she loved when I cooked for her. She came down to the park all the time. I'd call and say, "Baby, I'm cooking in the park." She and my grandson are on their way.

But then Fontaine passed in 2015. She was the woman that got hit by the WHAS truck and another vehicle uptown. The WHAS truck kept going. I lost my best friend. It was like, *It just can't be.* She was such a good person. I got hit hard. And then Angelina was

murdered in 2016 on Mother's Day, right in front of her son. She didn't deserve it. She didn't drink. She didn't smoke. If it happened to me, I could understand it. But she didn't deserve it.

They say it gets better, but that's a damn lie. It never gets better. Another thing I don't like—and I know people mean well, and I know it's in the Bible—is when people say, "She's in a better place." You're a liar. She'd be in a better place right here with me, with her daddy. She's not in a better place not being alive with me. So, it ain't no comfort.

Things always worked out hard for me. It's always been hard. I don't know why. It's just my cross to bear. I had stepped off the path in my twenties after my son passed. It just took me out. For a long time, I couldn't

From left: Derek's mother Helen Tyler, Angelina, and Alicia

stand to be around kids. I didn't hate them. It just bothered me. My calling was kids, and I really didn't pay attention. I slipped some kind of way. I got off my path. And I just never got back. Sometimes I felt like it was because I didn't do the right thing when I should have.

I know I should've worked with kids until I die. I still love them. It might not still be too late because the Lord let me stay around for some reason. I have a bullet in my ankle, and I've had a gun pulled on me: *click, click, click,* but it didn't go off. So, why am I still here? Why you take mine and leave me here? I wonder why. But I should've worked with kids.

I used to love to fight. I used to fight at the drop of a hat. I mean, real quick. I think I had a Napoleon complex because I was short. If something come up, somebody would say, "Get Derek," because I'd get it started. I'd hit somebody in a minute. I used to love it. There was something about getting in with that anger that I enjoyed. And once that anger feeds and you enjoy it, it grows. Then, after a while, I started learning. I kept getting in trouble for this, that, and the other. Once I could control it, I felt better. Because it's better being in control of the situation than it getting out of control.

I like being in control a lot better now. I like being able to talk my way out. I ain't got to battle. I can talk. Once you go to battle, you don't think anymore. You're just battling. But I enjoy peace. I enjoy smiles. I'd rather smile than frown.

My grief keeps me enough down. I don't need nothing else because that's enough. I've had a hard life. Sometimes I feel cheated, but that's just the way it happened. Sometimes I think I must've been a bad person in another life, and I'm paying for it in this one. That's how hard it's been. But I'm happy. I woke up. I fought my fight. Could I have done things different? Hell yeah. Who wouldn't if they had hindsight? A lot of things I'd do different. I wouldn't have lost that year, and I wouldn't have got locked up. I'd have seeked help. And just little things I would've done different because I was always in a hurry. But I'm at the second half, and I'm gonna do what I gotta do to end this book out.

The park is home. I feel safe and secure. I come up right there. The way my life is now, it is peace to me. I can go there, sit, turn that music on, and think of every-thing. *Whatever happens, I've gotta do what I gotta do.* I don't care how bad I feel the day before, I got to get up and thank God for another day and keep it moving. It feels like a safe area to me. I go right there, and I never have a problem over there. I've had arguments, of course, but never no real bad conflict. We don't come here to fight. We don't come to argue. We come to enjoy ourselves. To drink and smoke or whatever and just have a good time. This is peaceful.

We done made this our spot. I know it's wrong because it ain't my spot for real, but sometimes I come up there, and people be in my spot, and I'm like, "Man, why you in my spot?" In the whole world, I just want this one spot. I'll go around mean-mugging them and stuff. I'll be mad. Sometimes they don't know. And some people, I'll tell them, "Move."

Without the park, we'd all be doing our different things. Because you grow apart. We all be doing our different things. But that park, and those bicycles, that's something that pulls us all the way back together.

It's good people down there in the park. Come enjoy it with us one time. If you see a grill smoking on the 29th Street side of the park, come on down over there and sit down with us. Have a meal. Enjoy yourself. Drink a beer or pop or water. Whatever you desire. Come on over there and kick it. You'll find out you'll mess around and have some fun. And we ride bicycles on Tuesdays and Thursdays at six o'clock. Come on by.

When I die, I hope they can burn me up and throw my ashes all around Elliott Park, walking in four directions, pour me all over that son of a gun. I mean it. I'm settled on it. That's where I wanna be. Don't waste no money throwing me in the ground. Put that money in your pocket and take a trip on me. The park is where I'd love to be, which is probably what'll happen. They'll probably do that. My boys gonna come for me. ✦

Surrounded by Excellence

CARRYE JONES

Once, when my brother was in college, he received a letter from our father. Something he said in that letter has always stuck with me. He said, "Your childhood was happy because your mother and I were determined that it would be that way. If you live your life as you should, each stage is the best one. Your childhood and your late years should be the happiest times of your life." This has been very true for me. This is a happy time in my life, and I also had a very happy childhood.

I grew up at 1518 W. Chestnut St. My mother would say, "in the house between the two big trees on the south side of the street." We are sort of original Russell people before it was even Russell. My great-grandfather, John Martin Daniel, came to Louisville in the late 1800s from Stephensport, Kentucky. He was an enslaved person owned by his father Vivian Daniel, the richest man in Breckinridge County. If things had been different, our family would be millionaires.

Once my great-grandfather was freed, he moved to Louisville and worked as a porter at the Seelbach Hotel. We have a sense that he was able to get that really good job because of who his white father was. John Martin Daniel had nine children, and eventually he bought property for them. The family owned 1510, 1512, 1518, and 1529 Chestnut St., as well as property elsewhere. My husband and I own 1518 to this day.

My grandmother Carrie was a seamstress and made all my mother's clothes. I understand my mother was one of the best-dressed girls in Louisville in her day because her mother made all her pretty clothes. I'm named after my grandmother. She adored me. She died when I was eight months old. Still, there has been so much talk about how much she adored me, how she ran to greet my mother and father when they brought me home to the hospital, and how she rocked me in this beautiful sewing rocker I now have in my home.

Carrye's great-grandfather John Martin Daniel

I feel like I knew her. I feel like I can remember being rocked by her in that rocker.

We had a happy home life and were a close family. Being the oldest child, I felt very much adored my whole life. I was the first girl on my father's side of the family. My parents' friends were excited about me, and my grandparents were excited. My favorite aunt, Aunt Kate, lived across the street from us at the house my uncle John built at 1529 W. Chestnut St. We had the same birthday, and she would make me a lemon meringue pie to celebrate. My uncle Everett and Aunt Elma lived on our block, too. Uncle Everett kept his first wife Keturah's ashes in an urn on his mantel. He was blind, and I remember him reading Braille books. My aunt Hattie lived at 1512 W. Chestnut.

From left: Joseph P., Carrye, Margaret, and Joseph H.

Joseph Bowers with his four children: (clockwise from top left) Carrye, Joseph, Jomare, and Billye

She was a teacher and the first female trustee at Quinn Chapel AME Church. Her house was listed as a guest house in the Green Book, a document that Black travelers would use to find Black-friendly accommodations, restaurants, and other businesses.

School was wonderful. I went to Western Elementary School at 16th and Magazine. It later became William H. Perry Sr. Elementary School. We had wonderful teachers who were our family friends, and my parents were very involved. My mother did not work outside the home when we were in elementary school, so she was always there for us. My mother would sometimes come by the school and see how we were doing during the day. She'd go for a walk with my little sister Billye in a stroller, and they'd show up outside the fence. One day I really wanted to see her, so I prayed that Mommy would come walking past the school, and she did: my prayer was answered. And I think that was a turning point for me in my faith.

As children, we had play clothes and we had school clothes, and never the twain shall meet. During the summer, we'd play in our play clothes, then get dressed up for dinner before Daddy came home from work. We'd be really dressed up. After dinner, my mother and we kids would go for a walk through the neighborhood. We'd go over to Broadway and walk down Chestnut all the way to 26th. We knew people all up and down. Often people we knew would be sitting on their porches, and we'd just stop and talk. We enjoyed going to Page's Confectionery. Daddy bought me my first soda there. It was the first time I'd used a straw, and instead of sucking on it, I blew. I had on a pink pinafore, and I got chocolate soda all over that pink pinafore.

On Sunday afternoons, we'd go "pop calling." We'd get in the car and we might drive as far away as Newburg to visit people. Just pop in. You didn't have to call anybody and say, "Can I come?" You didn't have to have a playdate like children have today. You could just show up, and they'd be glad to see you. People just aren't that free anymore. There's a lot more pretense today.

Joseph and Margaret Bowers on their wedding day

Pas Si Bête Bridge Club at the Brock Building.
Carrye's mother, Margaret Bowers, is at bottom right.

Joseph Bowers shooting pool at the Brock Building

Carrye's parents, Joseph and Margaret Bowers,
often dressed up and attended social events

Your home was a place where you welcomed people, and other people's homes welcomed you.

The Black community was truly a community. We all lived together: the college president, the custodian, the housekeeper, the teacher, the principal, the ice cream shop owner, the house painter, the attorney who was alternate delegate to the United Nations, the barber, the accountant, the librarian, the medical doctor, the mortician, the secretary, the musician, the landscaper, the judge, the lawyer, the YMCA executive, the printer, the upholsterer, the mechanic, the gas station owner, the postal worker, the electrician, the plumber, the brick mason, the taxi cab owner, the caterer, the restaurant owner, the preacher, the tailor: these were the Black people in my neighborhood, in my life. We all knew and respected one another. You could see the possibilities because the possibilities might be embodied in your neighbor or church member. Everybody worked, and worked hard. Everybody took their jobs very seriously and did them very well. There was just this great work ethic and belief that all work is honorable, and that you learn something from every job that you do.

We knew our neighbors, and our neighbors knew us. That was a good thing about the area. They cared and we cared. If somebody died, they'd put a black wreath on their door, and everybody in the neighborhood would collect money to give to the family.

We had organizations that allowed us to do some very special things. There was a great club movement among Black people, and those clubs were really important to the demographic of people with whom I grew up. One of the reasons for the club movement was that everything was segregated, and we couldn't go into a lot of places, so we met in each other's homes. We socialized through those organizations. There were the Greek organizations, social organizations, and civic organizations. All those things were within our world, so we had great opportunities. Both my parents were active in their Greek organizations and had a very active social life. They frequently dressed up formally for dances and parties with their friends.

Louisville has one of the oldest Jack and Jill chapters in the United States. Jack and Jill was founded in 1938 by a group of Black mothers for the educational, social, civic, and recreational development of their children. There were chapters all over the country. The Louisville chapter was founded in 1954. My mother was in the first group after it was chartered here. We had age groups, three to five and seven to nine, and and so on: the little children, the Humpty Dumpties, the Lads and Lassies, and the La Teens. We had activities for each group every month. You would move up as you moved in age, so you got to know this core group of people really well.

Jack and Jill allowed us to be exposed and to get to know children of like-minded families. We had opportunities to travel. Both my parents were college educated, so they had friends everywhere. When we would travel, they'd look up a good friend, and we'd stay with that friend. When I was older, I would travel, and people would say, "Do you know somebody everywhere?" And I said, "Yes, I sort of do." Because we had to do that, we had to connect with each other and be close to one another to make life work well for us. It served us well during segregation. When you're part of these organizations, you walk into a town, and you network. It's an instant way to get to know people. When we traveled a lot with my husband's work, we'd move into a town and instantly be a part of that group because of the organizations, and then we'd make friends with them. And that makes all the difference in the world. We had a tremendous amount of exposure that really served us well.

Jack and Jill La Teens meeting, 1965

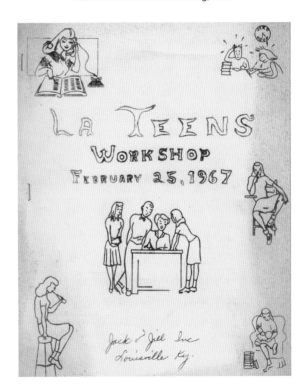

Jack and Jill is still going strong. Three of my children were teen officers in the Eastern region. My oldest daughter was the president of the Eastern region. My son was a treasurer, and one of my daughters was secretary. That's very important because my

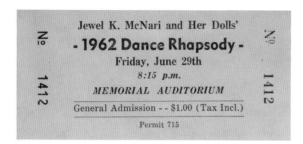

Ticket to Jewel McNari and Her Dolls' 1962 Rhapsody

father always said, "You need to be able to network." That's one of the real positive things about belonging to these national organizations.

When I was younger, Jack and Jill could reserve Memorial Auditorium just for us. We were exposed to events you couldn't go to if you weren't a member. I remember seeing a live theatrical performance of *A Raisin in the Sun* there. The stars were Sidney Poitier, Ruby Dee, and Glynn Thurman. Another time, we saw Marian Anderson and went to the stage door to get her autograph. I remember thinking she had such beautiful skin. She stayed at Dr. Jesse Bell and Geneva Bell's house when she was in town. We got to do a lot that the average white person wasn't even getting to do.

Another activity we held at Memorial Auditorium that was extremely important to our family was the Rhapsody—a big dance recital—of the Jewel K. McNari Dolls. Jewel McNari was the preeminent dance teacher in Louisville when we were growing up. She was a legend who trained generations of dancers. We'd have this big Rhapsody and these beautiful costumes made by excellent seamstresses from our community. We would go to their houses, we'd get measured for our costumes, and they would make these beautiful costumes. We didn't order them out of a catalog, as happened later.

My first solo was to the music "To a Wild Rose." I was about eight. I had a rose in my hand and this beautiful costume. There was a lady named Mrs. Seay who lived in Sheppard Square. We went to her home, and she would take us to her sewing room, where she measured me and created my beautiful costume so I could look like a rose.

Jewel McNari and I were very close, and being a dancer in her school really gave me a lot of self-confidence. It gave me poise and grace. Having a dancer's image has always been important to me. I danced when I was a student at Baldwin-Wallace College, and I continued to teach dance throughout my life. After I graduated college, I helped teach dance classes at the Plymouth Settlement House, which was a hub for Black people in the community. There were basketball teams, the Scouts, talent shows, cooking classes, dance lessons, all kinds of things going on for the community at the Plymouth Settlement House. People came from everywhere.

The Settlement House was connected to our church, Plymouth Congregational United Church of Christ. The church was a very important part of our lives. Most of the members of Plymouth were professionals. Recently, my husband Franklin and I were looking at a picture of the faculty of Central High School back in the '50s, and ninety percent of that faculty belonged to Plymouth Church. That tells you something about the demographic of people who belonged to the church. We were surrounded by excellence.

Our house was always full of young people. My father always said, "We welcome everybody to our house because that way, we know where our children are." My family renovated the upstairs, and it became our social place—a whole floor. The party room had this bar with a canopy, and we had tables and chairs in there. We had a record player up there, so our friends would come and dance to the Supremes and other Motown artists. The room was pink and green.

Carrye Jones during her time as a dancer

My mother was an AKA, and she loved those colors. There was an adjacent room where we could set up tables and have parties. We had a lot of good parties there upstairs at 1518 West Chestnut. Just really good times.

In the '50s, before they renovated the upstairs, my parents added a big addition onto the house so that we could all have our own rooms, modern bathrooms, and a modern kitchen. It took my dad a long time to find a contractor to build that addition. Finally, he decided on this white contractor from Portland named Mr. Sutter. My father thought a great deal of Mr. Sutter, and I think he thought a great deal of my dad. They agreed on what to do, and we were ready to break ground. On the day he was supposed to start our addition, we opened up the front page of the *Courier-Journal,* and Mr. Sutter had died.

Daddy said, "We're going to Portland to pay our respects to the Sutters." In those days, Portland was really racist. They'd call you a bad name, even the little kids. One day I was in the car with my mother in Portland, and these little kids who were younger than I was called us "niggers." But our whole family went to the Sutter's house, and when we walked in, the people just looked at us like, *Who are they?* You could feel it. My father and mother went right up to Mrs. Sutter and expressed their condolences to her and her family, and we left. That must have made a real impression on her because after Mrs. Sutter had settled her husband's arrangements, she told my dad, "We're going to do this job. It's going to be the last job we do." It gives me chills thinking about it. Mrs. Sutter and her son oversaw the completion of that job. And they did an amazing job. That addition stands strong today.

That's a very special story in our family. My father always said, "You cannot judge a group of people. Take one person at a time." He always taught us that. "You say Portland's terrible? What about the Sutters? Once a person gets to know you, that person cannot hold on to his or her stereotypes." You just get to know a person, one individual at a time. And you make an impact because not only will that person be changed, that person will change people with whom he is associated. He taught us that and I think it's true.

My father was really wise. He would say, "I pray that my children are innocent, but I know that they're not ignorant. Ignorance leads to a loss of innocence." Daddy taught me about the birds and the bees. He taught me that your word is your bond, that integrity is really important, and that somebody is always watching you. He taught me that there is a time and a place for everything. He taught me that communication is the key to life. He was a great communicator. He taught me not to have negative opinions about

Carrye and her friend Alice Kean in Tuileries Garden in Paris, France

other groups of people because you never know who you're related to.

People used to do graffiti on the viaduct there at 14th Street. He took me there and showed me all those words and told me what they meant. He said, "This is what these words mean. You should never use them. If you have a command of the King's English, you don't have to curse. People who curse just don't know the language. You can use the words in the English language to say the very same things, and they're magnificent words. You'll have friends who will curse, and we will never judge them, but I don't expect this of my children." How could I disappoint a father like that? This is the kind of quiet upbringing that we had. He was just special like that. He made sure that we were knowledgeable and that we would never disappoint our parents. And it's the same with my children.

People had great respect for my dad. He could get along with anybody, but he could also put you in your place in a very gentlemanly way. He just knew who he was, he wasn't intimidated by anybody, and he taught us that.

My mother taught us a lot, too. I remember visiting my mother's friend, who we called Ruthie, in Missouri once and watching my mother and Aunt Ruthie giggle all night. When I saw that, I realized that our ages go up, but our spirits stay the same. My mother also told us, "You should have friends of all ages. Between twenty-one and one hundred, you're all adults." She said it's important to make friends with people of all ages because you have to relate to everybody and you learn from one another. I've lived that way and my children live that way. When I was raising my children, some of my best friends were twenty years older than me, and they shared so much wisdom with me as a young mother. One of my best friends today is much younger than me. I'm older than her parents. When she was looking at schools for her children, I went with her and gave her my observations. And she helps me understand what younger people are thinking today. My mother was so wise about friendship and so many other things.

I went to Montpellier, France, in 1962 when I was fifteen with a group of local high school students

Carrye in England during her six-week trip
to Europe when she was fifteen

sponsored by the University of Louisville. We were gone for nine weeks. I turned sixteen in France and danced on Bastille Day in my toe shoes. The whole group was white except for me and my dear friend Alice Kean. We were friends as children, were in Jack and Jill together, and were classmates at Central High. Alice and I had made friends with two girls, Sarah and Sally—I remember their names to this day because Sally's father was president of Vanderbilt University. The chaperones, teachers from high schools here in Louisville, were prejudiced and did not want us to room with the white girls.

I wrote letters to my parents and told them about these chaperones who did not want us rooming with Sarah and Sally. My daddy wrote back and said, "Well, this is what you have to do. Since it's all about color, just put on your white glove and raise your hand, and you'll

be able to room with them." In those days, we wore white gloves when we dressed up. I'll never forget the way Daddy brought levity to the whole situation. My parents were so wise about race relations. Daddy would always say, "It's not you; it's them. Just consider the source and keep on walking. They've got the problem; you don't." And when you know that it's not you, it's that they're afraid or uneducated, ignorant as he would say, you just keep on with your life.

But we had a great experience. Just to think, we had enough confidence to do that trip. I was talking to some ladies, and they said, "Your parents let you go away for nine weeks?" I said, "*Let* me? That's the way we were raised! They weren't afraid. Why would they be? No, they wanted us to have experiences." My parents wanted us to have all the possible opportunities that we could have, and so they worked hard to make sure that we had them. And I know it wasn't easy. That trip cost seven hundred and fifty dollars, which was a lot of money in 1962. But my father was just determined that we would have opportunities and exposures. And there were other people in the community who wanted me to have the experience and helped finance that experience for me. They were good friends with resources, and I'm very grateful for that.

My father was a self-employed accountant and handled the finances of many of Louisville's Black businesses. He also worked in the post office. He finally became the director of finance before he died. The man had the same credentials his whole life, but he didn't get that opportunity until later when things kind of started opening up. He was always ready. It was very common to see educated Black men working for white men with no education. When I look at the paid corporate boards across the nation today, many white men on the boards are not credentialed, but the Black people on the boards are highly credentialed.

Margaret and Joseph Bowers on Chestnut St., ca. 1946

Joseph Bowers training U.S. Post Office colleagues on a computer

Margaret Bowers reading to granddaughters Elizabeth Mizzell, who is now the director of resident engagement at Byron Wellness Community in Fort Wayne, IN, and Grace Sanders Johnson, who is now an assistant professor of Africana Studies at the University of Pennsylvania

Likewise, my mother went to Wilberforce University and majored in English. She went on to get a second bachelor's in Library Science at Hampton Institute in 1935 as part of the school's last library science class and later did graduate work at the School of Library Science at Columbia University in New York. She was the children's librarian at the Louisville Free Public Library's Western Branch and the head librarian at both the Eastern Branch and the Shawnee Branch. My mother was president of the Top Ladies of Distinction group, a Kentucky Colonel, and a member of the Urban League Guild. Some of the white librarians did not have credentials.

Our parents raised us to be quiet contributors and good citizens. They had high expectations for us, and we didn't want to disappoint anybody. That served us well. We all worked really hard, and we each tried to be the best we could be. And the village cared so much for us, told us we could be anything we wanted to be, but that we would have to be three times as good. We had to learn to have a presence. That's why people from earlier generations were so well-educated; they needed to be in order to get any kind of job. Education has been so important to us for generations.

I went to a party at a white friend's house just a few years ago. A man asked me where I went to high school, and I said Central. He said, "I was wondering if anybody learned anything down there." In Louisville, Caucasian people have no need to know about Black people, so there's a lack of exposure to Black people and Black history, and really a lack of interest.

Most of the Black teachers I had growing up had graduate degrees. Lyman T. Johnson was my civics teacher. He was brilliant. Probably the best teacher I ever had. He taught us all the court cases and all the issues that were going on in America. There are people today that don't know anything about things like the

Day Law. People don't know what they don't know. What I see today is a lack of truth. But sometimes, people don't want to hear the truth.

We were always being educated by our elders outside of school, too. For example, my family was friends with Andrew and Charlotte Wade. They were in and out of our house all the time because they were really good friends. We used to go on picnics together. Mr. Wade and his father were electricians and their business was on 18th Street. They were our electricians. In 1954, the Wades wanted to buy a house in Shively, but no one would sell to a Black family. So their white activist friends Anne and Carl Braden purchased a house for them—though it was the Wades' money—then transferred the house to the Wades. The neighbors burned crosses on their lawn and bombed their house. It was a huge moment in the fight for housing desegregation in Louisville. My parents talked to us about it, and that really had an impact on me because they were our friends.

Then in 1955, Emmett Till was murdered. I'll never forget that. Then the Montgomery Bus Boycott happened. We heard about lynchings. So we were very much aware that horrible things could happen to us. My father and my mother talked a lot about it, too. We talked about those things at home. We even knew about the 1921 Tulsa race massacre.

We were also being educated in empowerment. My parents were always supportive of the NAACP and the Urban League. They always made contributions to the NAACP's Legal Defense Fund. When Woodford Porter ran for a seat on the school board in 1959, I would go with my parents to these meetings held by the NAACP. They always wanted me and my siblings to experience things like that. They were very intentional about us being aware of what was going on. At these meetings, people were instructed on how to vote

Cover of booklet created and circulated by the Wade Defense Committee

to ensure that Woodford Porter would secure enough votes to win: "It might say vote for two or three candidates, but only vote for Woodford Porter because every time you vote for somebody else, it takes a vote away from him." And he won. It was monumental. It's something I remember extremely well as a child. I think of it as the community coming together to make something really significant happen. That was a *community* effort.

When I think back on it and talk to my friends about it, our parents really protected us from the negativity. Were things segregated? Yes. But all of our parents were masterful at not letting that touch us. They protected us from being in parts of town where we might be called a bad name.

In 1961, high school student leaders began organizing civil rights demonstrations in Louisville.

At fourteen years old, I was an NAACP youth member and had been to NAACP youth conferences. Being very aware of what was going on in the United States, I was compelled to be a part of the movement.

My parents had always been protective of me. Still, they were always about integrity and doing the right thing, and at this time, they considered this the right thing to do. My father said, "I can't go out there because I have to take care of my family. I can't lose my job." You couldn't be beholden to the white man for your money because they'd snatch your job in a minute. I heard adults discussing this explicitly. That's why the movement was led by ministers. They weren't reliant on white money. They were dependent on their own people for their living. That's also why the youth were out front. My parents talked to me about it, and we decided that I would be the representative from our family since I was the oldest child. I felt proud to be able to be involved. It felt like it was really important.

We were trying to open public accommodations in Louisville. We were demonstrating to go into the movie theaters and the Blue Boar Cafeteria. Martin Luther King Jr. came to speak to us in the spring of 1961, and I'll never forget that. He was maybe four feet away from me when he was talking to us about nonviolent demonstrations. It was special to be at the feet of Martin Luther King, and that was before he became all he would become. It was profound.

When I was in the ninth grade at Russell Junior High, we'd go to Quinn Chapel every day after school to do trainings before the demonstrations downtown. Leaders like Raoul Cunningham and Arthur Smith, who had been our paperboy, and Frank Stanley Jr., the son of the publisher of the *Louisville Defender*. Rev. F.G. Sampson of Mount Lebanon Baptist Church would lead the proceedings. These high school seniors would

come into the church, and they'd come down that aisle on the left side. Those young men were so impressive. One of them was my future husband, Franklin Jones.

Everything was very well planned in those days. Nothing was ever random. We would discuss the plan and prepare at Quinn Chapel, then walk down to Fourth Street. Everything was well thought out. You learned a lot of critical thinking. We were *really* trained about how to behave when we went to demonstrate downtown: how to react if somebody tried to push you or touch you, what to do if you were arrested and put in the paddy wagon. They said if we got arrested, Black lawyers would make sure we got out that day. We were to be very dignified and nonviolent.

I can remember walking in a circle singing "We Shall Overcome" and "We Shall Not Be Moved" in front of the Palace Theatre. The little white lady who took the tickets just broke down and cried. Like, *It's not my fault.* She was teary because there was nothing she could do. We didn't bother her. We were just walking around in a circle, and she just cried and cried. It was all very deliberate.

My baby sister said to me recently, "You know, I took part in the civil rights movement. You know what my role was?"

I said, "What?"

"I washed your dishes. That was my role." In our home, we all had chores to do. If I was out demonstrating, my father told my sister, "You're going to wash the dishes while Carrye's out demonstrating for our rights. That's the role you'll play, Billye." We each had our part to play.

The department stores downtown didn't hire Black sales associates, and in some of them, Black patrons couldn't try on clothes the way white customers could. To get them to start hiring Black sales associates, we had a "Nothing New for Easter" campaign.

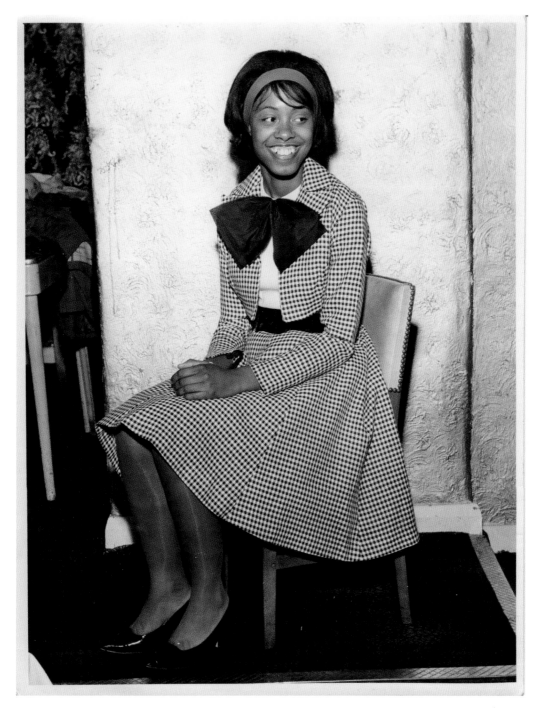

Carrye, age 15

Original pin from the "Nothing New for Easter" campaign

Black people would always buy a lot of new clothes for Easter. Everybody had new dresses, new bonnets, and new shoes. We knew that the way to get to people was economically. So we're going to take away the money from the establishment downtown. The NAACP made these buttons, and I still have mine: "Nothing New for Easter." We were going to hit them in the pocketbook. We had this big campaign, and nobody bought anything for Easter on Fourth Street. After the campaign was over, you started to see Black sales associates in those stores.

It's important to me that young people understand the shoulders upon which they stand, to know that they're in a community that was celebrated and formed by so many resilient people, and that they can do this too. When you know the history, you know what's possible for you. You also learn that there is often a backlash after a big step forward. We talk to our children and our grandchildren about that. It's important that they understand, too. My husband and I don't sit down in a restaurant today without thinking about a time when we couldn't do this. That's always in our heads.

Following those formative years, I graduated fourth in my class from Central High School and went to Baldwin-Wallace College in Berea, Ohio. While I was in college, my neighborhood back home began to be decimated by Urban Renewal, but I did not have a sense of that at the time. I came back home to Louisville in the summers. One summer, I had a job as a report coordinator for Urban Renewal. I was young; it was a summer job in an office. I was some kind of coordinator, keeping records of things that were happening. I didn't realize what was happening or the impact it would have on our community. I really did not. But when I saw those houses come down on the north side of Chestnut, that was devastating. Some of those were rental properties, but some were owned by Black people. Mr. and Mrs. Hammond—Elmer Lucille Allen's father and stepmother—lived across the street from my family. They had a phenomenal home with big stained glass windows and a kitchen with a fireplace in it. It was a beautiful house. And the city tore it down.

My husband and I discovered each other the summer after I graduated from college. I was in Joe's Palm Room with two of my girlfriends, which is something I very rarely did. He came in with his sister and her fiance. He was showing them around town. They sat up in the upper level with the beaded curtains, and after a while, he came down to talk with me. "Don't I know you from somewhere?" He knew my friend Alice, so I said, "Yes, I'm Alice's friend." We talked for a while. He's fluent in French—very smart—and he started reciting this Victor Hugo poem to me in French. He has a very deep, melodious voice. Then he said, "Maybe we can go out this summer sometime." That's how we first connected.

Clockwise from left: Billye, Carrye, Joseph H., Jomare, Margaret, and Joseph P. Bowers

For our first date, we went to see an Aretha Franklin concert at the Exposition Center. That was the first time I'd gone to one of those because our parents didn't allow us to go to what they called "rock and roll" shows. They would say, "You don't know who's going to be in those kinds of places. They might be smoking pot. The police might come."

Franklin and I dated, and then I went to work on the Dean of Women's staff at Albion College in Albion, Michigan, directing a residence hall. He was working in one of the big city social programs and would come and visit me up in Michigan. We were engaged the next March and married in Louisville on August 23, 1969. We lived in Louisville for six years before my husband got a Rockefeller Foundation Fellowship to get his MBA at the University of Chicago. We lived in Chicago for two years. Our two daughters went to Hyde Park Unitarian Co-op School, which was really special. In a co-op school, the parents are very involved, classes are really small, and a lot of individual attention is given to the students. Then we moved to Davenport, Iowa, where my husband was recruited

for a job at Vendix Corporation. That was really a very special place full of good people. The kids walked to school and then walked home for lunch, which was at least an hour. We had PTA meetings in our homes. It was utopian.

Eventually, we moved to the DC area, and we were there for a long time. Our children would say they're from Maryland. I got my master's of arts in teaching from Howard University, then taught in gifted education programs in Howard County, Maryland, for fifteen years. Then I transitioned to working in human resources in the school district.

We had so many opportunities there. We'd go to seminars and commencements at Howard and see all these notable people. We belonged to Metropolitan

Baptist Church, one of the biggest churches there at the time. Maya Angelou was there all the time. Rev. Jesse Jackson, Dr. Benjamin Mays, all these people were just *there*. We saw these people on a regular basis in different settings.

We would spend Sundays being tourists. We saw all the Smithsonians. The exposure that my children had because of where we were was really, really special. When Nelson Mandela was released from prison, he came to DC, and our daughter Carolyn, who shares a birthday with him, got to meet him. National news was our local news. My children had classmates whose parents were members of Congress, the Secret Service, the press, and much more. So I'm thankful that they grew up in the DC area. My daughter Margaret is a member of the Supreme Court bar, and her son Allan had an internship at the Supreme Court when he was still in *high school*. That's usually for young lawyers. He's a very outstanding young man and went on to attend West Point.

We always wanted to move back to Louisville, and after years in Maryland, that's what we did. My husband received a career opportunity, and I was offered a position with Jefferson County Public Schools, so we returned. His mother was here, she was aging, so it was good for us to be here for her. We like Louisville. We have friends here. We always stayed in touch with our friends and often came back to visit. So now we have old friends and we've made new ones. It's been good for us.

I am so impressed with the young leaders in Louisville. Our city is in good hands as we start to move forward. There are some excellent young people in leadership roles. The torch has started to pass here to these right-thinking young people, so that makes me hopeful there will be some positive change as we move forward.

Carrye and Franklin Jones with most of their children and grandchildren at their 50th wedding anniversary celebration

There's a lot happening in Russell. Some good things. There's money being poured into the community. There are a number of investors coming in and buying property. I'm kind of sad because I don't know where that's going to lead. I think it's going to displace a lot of Black people. A large percentage of people in Russell rent, and I don't know where those people will go.

There's Russell: A Place of Promise, and that's a good thing. Molo Village, developed by Rev. Jamesetta Ferguson, is phenomenal. To have somebody like her in the community is very positive. The Urban League has accomplished a great deal under the leadership of Sadiqa Reynolds. So I do have some hope. But I just wonder if it will ever become a community again where we can live, support one another, and enjoy amenities.

I can't drive up Chestnut Street without remembering beautiful homes, great friends and neighbors, and all the love and caring. I think about our family, the family built by Margaret and Joseph Bowers, their children, grandchildren, and great-grandchildren. You don't know who was behind those doors at 1518 West Chestnut. Forty-seven people are the progeny of that one home. My brother, Dr. Joseph Bowers, has been a practicing periodontist for nearly forty years in Albuquerque, New Mexico, and is a retired full-bird colonel in the Air Force. My middle sister Jomare Bowers-Mizzell is an interior designer, banker, and artist, a public TV show host in Fort Wayne, Indiana, and has served as executive director of the Northeast Indiana Small Business Development Center. My baby sister, D. Billye Sanders, is a prominent attorney in Nashville, Tennessee. She's a regulatory law expert and has been a trustee at Fisk University. Our children and grandchildren are just as accomplished. We're very blessed. We haven't had scandal or disgrace. We had wonderful parents who were so unassuming. They didn't boast about it; they just did it. We wouldn't be where we are if it weren't for them and for God's grace. ✦

More Than Just a Block Party

SHELLAINE TURNER

PHOTO BY DARCY THOMPSON

My husband Ronnie and I started dating when we were in high school. After graduating from Valley High School, we moved together to an apartment on Cane Run Road. When I was around twenty-three, I decided that I wanted to get a house. A realtor got me connected with Sam Watkins, who was the president of Louisville Central Community Center, which had a homeowner program. If you qualified and went through the program, they would cover your down payment on a new home. They gave us stipends every two weeks and took us on a little field trip down to Metro Council to see how laws work and how we can become a part of the community. As that process was going on, my house was slowly being built on 16th Street.

We moved in May 1994. I decided to follow my heart and have a family. Ronnie and I got married in 1996, and about two years later, we had twin boys: Nathan and Nicholas Turner. I wanted to make sure I was equipped to take care of my financial bills, so I went to Jefferson Community College and worked there as I got my associate's degree. I got school to pay for it because I worked there as an employee and received financial aid and grants. I transitioned from there to UofL, did a work-study, worked part-time, got assistance, and got my bachelor's degree. I did all of this while being a mom and a wife and making sure our family's needs were met, going to church, and just trying to be a good all-around neighbor.

When the twins were two years old, an incident occurred that led me to become an activist in my neighborhood. I was warming up my car one rainy day. I'd taken several items into the car and went back inside to get the twin boys, and I didn't lock my door. When I carried the kids out to the car, it was gone. I called the police to make a report. Three days later, the police gave me a call back to say they spotted the car

on 26th Street. I called my sister, and she came over to take me to get my car. I didn't have the keys because I had left them in the car, so I was standing there with my twins, looking at my car, and these young teenagers walked past. One of them said, "Ma'am, do you want me to move my car?" I said, "Well, that is *my* car," and the teenagers turned around and walked the other way into the alley. I called the police and said I spotted the car and the teenagers that took it. When the police came, he told me he was gonna go down that alley and talk to the boys, and if they give the keys back, he wouldn't take them to the Jefferson County Youth Detention Center. The policeman ended up talking to me too long, but the teenagers had thrown the keys by the garbage can. The policeman brought the keys back to me. They had left behind a rap CD in my car with foul music, and the boys' car seats weren't in the back. I looked in the trunk and found my car seats, so I was like. *Oh, they had a little humanity.*

I was upset. I was emotional. When I got home and had time to think about it, I decided I didn't want to be a victim. I needed to be an advocate and speak up and let other people know because if it happened to me, it could happen to somebody else. I needed to change the way I viewed my neighbors and neighborhood. I felt like we were just living here, and we really didn't know nobody. So I started a block watch to look after cars, houses, and property. That probably was in 1998. And then we just started talking from time to time. We would sometimes talk in the alleyway, and sometimes we got a little more comfortable at a neighbor's house. We started meeting outside of our home. Sometimes Joshua Tabernacle lets us go over there and talk. No one had phone numbers for each other, so we made a list. Then my neighbor Renia stated, "Maybe we should have a neighborhood party." I was like, "Yeah, we need a block party." I needed my sons

to see that people can get out here and take care of their community.

The goal was to introduce ourselves to each other for the security of the neighborhood. I was just looking for us to start watching after each other so that if a car is stolen, you will say something, or if you see somebody going in a neighbor's window, you can say something to the neighbor. I can call you because now I have your phone number.

I remembered from when Sam Watkins took us to sit in on Metro Council meetings that there were Metro Council funds for neighborhood organizations and things like block parties. So I thought, *Let me find out who our Metro Councilperson is*. I found out it was George Unseld, and I called his office, informed his secretary what we were going to have, and she said that was okay. We asked for a donation to purchase groceries for the block party, and they allotted us three hundred dollars. She said, "I'll meet you there at Kroger on Third Street and give you a card you can use to pay for your food." She told me that we also would need to go to Metro Council to request a permit, and I did that. The day before the block party, we just went to Kroger, and we got exactly what we wanted. Each year changes were made to the required paperwork, and additional documentation was required. I think it happened after the controversy with Councilwoman Judy Green's Green Clean Team summer jobs program for teenagers. That's when a lot of changes started taking place toward the end.

When I called for assistance for the annual 16th Street block party, I was told to come and get paperwork, fill it out, go do your grocery store shopping, then take your receipt and bring it back to us. I and a couple other neighbors did the shopping, and we purchased two baskets full of items. Then we had to put it all away until we came back the day before the block party.

Ronnie getting ready to string a banner across the street. Mr. William bought the banner.

Shellaine's sons Nathan and Nikolas helping Mr. William set up trash cans

Then Metro cut a check for the dollar amount on that receipt. Then we still would have to bring that receipt back to them and show it to them. The last time we had a block party, they said we needed to use a tax ID. So we went to LCCC around the corner and spoke to Kevin Fields, and he let us use their tax ID. Then we had to go shopping, get a receipt, and write down the items we were getting. Then we got the exact dollar amount back in the form of a check. It used to be just one sheet of paper, and then it went to stacks of paper. Now they want us to answer questions like,

Renee Wright's mother and Nathan Turner

Ronnie and a neighbor's cousin who was in town visiting

Why do you need this block party? How many people will be there? Paperwork after paperwork. Renia Wright was really good with always knowing what the dollar amount would be down to all the groceries. So she would always take care of that. She and Ms. Yvonne Bowler would go shopping, and I would fill out the paperwork.

Metro Council limits the money to neighborhood expenses. They would only pay for the food. But we still needed money to pay the DJ, buy prizes, and rent items such as a cotton candy machine. The rental place we used was in the Highlands area, and when it closed down, we bought a cotton candy machine and a casino wheel with numbers one through one hundred on it from them. Ms. Yvonne has that in her house.

The block party used to happen in August, close to the start of the school year. A couple of weeks before the block party, we went door to door to give out flyers to let people know which day the block party would be. If people were outside, we could talk to them about the block party. We put No Parking signs on the telephone poles.

This is always a busy street, so the city gave us permission to block it off from Jefferson Street all the way to Muhammad Ali. For just one day, we had time to actually get on our own street, to just walk on it and play and jump and talk to family and friends and dance. Kids got to play out in front of the street, and adults and kids would walk over from other areas of the neighborhood and enjoy the block party, sit in front of the neighbor's houses, or out in the street, or just walk up and down.

The annual block party would last until ten o'clock at night. We would start setting up at eight o'clock in the morning. City employees set up sawhorses to block off 16th Street from Jefferson to Muhammad Ali, then set up tents and barbecue grills. Music usually got

L-R: Crystal, Mr. William, Shellaine, a neighbor, and Reggie (Ms. Renee's grandson)

going at about ten or twelve o'clock. Ms. Mattie would cook. My husband would barbecue. We had a neighbor across the street, Melissa, who did face painting for the kids. Mr. William would have art activities ready for the kids. He basically wanted to see who could draw the best artwork, and then he would give them a prize. He would have really good prizes.

Mr. William Williams was awesome. He really got excited about the block party. He loved to see all of the adults and children interacting with each other. Mr. William was fun and also professional. He worked three jobs at one time. He took care of the food at Jefferson Alcohol and Drug Abuse Center downtown. He was a supervisor there. He also worked at Walmart

in the evenings and a call center. He raised his two sons. They moved in when they were teenagers.

He would get big seasonal balloons for the block party on sale at Walmart, like the Easter Bunny, Halloween ghosts and pumpkins, and Christmas ones. A balloon was put in each neighbor's yard all down the street. It was fun and festive, and different because each balloon stood six feet tall and represented the holiday seasons. It was really funny to walk down the street and see all the different balloons glowing in neighbors' yards. The kids were excited to look at the big balloons.

Mr. William played the Electric Slide, and we all danced, and he really enjoyed it. He smiled a whole lot and had a good time. He had all kinds of games that he

would set up. He did the limbo, and everybody loved it because he started up high and then went all the way low, and he had Caribbean music to go with it. It was really fun. He had little bitty goldfishes in little bowls that he would give out to the kids as prizes. Kids really liked that. He had a table set up with all kinds of gifts that he would give out, like buckets with bubbles. He would have balloons that you shoot darts at.

Mr. William made all the signs. He was always efficient when it came to drawings. He just had a lot of detail in anything he did. He made sure it was definitely

the best. He would pass out scratch-off lottery tickets. That's how we would make money. I would sell the tickets. Once I sold all the tickets, I would give the money to Mr. William. He used to hold all the money. And we would have a raffle, maybe fifty dollars every couple hours. I would do the raffle.

One of the games we played was called the Cake Walk. Each neighbor would make a cake or two desserts. And we would put that out on the table, and you could win a cake or pie or something like that. You could also put a quarter down, spin the casino wheel, and win a cake or pie or brownies if your number came up. Another activity was a watermelon eating contest for different age groups, usually in front of my house. You'd put your hands behind your back, and whoever ate the fastest and the most won a watermelon.

Renia's sister was responsible for the scratch-off tickets, and when your number is called, you win money. Each year the neighbors would put money together to have T-shirts made for the annual block party. We had a dance-off competition. Every year it got bigger and bigger. We could win a gift card to go to the movies or go get something to eat. It would go until about ten o'clock at night, then we would clean up. We had the kids help.

My son Nathan got involved with the block party. He was selling popcorn, pickles, and pop and was able to earn some profitable income. Mr. William would count it at the end of the block party, and we would see if we made a profit. Then we could get all items for next year's block party paid for in advance. The members of the neighborhood wanted to put any extra money earned in a savings account to help fund the following year's block party. We also asked people to give fifty dollars per household into a bank account. When someone passed away, we gave fifty dollars to the family and flowers. Once, we went out to Mike Linnig's as a neighborhood.

I became the president of the block. I initiated myself because I was always like, *Okay, I'll go ahead and do this.* I think we all have special gifts. After a few years I thought, *Well, let me drop back.* A new neighbor that moved in across the street, Marty, seemed like she wanted to pick it up, but then she said, "Well, I'll just be the secretary for it." I was trying to step back, but more and more, they kept pulling me back in. So I couldn't really step back because I cared. Every time I tried to step back, it seemed like it wasn't really stepping back.

Crew of Renee Wright's family and friends hanging out in front of her house

Right: Mr. William's son Lil Bit

Melissa painting kids' faces

Renee Wright getting the chicken ready. She always did the shopping at Kroger for the block party

Mr. William Williams

Anthony

Mr. William had a stroke, and after that, when he was confined to his wheelchair, he still wanted to participate in the block party. As he got more ill, he was unable to participate, but he was riding his scooter up and down the street. Every morning before I went to work, he'd be sitting outside, and he's still there in the evening hours. I said, "You have to be so hot." He said his blood was thin, so it wasn't as hot for him as I thought it was. When Mr. William caught COVID, he didn't recover. He passed away in June of 2020. He was probably in his sixties.

We haven't had a block party since 2018. There has been a lot of depression with the COVID, and a lot of people passing away. I would think they would like to bring back the block party to keep everybody connected and abreast of what's going on. I have a new neighbor who just moved across the street. I've said, "Hi! Welcome to the neighborhood," but I won't walk up to her because it's COVID. Usually, I would at least go over and talk, but I don't know about that right now.

The 16th Street block party helped to create unity and let us get to know people's personalities instead of just saying hi and bye. We got to know our likes and dislikes. Maybe they like the way their grass was cut, or they don't like the way their grass was cut, or they don't like the way you cut the bushes. They were able to voice their opinions to you. "Oh, really? I didn't know you thought like that." It was just good to know a little bit more about our neighbors instead of just going into your house and going back out to your car. The whole thing made neighbors feel a little more safe because now they have each other's phone numbers. If something's going on and I'm not here, they can call me to let me know if somebody is walking around my house. Ms. Mattie lived next door to Mr. William. She would say, "Somebody's walking in the alley" or, "Clean up the garbage." Sometimes you have neighbors that really

watch out for you. It's always nice to know that you can be a part of someone's life. Our car broke down one time, and Ms. Mattie came to pick me up from work. It's just nice to know that somebody will help you.

The 16th Street block party was about people just out having a good time, smiling, and family and friends coming out. It was just a really good time playing volleyball and dancing in the streets. That day was a nice celebration day. We have a lot of pictures of the neighborhood block parties we had. And we've met a lot of friends. We had good fellowship and just had a great time. ✦

Old School Renewed
Club Cedar and Cedar Cafe

DONNIE ADKINS
CLUB CEDAR

We were living in Indianapolis the night I proposed to my wife in 2011. I said, "Before we get married, there's something I want to tell you about. There's this club in Louisville called Club Cedar. If it ever comes up for sale, I want to buy it." My wife was sitting on the couch looking at her ring, getting ready to make a phone call to tell people she was engaged. She said, "I don't care what you do." So I couldn't have asked at a better time.

Fast forward ten years later. I hear that Club Cedar is coming up for sale. I was already on it. I was like, *Okay, this is not a test.* Looking at this place as a customer and dreaming of buying it was one thing. Looking at it as an owner, it was, *What did I get myself into?* We rolled up our sleeves. It's still a challenge every single day to make sure that we're doing what we need to do and doing it correctly. But I love it. I'm super excited about it. I won't go into it, but had I not bought the club, it would no longer exist. Period.

At first, the reception from the old-school regulars was a little icy. They all thought I was this outside guy coming in from out of town to buy their club. I had done some TV interviews about the club at that point, but I guess they didn't see the first part of the interviews because they didn't believe me when I told them

I am from Louisville, Kentucky, born and raised. Came up in Southwick and later in Russell.

We had the average low-income household just like everyone else. Pops wasn't around, and Moms had four of us boys. I was the oldest. I always felt like I needed to somehow make a way out of no way. Unfortunately, I got into some problems, and my mom felt like she could not handle us at the time. So she shipped me and my oldest brother off to live with my dad in Atlanta. We stayed in one of the worst housing projects there for several years, and I came back to Louisville in eighth grade. We ended up in Russell. Got Section 8 at 24th and West Muhammad Ali.

I got into and out of trouble growing up and even did five months after me and a buddy stole his aunt's car and got into an accident. Once I got out, I knew that I had to change my life because jail was not the place for me.

I got a job at the Housing Authority and worked there for almost ten years. During that time, I went to business school and got a degree. I guess somebody noticed that I was working on moving up, because the Housing Authority asked me to apply for a management position and promoted me. They told me I was the only person in Housing Authority history to be promoted from maintenance to management. I went from picking up trash in Park Hill, fixing sinks, and wearing steel-toe boots every day to wearing a suit and going to an office job. True story: when I got there, I

David Duncan and Donnie Atkins, owners of the Cedar Cafe and Club Cedar

didn't know how to use a printer. I had to hang out by the photocopier, and when people would print stuff, I would just be talking to them, but I would be paying attention to what they were doing so I could learn how to use the photocopier.

I was hooked, though. I couldn't get enough of education. After I was promoted, I went to night school and got my MBA, and within a ten-year time frame—from age nineteen to twenty-eight—I had my own house and two cars, two kids, and I had a graduate degree. I was like, "Alright, it's time to go to corporate America." Every single moment in my life has been a step.

I worked at Humana for several years, which is where I met David Duncan. We were solid from the first day we met, and I call him my brother. Dave and

I would come hang out at Club Cedar after work to unwind and pontificate. I'd say, "If I owned this place, these are some of the things that I'd do. I'd change this or that. You could run the kitchen. We'll have great food, great drinks." And so on. That was in 2007. When I bought Club Cedar in 2020, David took over the kitchen and opened Cedar Cafe.

I came in here and cleaned it up, made it safer. And I kept a lot of stuff the same. With some of our customers, change is not always welcome, and I understand that. So I've tried to make small, incremental changes so that they can see a benefit. We did have to raise drink prices, which were grossly undervalued. They're still super cheap, if you ask me. One of the first things we did was pave the parking lot, which was a

Donnie Adkins, owner of Club Cedar

gravel dungeon, potholes everywhere. It was horrible. When we blacktopped it, you would have thought I'd given every customer a hundred dollar bill. That's how proud they were of this place. That's when I said, "This is going to work out." The ideas I have in mind are not going to do anything but take it to the next level and make people proud. I want this to remain the place that they call home. And I want this to be a give-and-take relationship.

When I think about the future of Club Cedar, I want to give back to the community. This past summer, I got the idea from the Black Panthers back in the day about feeding children. We started a free lunch program from 1–4 p.m. every Monday during the summer. All JCPS kids can come here and get a free lunch, no questions asked. We're also doing a backpack drive. I don't want people to have to come out of their

pockets for this stuff. We start to get into what Russell really is and what Russell was, and what Russell can be. You can't go anywhere else in the city and get the same kind of love that you can get from a Black business.

Sometimes it feels surreal.

When I come to the club, I like to come down 24th from Muhammad Ali because it reminds me of what I used to do. I used to go to this little grocery store on 26th. My brothers used to get their hair cut by someone on 24th and Madison. I remember someone who used to live in this one particular house; now the house is vacant. It's up to people like myself and other community partners to figure out how to bring Russell back. Russell is booming. You'd have to have been under a rock over the last five years not to understand where Russell is headed. I want to be a part of that. I want my name in the mix.

David Duncan, owner of Cedar Cafe, and his daughter Daviona

DAVID DUNCAN
CEDAR CAFE

Back in 2017, I started working as a life insurance broker. I worked for that company for about two weeks before they told me not to sell any life insurance policies in the West End. It would be illegal for them to just come out and say, "Don't sell policies to Black people." But if you're saying, "Don't sell policies in an area that's ninety-five percent African American," that's exactly what you're saying. That didn't sit right with me and everything I believe in, so I ended up leaving that company. If you're alive, you need life insurance, and it's maybe even more important in under-served communities west of Ninth Street. So I started doing my own thing, selling policies myself, and that took off like wildfire.

I live in Russell and felt like people connected with me and trusted me. When people who are not from your community come in and try to sell you something, it can feel like they're trying to get over. I had enough equity built in that people knew when I showed up, it wasn't a hustle. So, since 2017, I've been building up and maintaining my clients. A big part of my business is being able to get in front of people face to face, so when COVID hit, the life insurance slowed quite a bit. But I still had to feed my family.

I'd always had a culinary side. I like to cook. And I had always wondered if I could make a livelihood out of selling food. I would cook for friends and family, and they'd say, "This food is delicious!" but I think if you're cooking for people for free, they feel obligated to say, "This is the best food I've ever had!" I wanted to know if it was true. I saw some folks on social media selling

dinners during COVID, and I was like, *I could do that.*
I'm gonna start selling dinners from home. I did steak,
chicken, lamb, and sides once a week, and it was really
successful. I developed a strong following.

All the while, my best friend—I actually call him
my brother—Donnie Atkins and I were meeting at
Club Cedar once a week. We called it Man's Mondays.
We'd come over there, hang out, and talk about politics,
corporate life, or what was going on in the streets.
Donnie would always say, "If I ever had the opportunity to buy Club Cedar, I would."

At the time, it was owned by the Turner family,
who had owned it for like forty years. It was a legacy
story. Earl Turner—God rest his soul—was the
founder of Club Cedar. He was a Louisville legend.
He was ahead of his time as far as being a Black busi-
nessman in the climate he had to navigate. Earl passed
away, and the club went to his sons. Unfortunately, one
of his sons died tragically, and the surviving brother
wanted to exit the business. The owners had known us
just from being around the club, and I introduced them
to Donnie and then stepped out of the way. They did
some negotiations and finally came up with a number
they both agreed on.

So, Donnie's buying the club. I'm selling dinners
out of my house. COVID is going on. There's a lot of
moving parts happening at the same time, but it was
just a foregone conclusion that I would operate the
restaurant part of Club Cedar.

December of 2020 is when Donnie acquired the
business, and I began to lease the kitchen from him.
We started this in the middle of a global pandemic.
Sure, it was super risky, but things came together.
Donnie owns the physical building and Club Cedar,
the bar part. Then Cedar Cafe is the part that I own.
They're two separate businesses operating under
one roof.

I live on 20th and Muhammad Ali. I can walk
to the club. When you live nearby, you kind of have a
pulse of the community and what's needed and what
isn't needed. It is important to have people who are
living in the neighborhood who also have business
interests here.

Club Cedar has been a mainstay in our community for forty-plus years. Everybody already knew the
name. It was like buying into a familiar franchise. It
was already established. One of the things Don and
I tried to do was try to maintain the integrity of the
bar and the restaurant as well as propel it into modern
times. People were familiar with it; they knew where it
was located, where to get food, how the food tasted, all
of that. So I didn't take anything *off* the menu because
that just wouldn't make good business sense. If you
bought a McDonald's franchise, you wouldn't take Big
Mac off the menu, right? Club Cedar has been known
for bar food: fish, chicken, burgers, wedges, that type
of stuff. This is what people have grown to love and
expect, and it works. I added some things to the menu
like some salads, a quesadilla, steak, and chargrilled
oysters.

Some of my regular customers have been coming
in for the last thirty-five years. There's a legacy here.
This is like the Black man's country club. Whether
you're from Chickasaw Park or Lake Forest, if you're
Black, you've heard of Club Cedar. I would task anyone
to find a Black family from Louisville who doesn't have
some family member—an aunt or uncle or granddaddy—who's been here to eat or to party. And that's
from now to forty years ago. That's important.

People come here to eat, drink, and be merry.
That's not something that Donnie and I did. This
was already built in. It's important to us
to keep that consistency and just keep that legacy
going. ✦

A Conversation With Myself, or Maybe With God

DEMETRIUS MCDOWELL

There's this thing that we say: "Being Black is dangerous, but man, it's lit." I grew up around Sheppard Square and then later in Southwick. In the projects, even though you might have to duck from a few bullets and be cautious of who you talk to and how you walk, you're gonna have the time of your life. It was a dangerous time, but there's definitely parts of my childhood that I wouldn't take back.

I feel like Black kids who come up in that scene have PTSD that we don't even notice. As kids, we see too much. We grow up too fast. We're not pampered or shielded in any type of way. Not to take anything from the middle class, because their parents worked hard. I can't take anything from people who did what they were supposed to, but we don't have those examples. We can't get our foot in the door. We have to get through so much before we can even get the opportunity to succeed. So, for a lot of kids it's like, "Fuck that, gimme a bag. I'm gonna sell some dope and get some money."

At thirteen years old I started snorting powder cocaine. Dealing with the shootouts I was in was easier when I was high. My era was the late '80s during the crack epidemic, so I definitely knew to stay away from crack. Just like heroin, anybody that tries it, you're about to be hooked. I didn't drink. I smoked a little weed and tooted powder. We were hanging with twenty-one-year-old guys, and I was hustling these streets, getting my money.

I got my first adult charge at thirteen years old when I took a gun to Southern Middle School. A little dude had brought a gun to school and threatened my cousin. My cousin was a good guy, and I was that bad kid. Only reason I came to school was to let this guy know I'm out here carrying too: *Hey, they didn't stop making guns after they made yours.*

Demetrius' great-grandparents settled in Smoketown in the early 1900s

I don't know how it would've turned out. Maybe God intervened. I cut class and was walking the hallway and the principal caught me and sent me to in-school detention. I fell asleep and a chrome Lorcin .380 fell out of my pocket onto the floor. The teacher said, "What is that?" I said, "Oh, it's just a BB gun." I turned around like I was gonna give it to him and then ran out. I didn't get caught until two or three days later. The charges were minor in possession of a handgun on school property and minor in possession of a handgun. Back then, for anything gun-related, you were charged as an adult at age thirteen and over. So, that's what went to circuit court. I was facing one to five years as a thirteen-year-old for felony charges.

Eddyville Correctional Facility, 1998

clear. I didn't go to school at all for a year because I couldn't come on JCPS property with a felony gun charge on the books. I was in school in the streets, bouncing around, sleeping on couches at my auntie's house or in Iroquois Housing Project, or at this crack house on 35th and Broadway. That's when I first really got into selling drugs. I was working for somebody and I was the little guy learning the ropes. I got five dollars on every twenty-dollar sale. I wasn't making any profit. I didn't have the clientele who were buying fifty or a hundred dollars worth.

Mom was trying to keep her hands on me, but I'm a young Black man: it's hard to raise us. You have to be tough. You can't really be listening to everything your mother's saying. You're *supposed* to, and the mothers try as best they can, but you just can't get through to a young Black man who's out here seeing all of these influences and his father's not around. I can't take nothing from my mother. She did everything she could with what she had, just like most mothers. There ain't no bad moms. What looks like a bad mom is just a woman that went through her shit probably because of some fucking man. Every woman has been done wrong at some point, whether a scary moment of somebody trying to take advantage of her or some guy manipulating her to feel loved when she wasn't. Us men, we can't handle that. But women are way stronger than men. They're powerful. A woman takes all of that and comes back from it. They're put here to love. It's just their nature.

A month after my eighteenth birthday, I caught a robbery charge. I'd never done time before. I was going to juvie all the time, but my mother would come and get me out. Now they're telling me, "It's a ten-year sentence. You gotta do two years before you even get an opportunity for parole." I held my newborn son when he was born on February 10 and got locked up

They say possession is nine-tenths of the law, and since I ran, they never actually caught me in possession of a gun. They just saw what it looked like, and I said it was a BB gun. They never could prove anything and that's why it eventually got pushed back down to juvenile court. But it took two years for that case to

two weeks later on the 22nd. My daughter was born a month after I was locked up on March 28. I did four years in the penitentiary.

When you first start your time, you're angry. But, who can you be angry at besides yourself? I had to take accountability for what brought me there and then focus on what was going on on the inside versus what was going on on the outside. I had to be tuned-in, get a routine, try to get some type of education and just learn from other men inside. The hardest part was not knowing when you're going to come home. You get used to it, but you don't get comfortable with it. You always want to come home.

I got out when I was twenty-two and came home with two kids. The only thing I knew about being a parent is that my father was never around, and I wasn't gonna be nothing like him. I wanted to be there for my kids so they could have someone they could learn from instead of getting pulled into the wicked ways of the world. The world's mean, but at least I'd be teaching them from love. But I didn't know whether or not I could provide for them. Everything I was doing was supposed to be the opposite of my father, but the life-style I chose to take care of my family meant I was not as present as I could have been. I wasn't there for them emotionally. You say that you sell drugs so you can support your family, but if you go to the penitentiary for four years, you could've made as much had you went to work for four years.

For the next ten years, I was selling drugs and in and out of incarceration. I'll put it like this: For the last twenty-two years, the first time that I *wasn't* either serving time, on parole, or serving probation was last year. That's my whole adult life since I was eighteen. We say, "We're products of our environment," but that's a cliché. It's something we say to justify what we're doing.

Demetrius with his mom, Regina McDowell, at Eddyville Correctional Facility, 1995

Demetrius at the Marion County Adjustment Center with his kids, Demetrius Jr. and Demeisha, ca. 2000

Demetrius' cousin Glori and his mom, Regina

Regina, ca. 1980

I started applying my crack hustle to a heroin hustle. I got up every morning at five-thirty like it was a job and made a $20,000 stack in two months. Once you get a heroin addict that's spending $150 a day, you have him every day; they can't miss or they're gonna be sick. Just imagine twenty people calling you every day with a $150 habit; you can count your money before it comes. I never left anybody dopesick, though. That

was my thing. If you're sick, give me a call. Even if you only have ten dollars, I got you. It's your relationship to your customer and your product. If your product's good, it's gonna sell itself. The younger generation doesn't get that. They're coming in thinking that you're supposed to cut everything to make a dollar, so they use fentanyl. That's how you mess around and end up killing somebody.

I made six figures in a year when I applied myself. I had like $200,000. I wasn't out here caught up in clichés about gold chains and cars and stuff. I was stacking my money, and the money was beautiful. But I was justifying it with the clichés of our community: doing the things that are in my environment to make money and calling it a job, saying that I'm doing all these wrong things for the right reasons. That was just bullshit.

The last time I got arrested was in 2015. The cops did a round-up. The messed up part about it was they didn't catch me with anything—didn't find a baggie, a scale, nothing—but charged me with trafficking heroin. "We know you're doing things because we've seen the bills. You're paying your mother's bills, you got this apartment, but you live out there, you got a safe and two different cars." They hit every place that I had ever been and there wasn't nothing there. If they had waited ten minutes, they'd have had me because I was going to my stash, about to grab what I needed for the day.

We're in the same game, they're just the opposite of me: *I deal drugs, you deal with drug dealers. Your job is to catch me, mine is to get away.* I understand the concept of both of our jobs, and yours is to get information from me, and mine is not to give you no information. I had a sense of achievement for the way I chose to traffic, the moves I made, the people that I followed, and the places that I frequented. None of those places and spaces were raided. I patted myself on the back for knowing how to move. I guess it was a little bit of cockiness to find out that the evidence that the police had wasn't good enough to convict me. It took six years of pre-trial, grand jury, and another trial before the case was settled and I was found not guilty.

Every time I caught a charge or was on parole, I had to sell more drugs to fight the charge. Nine times out of ten drug offenders is still trafficking while going to court. And the police always do a follow up investigation. They try to stack the deck on you. So I had a conversation with myself. Maybe it was with God. It was one of those times you say, "God, if you get me out of this, I promise I won't do it no more." This time I actually committed to that.

Coming into dealing drugs, you know you're gonna spend the rest of your life in the penitentiary or you're going to die. And I think it was one of those things where God intervened. Thinking back—and definitely being spiritual now—that's the only thing that could have convinced me to stop.

So at thirty-five years old, I had a moment of clarity: *You have more in your possession than the fifty-year-old men in your environment. You have financial stability, but you already have ten years in the penitentiary.* I lost a lot before I ever won. Missed four years at the beginning of my kids' lives. How much is enough to reach your ultimate goal? You willing to pay with your life or your freedom? So I just stopped cold turkey, and it worked out. It was a good thing. I don't miss the money. I know how to make it legally now. I bought some houses, and I was done. I was done with the streets.

I'm glad my mom saw me transition out of that life. My mother was my best friend. I didn't have any secrets from her. That's what hit me hard; I have a person that, right or wrong, was gonna defend me with her last breath. She knew what I was doing. But, she also saw me trying something else, buying real

Demetrius on the day he beat his last drug charge in 2016

estate and trying to start small businesses. I went out and bought zero-turn lawn mowers and a twelve-foot trailer that I parked on the side of a house instead of pulling up in a '66 convertible Deuce and a Quarter with loud music. She saw that transition. And I talked to her about doing something different than what I was doing. As parents, we don't want to leave this world without knowing our child is in some type of position to take care of themself without us. And I think she saw it. I still have a screenshot from a Facebook post from Valentine's Day in 2015. She was at church, and I snuck up behind her and surprised her and joined her

Demetrius and Regina at a family gathering in 2006

Clockwise from left: unknown, Jesse, Keeshawn, Niya, Jelise, Demetrius, 2017

at church that day. She posted about it, saying, "God blessed me letting my son come to the church," and saying how proud she was of that. She saw me in a different light.

My mom, Regina Ann McDowell, died in 2016. They talk about the five stages of grief. Believe me, I went through all of them, and I just came out of my grief fully this year. The first year or so, I self-medicated, distracting myself from it, dabbling in different drugs, waking up with a bottle. I stopped looking at pictures of Mom. I pretended like I was still locked up and hadn't seen her yet. I watched a whole lot of stories on TV and just dealt with myself a whole lot. I was trying to figure out, *How do I move on from somebody I knew my whole life?* And I couldn't find my way. I just couldn't find the motivation. I felt like I shouldn't be happy without my mother. It's messed up to be carrying on like she's not gone. I cried for five years.

But one day I said, *Man, come on, this ain't you.* I knew she wouldn't want me living like that. I'm never losing another mother. I'll never be that hurt again, so what else can you bring at me? So I finally made peace with that. I'm already in the mindset that things will never be normal again without her, so I'm just searching for a new normal. So, that's what it is. I'm all right. I'm at peace. I'm good.

I stayed busy. It was like I was manic depressive. I was getting into so much stuff, buying this house, that house, investing in this restaurant, this corner store, being a jack of all trades, but a master of none. I bought a little corner store in Portland. A girl was trying to get out of her lease, so I made a deal so she could walk away from the lease, and I bought everything in the store. These kids from the neighborhood started coming in, like fifteen teenagers at once. They were probably coming in to steal. I used to do the same stuff. I stole from so many stores that if somebody is stealing from me at this point, it's a hood tax. Write it off.

They all thought I was a drug dealer because I had a 1970 Cutlass 442 or a 750Li BMW parked out front and I had gold teeth in my mouth. All that was eye candy for them, I guess, and they ended up hanging around, asking me questions. "We know you sell dope. Why else would you be doing this? This store's a front." I had to tell them, "Come on, that's not the only way that you can get money." I showed them my LLC paperwork and stuff like that. "I actually am legit. Hang around me. If you see me selling drugs to somebody, I'll give you a thousand dollars." And that was an incentive for them to hang around. We got to be real cool friends. I got to know Lee, Keeshawn, Jesse, Jelise, Niya, and Noah personally.

They started asking to work and I'd let them clean up, give them a couple dollars for that. I'd let them come in and mess with the register, charge people. They didn't want much except for the accomplishment of having a little job at the store. They just wanted to be a part of something. You get the same pat on the back when you do something positive in the neighborhood as you would if you were selling drugs. And they got recognition for working in the store and being around me. I had their attention, and they were taking heed of the things I was saying, and I listened to them. I was just teaching them to be responsible and accountable for their own actions.

My own kids, my sons and my daughter, took everything I told them as preaching, and they couldn't wait to turn eighteen. I was always the disciplinarian. When I spoke, I was not so sensitive. It was direct: *This is how the world can be and this is the reason why I'm telling you these things.* They couldn't take the advice because it was a scolding. I was just trying to drill the point into them. I didn't figure out a way to give them something other than the raw and uncut version. I wasn't patient with them.

But these kids I met at the store were asking questions. They wanted advice and I wanted to give it to them. I felt like, if a child is asking you questions, and

Outside the corner store with his Cutlass 442, 2018

you're in a place to tell them something that's gonna keep them from going down the road that you were on, why not? So, I was able to play that part. Like, *I ain't the grown up that's telling you what you should or shouldn't do. I'm just telling you what I've done. I haven't lied to you. I'm accepting you. You have a voice with me.* It was almost therapy for me dealing with kids because they were listening and I was doing something good. When we do something good for somebody, it makes us feel good. It feels good to be wanted, needed, and responsible for somebody. I thought, *Well, this is something I can do.*

At the time, the city had started a Cure Violence program where they had got $1.7 million for a grant. I knew somebody who worked at the YMCA. She told me they were hiring convicted felons—guys like me in the neighborhood—to negotiate cease fires, mediate retaliation for gun violence, and act as an interrupter

Chestnut Street YMCA

before things went too far. "You might wanna come up here and sign an application," she said, "because what you're doing with those kids at the corner store is what they're trying to do."

I felt like it was an opportunity, and I was hired as an interrupter. We was supposed to mediate and try to get in touch with certain people and try to stop the violence, cure it from within. It's not easy to get guys that have influence in the neighborhood through violence or drugs and change their whole perspective. I *was* that guy. And a lot of us ain't gonna come in here to talk because it's almost like dry snitching. If I tell you something, and you, being ethical and all, tell the police, then I've gone and told on somebody. You ain't gonna get too many guys that want to come here and have that conversation.

They hired a female and maybe three other guys to be interrupters. When one of the guys was arrested on a rape charge, that was the end of the whole program. It could've gone differently. But you can only get so far with pep talks anyway, though. You're never going to get to the root of the problem by trying to get kids

to come in, sign their name, and sit in this program or that program. Find me a shooter out here with a gun who went through a program voluntarily and was changed by it. You have to form relationships.

Even though the Cure Violence program closed, I had some ideas I was getting into that I wanted to implement. I thought, *So what if the program didn't pan out? I'm a hustler. I'm a learner. I'm a watcher. I'm gonna find a way to do this.* At that point I'm three years out of the game and haven't sold nothing. I'm still living off my proceeds, my houses. I have a legitimate income. I own my own stuff. So, I'm really a boss. I'm not a gangbanger, I'm not a dope dealer. So, that's where I came up with the name Bosses Not Bangers. Let me take this and see how I can transition from what I used to do—selling dope and maneuvering through the streets—into a program consisting of dealing with people from the street, building fellowship, and leading kids away from the lifestyle that I used to lead.

What better way to learn and figure out what I could implement than to be around an organization like the YMCA? The Russell neighborhood is definitely a hot spot for crimes, and there's a lot of kids in this neighborhood. So I took a job at the front desk at the Chestnut Street YMCA as a Trojan horse. The way I thought of it was, they have a gym, and that's the catch. It always kept my age group out of trouble. The gym is how you get them in the door. Then you find out what they need *from them*—not what you *think* they need—and try to implement something. You gotta mix the medicine in applesauce for kids. You gotta make them think the education or whatever life lesson that they're getting is cool.

I started letting kids come in on my shift to use the gym. Baxter Center's gym is not open anymore in Beecher Terrace. So, you get those kids that come from that side of Jefferson coming over. They're coming from

Henry Greene Apartments, Broadway, Phase I and Phase II of City View; all of those kids are coming over here.

They were in here after school, and then during the summer I started letting them stay late. They were in here until nine, ten, eleven o'clock at night. They'd be standing out in the lobby and I was getting to know them while they were talking to each other and I'd listen to their conversations. I'd jump in from time to time like, "Can I say something about that?" and give them a little guidance. I thought, as long as I was being up-front with them, not dumping on them, I could get the kids to trust me and hand them over to some people who could help them. You can't just scold them and chastise them, because nobody's receptive to somebody in your face being aggressive or making you feel less than. I learned their names. They remember my name. Any time I had an opportunity to get them engaged in something, I'd refer them to the right educational resources or other organizations that could help them out with whatever they were lacking.

So, that's been my job at Bosses Not Bangers, to soften up the youth who come from my background. We get discouraged when we talk to educated people; we don't feel like we belong in the same room, so we kind of shut down. We can only relate to the environment that we come from. Somebody like me being on the inside can peek my head up and say, "Come on in, the water's fine. They're giving out resources here." It's a way to get help without having to know everything. Just kind of lead the horse to water, letting them know that I'm always here, and it became a thing.

The YMCA heard that I was letting them in the gym on my shift. Some of the kids was coming back when I wasn't here like, "Oh, we was in here last night." So, some of the employees got wind of it and went back and told the management at the Y. I said, "Well,

First group of Bosses Not Bangers participants

The corner store crew with coaches from Central High

Demetrius and Master P, 2022

I've already been taking care of them, and nothing happened. It's just guys playin' basketball, and I haven't had any type of incidents." So, instead of getting fired from the desk job, the YMCA gave me a contract to do outreach. That was the first contract I got for Bosses Not Bangers.

I turned Bosses Not Bangers into an outreach organization to get rid of that whole cliché about being "a product of my environment," which is how we justify some of our wrongdoing. Where we come from, if you're doing a little bit better than those around you, that's enough. When you're in an environment of impoverished people who aren't used to having much, once they have a little bit more, it's a sense of accomplishment, and that doesn't challenge you to do more.

You can ride out your days in your comfort zone with no challenges. But there's so much more to life than that. We don't experience it if we don't come out of our neighborhoods or get away from our family members who have settled for being has-beens. We don't know that there's more because we stand in those comfort zones being products of our environment.

I want to change the perspectives of the youth in our community through mental health support and entrepreneur mentorship, and developing fellowship, whether it be feeding folks, helping kids get jobs, providing space for people to meet or whatever. I've developed relationships there through the programming and now I'm someone people feel comfortable calling. When things happen in the community, I hear about it because I have close relationships with people in Louisville. I'm not a stranger in these neighborhoods.

I got my nonprofit designation recently. I really appreciate the opportunity that the Chestnut Street YMCA gave me. Freddie Brown, the vice president of diversity at the YMCA, took that chance knowing that I'm a convicted felon. He gave me the opportunity to learn from people who had already been doing the work. I've been learning my craft, trying to master it and provide resources and opportunities as they come to me. Youth development is my job now.

My thing is keeping them alive long enough to establish themselves as bosses. "Squash the beef. Get the money." Let go of your petty differences if you're trying to excel. If you're getting your money, you ain't out here just looking for the gangster part of things. It's hard to stop somebody from drug dealing because it's definitely lucrative. When you're coming from a starving household, and you don't have anything in the refrigerator, how do you tell somebody not to eat that steak? Just don't kill nobody just to get the money. A lot of our kids are trying to adopt the gangster lifestyle without any idea what it's really about because they can be a gangster on social media, and then come out here and mess around and get into an argument or shootout. What comes behind that is jail or death.

I'd never done outreach before. There was a learning curve. My thing has always just been, *Do it and go. Run and gun.* But I had to learn that things have to be done a certain way: policy, procedure, and accountability. Letting the Y know what I plan on doing and how I plan on doing it. You can't just be taking on the responsibility of peoples' kids with no type of curriculum or responsibility of how you're gonna do it.

One of the first things I did was reserve the computer lab. The pandemic came from out of nowhere and a lot of parents didn't know what to do. Nobody knew that JCPS was going to shut down. Kids were doing school remotely and online. I thought that if I could get the behaviorally challenged kids, get their curriculum from their teachers, and get a monitor to help them sit still and tutor them if they was lost, we could keep them in line with their teacher. That was another thirteen kids I met out of nowhere and they kept up with the NTI curriculum.

I've met a lot of people. I was able to get an outreach job through the mayor's office, the Office of Safety and Healthy Neighborhoods. I've done a collaboration with Goodwill, KentuckianaWorks, Compass Rose, and the Indiana/Kentucky Regional Council Millwrights where I was able to take some youth to learn carpentry and get a job before they turned eighteen. They start out making around eighteen to nineteen dollars, then in ninety days they go up to twenty-three dollars.

I got an office for Bosses Not Bangers down on 20th and Broadway. I felt like in my line of work, there might be some people who might want to talk in private or who I wouldn't want to meet at the YMCA. So I have an office in the Russell neighborhood.

Bosses Not Bangers event at Shawnee Park, 2022

Community conversation between former drug dealers

I planted a seed there. I've got a lot of backpacks, food, clothes, and hygiene stored there too. If somebody needs something, it's just seven blocks from the Y, and I can run over there and grab a backpack for somebody. People can use the office for group therapy conversations, meet and greet, and developing relationships.

I've built a program called Bosses, which is a SummerWorks program. What it does is put our kids back into the Russell neighborhood learning how to pick up a trade working for small businesses. The small business thrives because you get free labor. This child wins because they're getting paid, learning a trade,

Demeisha, Demetrius, Demetrick, Demetrius Jr.

and getting experience on entrepreneurship from an entrepreneur. And, it gets their wheels turning about what they might want to do before they go out here and grab some drugs to sell. Right now there's thirteen and fourteen-year-olds that are cutting grass for my buddy's lawn care service. Whether they're raking up the grass, putting it in the brown bags, or running a lawnmower, they get paid for that versus going out here and getting in some type of trouble. I interact with kids from Russell at the YMCA, and they're getting the first opportunities in the Bosses program. I tell them, "I got some guys who need help. Y'all wanna be involved to make some money?" Of course they do. They just need five dollars to ride those scooters for a few hours, pay a cell phone bill, or go to the corner store.

I started another program called Dear Mama

after I was invited to speak to Mothers of Murdered Sons and Daughters, a support group for women who have lost their kids to gun violence. These women go through so much after burying their child. A lot of times these murderers get off with probation after three years. Then they're on Instagram bragging about what they did. The victim's families relive it every time they just happen to scroll online. I offered their group a place at the YMCA for mental and physical health. Now they have their meetings there and even started doing Zumba together at the Y.

I was inspired by these women, and talking with them gave me a different perspective of what I want to do with Bosses Not Bangers. These are the people I need to work with when it comes to controlling gun violence and what's going on out here. They say, "If we

In 2022 the Mayor's office awarded Bosses Not Bangers $10,800 for programming including the Safe Summer Bash. Demetrius and BNB participants present Mayor Greg Fischer with a plaque of appreciation.

stop our babies from dying, we stop our mothers from crying." If we could get the message out there that, "This is what your mother's gonna go through if you keep acting the way that you do in the streets. Your mother's gonna grieve like this. She's gonna be wandering through this world not knowing what to do with herself because she lost everything she thought she should live for." I started some programming where the young men I meet out in the streets can be mentored by these mothers. To hear these mothers talking about losing their children can give the kids a different perspective on what they're doing. The last thing any of us want to do is make our mother cry. So, if you're seeing a grieving mother weep for her child, then you can put yourself in her shoes. You don't want your mother to go through the experience, so you straighten up. A

couple times the Dear Mama group has gone out and walked the neighborhoods as a community event and an open conversation. I've gotten some funding from the mayor's office for that.

I took a lot from the streets, and I'm ready to give a little back. I can't say I can repay for all the mischief I got into, but if I'm willing to talk to some kids, hire me, because they're not gonna talk to you. You don't look like them, you don't talk like them, you don't understand them. They're not gonna talk to you. If they have drug-addicted parents, or are neglected by their mother, or just have an absent father, that's the part I can relate to them with. Instead of resenting adults for not being there or lying to them, they're listening to me, and I'm teaching them to take responsibility for their actions, to think, and to tighten up. ✦

Tailor Made

RAMERIZ REED

They say home is where the heart is, and though Louisville is my home city, it's Russell that has my heart. That's where my life started, at the Village West apartment complex. It was Sunday, December 14th. My childhood was great. My parents did their job as far as clothing, sheltering, feeding, nurturing, and encouraging a child.

We lived in Village West for a number of years, so of course, I attended Coleridge-Taylor Elementary School, which was next door to my house. It was there that my family was informed of my "severe ADHD," and I was placed into behavioral disability classes. I had a lot of extra untamed, raw energy. I wasn't able to focus or sit down, my mind was constantly racing, and everyone was like, "Something's wrong with you." But art and science were my go-to things. If we were finger painting or clay-making in art class, I was able to channel my energy into that. In science class, when I learned about all the different molecules and reactions and stuff, it entertained me, kept my attention, and allowed me to focus all of my energy.

My grades and behavior may not have always reflected it, but I rather enjoyed school. I was quiet, yet loudly inquisitive. I truly enjoyed and still enjoy learning. I am a sponge for new information. I'm intrigued by riddles, puzzles, patterns, and sequences. I love a good brain teaser; it's cathartic and just flat-out entertaining. Learning is the most intrinsic part of my life. I love to learn and always have.

As far back as I can remember, I was always sewing or designing in some form when I was a kid. It's an inherited talent because sewing is something that my paternal grandmother had done. She would sew her and her family's clothes—and I have my fair share of aunts and uncles. When you have family pictures coming up, and you can grab two or three different colors of fabric and make an outfit for each person in the family photo, that's what I consider sewing as an art form. Sadly, I lost my grandmother at a very young age. As I was coming in, she was going out, so to speak. She had other engagements. I was always designing with my sister's cousin Carolyn, who was a seamstress and an artistic genius. We would make paper dolls and design outfits, put little tabs on them, cut them out, and put them on the dolls. It was really neat. I suppose I was born to make clothes.

In eighth grade, I had a home economics class. One particular day, we had to sketch an outfit, and I was like, "I like this!" We only had to make one outfit, but I came back with three or four pages.

All my friends were like, "You only had to do one."

"Well, I've got four!" It stuck with me since then: *I want to design clothes.*

Both my parents have always supported my interests, but somehow or another, I was scared to tell them that I wanted to be a clothing designer. I don't know why I was so nervous. I am a very vocal person. Communication is my strong suit. I remember the day I told my mom; I showed her my designs and said, "Do you like these?"

"Yeah, they're really nice."

"That's what I wanna do. I want to be a clothing designer."

And then she's like, "Okay." It wasn't much of a surprise to her.

I was like, *What was all the cloak and dagger for?* After all, she had always made us hem our own pants. At the time, I'm pretty sure my siblings thought my wanting to be a designer had something to do with my huge Mariah Carey obsession. I am a superfan. I just love her music. Since I started designing women's clothes first, my sister would be like, "Oh, is that gonna be the dress you send to Mariah?"

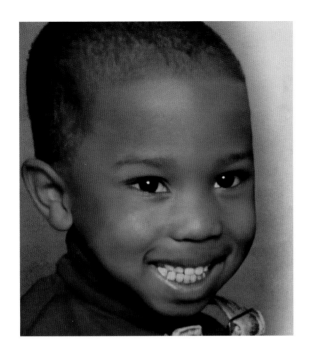

I'd be like, "Maybe. You can get out." I still believe that someday Mariah "The Queen" Carey is going to wear one of my designs.

By the time I was nineteen, I started to sew my own T-shirt designs. I'd take the sleeves off one shirt, stitch the other sleeves onto the shirt, and then throw a collar on it. To me, I'd made my own T-shirt. But then one of the haters was like, "Well, cutting up T-shirts and putting them together is not making your own shirt." That resonated with me. It wasn't until maybe a year or two after when I'm like, "You know what, no wonder I haven't forgotten that comment. They're right."

After that, I would actually sit down, draw out the T-shirt that I wanted to wear, and then cut the patterns out of the fabric. I don't remember the very first one, but I remember when they first started happening. That was super awesome. People would say, "I like your shirt."

"Thanks. I made it myself."

"That's really neat."

And then, by sticking with it, I was able to progress and continue to move forward in my craft.

By the time I was twenty-five, I felt like I was running out of time. "What am I gonna do with my life?" I thought, "You know what, I'm just gonna sew." I focused more on my work, but I didn't feel like all of me had fully come together and agreed on this. I was always kind of tugged towards it, so I ended up getting my GED, and by the time I turned twenty-eight, I realized, *I've been an adult for a whole decade. I could already have a doctorate. I'm good at sewing, so that's what I'm gonna do. That's my career. Buckle down.*

My work has matured and expanded over the years but still kept the same shape. More refined, more polished, but without losing its edge. I've had many instructors. There was this one lady who used to have

this shop in the 2500 Building on 25th and Broadway. When I first met her, I went in looking for a job, and she was doing some alterations on someone's shirt, just a simple button-down. She was bringing it in some, and she said, "Make the inside just as pretty as the outside." I always held on to that because it applies to life, too. Make the inside of your home or your head or whatever just as pretty as the outside.

My dad says that your work is only as good as your craftsmanship. When people go out and buy stuff, I would like to think that they would expect their things to last. If I need my mee maw's picture printed on my T-shirt, I don't just want it there for three weeks. I want it there as long as I have this shirt.

I do pretty much everything. It could be a simple repair, a hem or zipper, or a full original design. I may

get two or three calls the whole spring and summer for wedding alterations. Usually, I get calls for other stuff like hats or other accessories for the Kentucky Derby or last-minute birthday parties. There are really no decorations for Thanksgiving, but I'll get calls for it. "I need my chairs to be reupholstered." "I need a wreath." "I want to know if you can put our names on the napkins." I get more exposure, and I'm always learning something from it, so I'm like, "Hey, I'll take it."

Clothing is art, and not everyone has the same taste in art. Even if I don't like something I make, someone somewhere is gonna end up liking it. I like sugar and butter in my grits. Someone else may like salt and pepper. But that doesn't mean we both don't like grits.

PHOTO BY DARCY THOMPSON

I got my first apartment in 2008. I had never lived in income housing. I lived in Iroquois first. I had never even heard of Iroquois, and I didn't know what a project was. When they tore Iroquois down in 2012, I moved to Beecher Terrace. I knew some people but not many. I was new in the neighborhood, but I knew the area and was glad to be back downtown again. I thought that was pretty awesome.

When I first moved to Beecher, I was on three months of home incarceration for breaking one of Kentucky's deadliest sins: driving with no insurance. If I needed smokes or something, I would try to run to the store and make it home before my bracelet went off. It was boring being on house arrest. There wasn't anything to do. When I ran out of stuff to do, I dug up my front yard to plant some Kentucky Bluegrass

seeds. I come from a long line of do-it-yourselfers, and my dad's trade is construction, so I'd re-caulk my baseboards, replace electrical sockets, repaint the walls, or whatever. I had nothing to do but find stuff to do. Neighbors were like, "He's been there like two months. He really doesn't talk to anybody." And then, eventually, they just kind of started saying, "Hey, I'm your neighbor. How you doing?"

It really truly was a community, and I had friends of all ages. There was one friend of mine a couple of doors over who had a son who was maybe three or four. He was just a little bitty bean sprout. Once for my birthday, he got me a little sewing kit with the little hand needles in it and some threads and stuff. Then he surprised me with another little sewing kit. I'm like, "You know what, as soon as my business takes off,

I'm paying for your whole college, kid." I consider him my biggest supporter. It was neat. Of course, I know his mom picked it out, but he still gave it to me.

There was a sixteen-year-old boy that used to live in the building who was so incredible at drawing. I called on him a couple of times to help me with some of my pattern-making. He could just look at something for a second, shut his eyes, and then just go and draw it out exactly like you see it. I had a friend who was like a human calculator. You could ask him the percent of anything, the distance or calculation of something, and he'd give it to you right off the top of his head, and if you checked his work, it was usually right. That's a talent.

No one really ever focused on the youth up there. We had some of the most incredible dancers. The Africans were super awesome. You could go past and see the Africans and their version of football. We call it soccer. When I saw their skill, the things they could do with their feet, it was like, *Why don't Beecher Terrace have a soccer team?* No one really focused on our youth, and a lot of the youth were super smart, well-to-do people. They weren't all thugs, monsters, and Neanderthals. They weren't all gang bangers or trying to steal your granny's pearls.

Still, Beecher Terrace was known for its violence and its murders. The local TV stations talked about the murder rate, mentioned someone that was killed in Beecher Terrace, or that Beecher Terrace had thirty-six murders. They didn't mention how it was never Beecher Terrace residents that were being killed or doing the killing, though. They never said that part. Apparently, violence sells. But the truth is worth what

nowadays? Yes, Beecher Terrace was crime-ridden but not so much among the tenants. When I didn't like my neighbors, I just didn't talk to them, and they didn't talk to me. But there was never any shootout or nothing like that. No one mentioned that, and no one mentioned none of the talent that was down there. I met so many incredibly talented and smart people in Beecher.

People would think, "Oh, the folks in Beecher Terrace, they're all bottom feeders and dumb," or just whatever negative thing you'd think about them. But no, it was a lot of good people down there. They were not gonna see you go without something. If you needed something to eat, you just asked any one of your neighbors. More likely, your neighbor would say, "I made some pork chops and macaroni today. Do you need a bite to eat? Are y'all okay?"

Beecher Terrace was the only place in the city where you could bring your family, your girlfriend, your son, and your daughter, and get your hair cut, your daughter and her girlfriend's hair done—styled, cut, braided, or whatever—and be able to get your pants altered and probably catch someone selling some household cleaning supplies. Had not everyone else brought their crime to Beecher Terrace, it would have been one of the most family-oriented places in the city. Almost everybody has a direct relative—not an auntie who raised them or a step-granddaddy, but a direct relative—that lived in Beecher Terrace.

In the springtime, with the Kentucky Derby festivities like Thunder Over Louisville, everyone usually flocked to the Russell area. And everyone usually knew someone that lived in Beecher Terrace who they could

hang out and barbecue with out front or in Baxter Park. Overall, Beecher Terrace was really tight-knit. Not like, *No outsiders!* or, *No person from 22nd Street come over here.* Tight-knit as far as, *I live here, and you're my neighbor here. Why be hostile or uppity with each other?*

But then the city decided to tear down the entire Beecher Terrace complex and build a new development. The residents were told that we would be relocated before our buildings were torn down and that we would have an opportunity to move into the new development when it was finished.

Moving was bittersweet because a lot of the folks had become friends. Your friends were moving away. "Oh, I'm gonna miss you, friend." But it was great because it was like they were on to their fresh start, their new beginning. For a second there, I did miss everyone. As Beecher started getting vacated, we started seeing squatters, folks we had never seen before, staying in empty apartments. It was eerie. Not even coming from a trauma place, but just coming from an observant place. Like, *Hey, that's not right. What's going on here?*

"I've lived here twenty years, and I've never seen them."

"Me either."

It was just weird. New faces and old empty places.

They started to board up the doors and windows, but a lot of folks came and started breaking in. They weren't just breaking in to live inside of the unit, they were breaking in to steal the features like the doors or copper or whatever they could get their hands on. Beecher did not protect the property, and it became extremely unsafe—physically unsafe, spiritually unsafe, and mentally unsafe. It was a ghost town, especially at night. A lot of us that were still left quit coming out after a certain time. When it was still standing and people was living there, you knew what to expect, you knew who was who for the most part, you knew what was what. But then, when you had a whole side cleared out, and you had squatters, it got to a point where they were finding dead bodies and addicts in the vacant apartments. It was intense and pretty heavy.

My closest friends were all mostly gone except one who lived right there in the alley by my mailbox. She and I were the last two standing. It was comforting to have her there. We were in it together. We still were able to watch out for each other. She was like a blanket of emotional support and security. She was the best.

I was finally able to move to a new apartment. The process of looking for a new place was completely unorganized. Even now that it was coming down, people were still facing a backlash from the stigma of Beecher Terrace. A lot of people were getting Section 8 housing vouchers, but a lot of the property owners pulled their names or certain properties off the list.

"I'm calling about the three-bedroom I saw on Parkway. My previous residence was Beecher Terrace."

"Beecher Terrace? Well, I don't know if it's available. We have to call you back."

There were more people looking for places than there were places for a while. I kind of blame the city because when we moved, a lot of folks had the option of scattered sites or Section 8 vouchers. But then it didn't seem like there were enough Section 8 properties, or not enough that were readily available, because there was a massive surge of people moving from Beecher at one time. I signed up for both the Section 8 voucher and scattered sites but then had to figure out which one was going to be best for my financial situation at that time. I originally wanted the Section 8 option and got it, but then you apply for three or four different places, and it could cost you like two hundred dollars in application fees, and you're not even getting the places. That money is not refundable. Then with all the credit checks and background checks they do that keep popping up—a hard inquiry, a light inquiry—that kind of messes things up too.

So when I talked to the Housing Authority, they're like, "Well, you still have to move." I was one of the last people on my whole side of the projects. "We can probably try to find you something on scattered sites." And then they showed me this apartment in Crescent Hill, and I was like, "Great, I'll take it," because I liked how it had a lot of windows.

Moving all my stuff out of my apartment went really smoothly. I had everything already boxed up nice and neatly, the whole apartment inside of one room. I already knew the order things was going to go in the truck. I moved, but I still had the trauma and the PTSD from how scary everything had gotten as Beecher emptied out. A lot of people don't like to admit when something's traumatic, but that was very traumatic. So when I moved here, I was able to actually deal with that and work through it. I wasn't just healing from Beecher; I was healing from everything up until Beecher. I slipped out of survival mode into normal mode, and I was able to let my guard down some.

During the pandemic, I got my first official contract with the Housing Authority. They needed some face masks made, and Markham French was like, "Call Rameriz. He sews, and he's a Beecher resident." I single-handedly made five hundred cotton face masks. The contract was from May to December 2020, and I

ended up finishing it in July or August. They wanted solid colors. I put the colors together that I liked the most and went from there. I made them reversible, with one color on either side and different colors on the outside so you can remember which one touched your face.

Each mask took less than twenty minutes. I work alone, so I'd cut out like fifty of the front side, like fifty red ones, then fifty white ones and then go through and stitch them all together. I had a nose guard in there and I'd stitch that in first. When I flipped it right side in, it was pretty much finished. Then all I had to do was iron it down and add the strap.

Right now, I'm untangling all my projects and plans, and I'm trying to get them in the right order. Most of my designs are couture. Red carpet stuff. If I come up with a gown, then I want there to be just one of those in the world, and it's going to be made specifically for you and your body measurements. There will never be another one. Now when it comes to my T-shirts, there's more than one. They're more mass-produced.

The biggest, most lucrative, and most beneficial project that I've been working on that's really going to last is myself. I'm working on me, expanding mentally, growing spiritually, and making sure I'm still physically fit. Because mental health is more important than anything. If you're not right, nothing that comes from you is going to be right, and your family won't be right. I've learned so much about myself. I learned how to shed parts of myself that I created just to survive or created to get through this, that, or the other. I've grown tremendously. It's my favorite project right now. It's something that I get to do every day for the rest of my life. I was able to go deep within and face my shadow side, to stand neck to neck with the dark night of the soul, and beat his ass too. All on my own. Well, I can't say all on my own because I had my spirit guides with me, my ancestors, and everyone else rooting for me. But physically, I was alone. It's the biggest and best project I've been working on.

Since I'm so far ahead on my spiritual journey, I have some other products. One thing is creating spiritual baths and spiritual cleaning products to clean your aura and yourself. You need sea salt because it's very cleansing for your energy. It's pretty much just herbs, sea salts, fresh lavender, oatmeal, and eucalyptus leaves. You can have them dried or crushed, but I like to have them dry because they're easier to clean out the tub. It is going to be targeted and packaged for men because nearly everything is targeted for women, as if self-care is a womanly type of thing. I'm trying to remind men that you really need to clean your energy and your aura too.

I'm also working on designing my own tarot decks. The first one is my tailor's deck. I want to be able to incorporate my love for sewing and my infatuation with photography into my spiritual growth. It'll have pretty much the same meaning as the regular tarot but be worded in sewing terms. Someone else is working on it with me. She's a spiritual guru lady with over a hundred decks of her own, so she is giving me pointers and pretty much funding it. One of my cards says "Tailor Made." In my deck, that's more like the Emperor or the Empress in a standard tarot deck, because it means you freakin' built it on your own, you're at the top of your game, and you are specifically tailor-made for yourself. Another card is "Loose Thread": it's time to cut some shit away. Then there's "Tape Measure": it's

time to measure some shit out. How far do you see this going? And "Broken Needle." Usually, when you're sewing and your needle breaks, either your cloth is too thick, you're going too fast, or your tension is pulled too tight. Either way, you need to slow the fuck down and pay attention to what you're doing, or your needle's gonna break.

Since leaving Beecher Terrace in 2021, life has been good. But it was good then. I suppose it's been slightly better. I've accomplished more, grown more, because I never miss an opportunity to grow. I'm still standing. I'm still smiling. I'm still whole. I'm stronger than ever.

The new Beecher Terrace is Beecher Terrace in name only. I think they did a wonderful job building it, the design is okay, but it's no longer owned by the Housing Authority. It's owned by a company called McCormack Baron Salazar which is conveniently located out of state. They said I have a lifetime preference if I ever want to move back. I'm like, "Okay, well, I don't know Salazar and all them, but I'll give it some thought." I do miss living downtown; I miss living in District 4, in the Russell area, and all the community endeavors that I participated in there. I'm still an honorary member of the Beecher Terrace resident council. But my current apartment in Crescent Hill is the spot where I'm supposed to be. I can focus on my work and my career with no distractions from anything or anybody.

Though I will never see the Russell that my elders speak of, I believe it can be remade by my generation. It has all the ingredients to outshine the rest of the city. We can bring more programs to teach self-reliance, like gardening, home economics, STEM programs, and financial literacy classes. We have all the tools we need to make it happen. We just need to make *us* happen. And I know my generation will do it.   ✦

My Noble Neighborhood

KATHERYN D. HIGGINS

My parents bought their home on West Chestnut Street on September 1, 1946, right after my father got out of World War II. We're celebrating over seventy-five years in Russell in this house. I grew up here. This is where my parents lived until they died.

I prepared dinner for my family on the occasion of my parents' 60th wedding anniversary. I roasted a duck by scoring the skin, seasoning with five-spice powder, rendering the fat, and baking it. When my parents, my brother Martin, and I sat down, my father had a present for my mother. He had saved every note she had ever written him. He gave her a stack of three-by-five postcards with two-cent and three-cent stamps tied up in string. I was touched. The ink was brown, and the paper was sepia-colored. I looked over my mother's shoulder as she read them. She put her hand over the cards and said, "You can't read these." My father said, "You cannot read these until after we die. You cannot know how silly we were."

My mother, Elnora Tolliver, was born in Monticello, Arkansas. My maternal grandmother, Parthenia Tolliver, was born in 1879. I believe that she married when she was thirteen. She raised four children by herself during the Depression after my grandfather fell ill and died when the plague came through town in 1918. A domestic worker who had maybe a sixth-grade education, she was a wise, hard-working, Christian woman who was good with money. She bought property for each of her children. My mother had to leave home to attend high school because the one in her town did not accept Blacks. They all eventually moved away because there wasn't any opportunity in Arkansas for African Americans. I saw that firsthand when I went back to Arkansas as a grown woman pursuing some business opportunities. They had to leave.

Frederick Higgins, 1943

My father, Frederick Higgins, was born in Plaquemines Parish in New Orleans, Louisiana. The abject segregation and treatment of Black people was so bad that my father wouldn't even talk about it. When I explained to him, "You need to tell me this. This is history," he would go silent. My great-great-grandfather Bill the Blacksmith was a slave in Louisiana. Apparently, he was highly favored by the family who owned him, so much so that he was buried in the white person section of the family plots versus the slave section on the Bayhi plantation. Harriet Tubman died in 1913. My father was born in 1917. That's how close I am to slavery: four years. Within this time frame, slavery does not seem to be in the distant past.

My father was a sergeant and clerk at Fort Knox, Kentucky. He wasn't career Army. He enlisted in May

Elnora and Frederick, 1943

officer was career Army, and he had been waiting for this moment all of his life. He ran around saying, "We're at war! We're at war!"

At Fort Knox, my father trained a Tuskegee airman, Lee Archer. It was basic training. They were coming around recruiting Black soldiers. I said to my father, "Why didn't you become a Tuskegee Airman? Your name could have gone up in lights. You would have gone down in history." He said he liked his job at Fort Knox, number one. Secondly, he was afraid of flying. I thought that those were good reasons. He was honorably discharged in 1946. My parents then came to Louisville, Kentucky, and bought the home where I grew up. I'm proud to say that the home remains in my family. They always meant to move on; however, they died there.

When my father gave me his war diary, I read it from cover to cover. He started writing in it when he went into the service. The last page talks about his discharge. He would have his fellow servicemen sign it, and women would sign also. One woman wrote, "I'm not a fish, but you can drop me a line." Cab Calloway signed, saying, "Hi de ho!"

My mother inscribed his diary on the day they became acquainted, August 29, 1941. She wrote where they met, her address, and signed her name. Later on, my father wrote, "On the bus from Columbus I met a very charming ER nurse from Tuskegee." That was eighty-one years ago. They were in separate cities and didn't date in person. They wrote back and forth. He invited her to visit him at Camp Wheeler in Macon, Georgia, as he had invited other women. He says he promised them all a visit.

He had another girlfriend at the time, Leotha LeFrance, who had come to visit him at Camp Wheeler. In his journal, he wrote about how they'd had a wonderful time. He mailed her a letter that would be in

1941, thinking that he would go into the Army and come back out shortly. However, when the Japanese bombed Pearl Harbor in December 1941, he realized he was going to be there for a while. His commanding

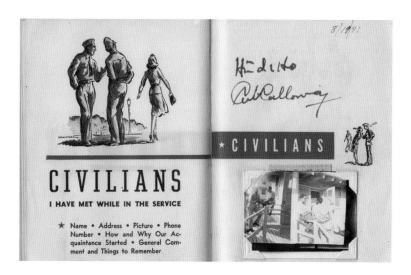

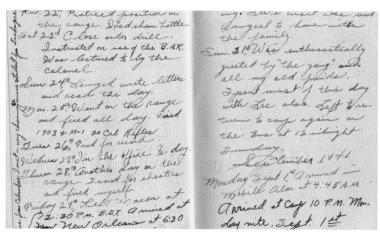

New Orleans by the time she returned home from her visit. He went on and on and on about their meeting. Not long after that, maybe ninety days later, he's married to my mother! I said to him, "What happened to Leotha?" He said he had been getting ready to go overseas, and before he left, he wanted to have accomplished as much as possible in case he didn't come back. My mother came to visit him, they got married, and there you have it.

Her version is different, though. She says that while she was a student at the Tuskegee Institute pursuing her nursing education, soldiers would come on campus for R & R. My mother was dating another young man, Riley Sally, but she and my father met and later married in Macon, Georgia. My father's transfer to Fort Knox brought the newlyweds to Kentucky. My mother stayed in Louisville because there wasn't room for her at Fort Knox. They always meant to move on after he got out of the war, but they settled down, worked, and raised their children here in Louisville. She came home one day to find a soldier's cap on the stoop. She always believed that it was Riley's hat,

Nazarath College, Graduating Class, 1952

Elnora's high school graduation

that he found her in Kentucky and came to visit, but realized she was married and kept on moving. I don't know where Riley is or what happened to him. I would have loved to have met him.

In their later years, I asked about their first impressions of each other. My mother said, "I thought that he was Mr. It!" My father blushed, dropped his head and said he was misled (his words) by her uniform. In those days, nurses wore stiff white headwear, starched white dresses with white stockings, and white shoes. My father was not the only man to make the observation that she looked uncommonly beautiful in her nurse uniform. When I asked him what "Mr. It" meant, he said that he was always gentlemanly and presented himself in that manner. That statement cannot be disputed.

My mother had a nursing license in Alabama, obtained her Kentucky nursing license, and nursed at the old General Hospital, Methodist Hospital, and the old Red Cross Hospital in Louisville. She soon realized she was not going to be afforded the career opportunities she wanted because of the color of her skin. Therefore, she changed her career to teaching, one of the few professional careers available to Black women in her day. She earned her Master of Education degree at Nazareth College and became a public school teacher. Initially, she was paid less because of her gender and her race. Her first teaching assignment was at Virginia Avenue Elementary, then F.T. Salisbury Elementary, followed by John F. Kennedy Elementary in Southwick. She retired from Auburndale Elementary after a twenty-seven-year career in elementary education.

She taught Muhammad Ali's brother at F.T. Salisbury Elementary School at 2204 Magazine St. It's an apartment building now. The teachers were required at that time to visit with the students in their homes. She made a faculty visit to Cassius Clay's family while my father sat outside in the car. My mother said that when they would go on field trips from school, they couldn't get up the block without Cassius Clay getting into a fight, so a teacher would have to take him back to school. Of course, he turned that into greatness, becoming Muhammad Ali, the heavyweight champion of the world and a humanitarian. She knew him when he was a pugnacious young man.

She was a fourth grade teacher who never wanted to leave the classroom. I am told that my mother was gifted in helping children learn how to read. Every year she'd get the students who couldn't read. If you can't read by the time you're in fourth grade, then you have quite a bit of catching up to do. She helped them to overcome that deficit. My mother taught a boy named Scott. When she got him in fourth grade, he didn't know his ABCs. He ended up getting a scholarship to Speed Scientific School at the University of Louisville. His parents did not forget my mother and invited her to Scott's high school graduation. My father and I went with her to the ceremony. Scott became an engineer. My mother was a modest person. She said, "Well, I just caught him when he was ready." She didn't take too much credit for it.

After the war, my father was hired at the post office. He would talk about how, at that time, you had Black men with all kinds of college degrees—doctors and lawyers—who couldn't get hired for any jobs except at the post office. He also obtained his mortician's and funeral director's license in 1949 and worked at Rose and Higgins Funeral Home just up the street from our house. He worked both jobs simultaneously until his retirement from the United States Postal Service in 1980. After that, he worked until age ninety-six at George R. Mason Funeral Home. He had a reputation for being very skilled. In his later years, they said, "He's good, but he's slow." I thought, *Well, it's not as if the people he's working with are in a hurry.*

Elnora Higgins, 1974

Katheryn and her brother Martin, 1970

Katheryn's high school graduation, 1975

When the Archdiocese of Louisville started its diaconate program, my father was in the third class. After his ordination in 1978, he was assigned to St. Charles Borromeo, later renamed St. Charles Lwanga. This church was a block from my home. We walked to Mass every Sunday. Unfortunately, the church and the school closed over thirty years ago. Later he was assigned to the merged St. Martin de Porres at the Holy Cross church site. When he died in 2015 at age ninety-eight, my father was the oldest deacon in the Archdiocese.

Russell was a middle-class African American professional community. The lady who lived next door to us, Mrs. Lillian Henderson, was the principal at Coleridge-Taylor Elementary on Chestnut Street. Mrs. Henderson was a gracious, well-educated lady, and my parents would exchange Christmas presents with her. Most of my neighbors were teachers. The lady who lived catty-corner to us, Mrs. Lena W. Warders, was the principal at John F. Kennedy Elementary in Southwick, where my mother taught. Her husband, Jesse P. Warders, was the Kentucky legislator who introduced the bill to create the Kentucky Civil Rights Act.

Chestnut Street is where civil rights icons lived. I knew them personally as a child. Mae Street Kidd, one of the first Black women in the Kentucky legislature, lived just three blocks up from me. We'd see her walking down the street. She was a tall, stylish lady with blond hair. She introduced the Equal Housing Bill and the bill to make Dr. Martin Luther King, Jr. Day a holiday in Kentucky. Samuel Plato, a Black architect and one of the first Blacks to design post offices and federal buildings, also lived on Chestnut Street. My father buried Mr. Plato. Henry Hall, the founder of Mammoth Accident and Life Insurance Company, one of the largest Black-owned businesses in the United States at one time, lived here on Chestnut Street.

Then there were Robert and George Berry, who published the *Kentucky Reporter* newspaper. There was Sarah Bundy, who was brought to Louisville to integrate the Girl Scouts for African Americans. There was Harvey Clarence Russell, who was dean at Kentucky State University and held positions at various educational institutions in Kentucky. He's who the Russell neighborhood is named for. There was Jesse B. Taylor, the first African American homicide detective in the South. He investigated the murder of Alberta Jones, who was one of Muhammad Ali's attorneys.

My neighbor two doors down, Mr. Childress, owned a bar in the Black business district on Walnut Street. His business, like all of the others on Walnut Street, was destroyed by the city of Louisville's Urban Renewal program. Some called it Negro removal. His investment in his thriving business was demolished by the city. Instant poverty results when your investment and livelihood are destroyed. Tragically, Black history is discarded, disrespected, lost, or put into storage. We know that a red line was drawn around the Black neighborhoods on the real estate maps, and the city and banks would not invest in them. This was the start of a pattern of consistent disenfranchisement of west Louisville and its residents in the twentieth century through inequitable and unfair policies. My neighbors, my parents, and I have constantly faced outside forces and systemic racism that have negated our hard work and our investment.

My parents lived west of Ninth Street. They experienced the effects of redlining. I remember when they couldn't get a home improvement loan. The bank wanted them to get a second mortgage. Today, a second mortgage is commonplace; it's considered a home equity line of credit. Back then, if you were applying for a second mortgage, it meant that you were close to bankruptcy. My parents were not even close. It was

Louisville Free Public Library panel of influential Louisville Women. From left: Katheryn D. Higgins, First African American and first female engineer at the Louisville Water Company; Barbara Lewis, first female Dean of UofL's Brandeis School of Law; Shirley Cisney, National Teacher of the Year; Moderator, K. Shaver, owner of K. Shaver Advertising

Katheryn and Pepper English, ca. 1987

Katheryn with Former Lt. Governor and former Louisville Mayor Wilson Wyatt, 1985

Louisville Water Company, ca. 1987

engineering and finance. I've served on the business school alumni board and was president of the alumni board at the Speed Scientific School. After college, I started working for the Louisville Water Company. I was the first African American engineer, the first female engineer, and the first chemical engineer there. I'm one of those hidden figures. I retired after twenty-one years.

My brother and I sought to emulate my parents' example of hard work and sacrifice. They prepared us to excel. They knew we were competing in an unfair fight. My parents worked hard all of their lives. They secured a mortgage, and then paid off their house. They intended to build equity and an inheritance for me and my brother. Even though my family and I have paid taxes on this house since 1946, my inheritance is being undermined by a computer in the PVA office downtown. In 2019, the value of my house declined by $6,000. When I asked why, I was told that the value was computer generated. Later it was revealed that all property values in the West End of Louisville had been lowered. External forces are destroying the neighborhood that was created by long-term residents, some quite notable, who built Russell over multiple generations. The decision of the Catholic Archdiocese to close the church and school on my street contributed to the downward spiral of my neighborhood. These setbacks, economic and otherwise, have continued over many generations.

The second generation of redlining is the unpermitted halfway houses saturating my neighborhood, and the destruction that they bring to their surroundings. A friend and I have identified eight illegal halfway houses on 26th and Chestnut. They've deteriorated the value of her house so much that her mortgage is underwater. She went to college. She's a Ph.D. student. Her father was a fireman. This is not her doing. It's being

because of where they lived and the color of their skin. They refused to accept the terms. They weren't a poor risk. My father served his nation in the Army. He was licensed as a mortician and worked for the United States government. My mother had earned multiple academic degrees in two disciplines, completed a ten-year career in nursing, and a twenty-seven-year career in elementary education. They both went to work every day, they raised their children, and their children went to college.

My brother attended Aquinas Elementary school, Flaget High School, and Trinity High School. I attended Sacred Heart Model School and Sacred Heart Academy. I was one of a few African Americans in that grade school and in that high school. I completed degrees at the University of Louisville in chemical

brought to her. This is a problem put on the West End, not generated by the West End. It's not by accident. It's by design that these houses are losing value. Anytime you have eight illegal halfway houses on one city block, you're condemning it to death. My block has been branded as inhospitable for families and businesses. I talked to someone at a social services agency who said they're not putting any families on my block anymore because there are too many halfway houses.

Investors come from outside of Louisville and purchase properties whose values have been artificially depressed. They buy large houses in my neighborhood, divide the rooms with bed sheets, and rent those spaces for eighty-five dollars a week. It's not even a room. That's not up to city codes and regulations. The city doesn't enforce the law, to the detriment of the neighborhood and the renters.

In 2017, the building next door to me opened as an unpermitted sober house. CBS News aired a nationally televised piece about the owner. The premise was that a formerly homeless man was establishing a rooming house for the homeless. He said, "I'm eighteen years sober, and this is where God wants me: in a bad neighborhood in west Louisville." That was an insult. That statement displayed a lack of knowledge about the rich history of Russell. Civil rights icons lived on my street. He came from New Jersey to my historic neighborhood, bought a building with a depressed property value, and started piling people in there and making money as a landlord. He obtained people's social security numbers and signed them up for government checks. To my knowledge, he had no previous experience setting up or running transitional houses. His background was that he was once homeless himself. No services were provided and no effective supervision was given to the residents. They exhibited behavior inconsistent with sobriety. The mayhem spilled over into the

ca. early 1990s

neighborhood, compromising the quality of life for long-term residents.

Most of the residents in these transitional houses are not from Louisville; certainly not from my neighborhood. Russell is 96% Black. The house next door was almost 100% white. It was supposed to be a sober house for men. A woman overdosed on drugs in there. So how sober is it? I saw drugs being distributed from that building. One of the men would come over to store his liquor bottles in my water meter vault. If those men were getting the help the sober house owner said he was giving them, they wouldn't have come over to my house asking me for food. One man came over waving his arms, having some kind of fit. He ended up writhing around on the ground in front of my house.

Katheryn and Frederick

Deacons marching into Louisville Gardens
for the installation of Joseph Kurtz as Archbishop
of the Archdiocese of Louisville, June 2007

Another lay down in front of me as I was trying to enjoy a Sunday afternoon on my porch. When I asked him to move, he wouldn't. I called the police, who told me they couldn't do anything about it. Finally, the man asked me to call an ambulance, which I did.

The sober house owner didn't live there. He was getting money and donations to run his illegal operation, and I was getting the hassles. He then had the nerve to say that I wasn't sympathetic to the homeless. He asked me, "What have *you* done?" What he didn't know was that I helped feed the homeless at a local church. We served people a home-cooked breakfast of hashbrowns, eggs, grits, bacon, sausage, donuts, milk, juice, coffee, and cereal. They come in, sit down at tables, and dine. We don't put food on the sidewalk and expect them to pick it up and eat off the concrete. We treat the homeless like the people they are. I'm not unsympathetic. Nothing could be further from the truth.

The sober house operator went before the board of Zoning and Adjustment to get a conditional use permit. Even though the application was denied, the residents remained, and the city did not enforce the board's decision. If this were Cherokee Road instead of Chestnut Street, the operation would not have opened to begin with, much less continue unregulated for four years. Things are allowed to happen in my neighborhood that wouldn't happen anywhere else in Jefferson County. The patrons and churches who make these donations don't live in this neighborhood. Contributors can have compassion for the homeless and people struggling with addiction as long as they aren't inconvenienced. These benefactors drive home to their neighborhoods miles away and get a good night's sleep. One time I was outside working on my car, and one of the guys from a house came over and asked me for sex. This is not the neighborhood I grew up in. There's no reason for me to be disrespected like that on my own block.

Grievously, it would seem that my neighborhood has been characterized as a dumping ground. Anything you don't want elsewhere in Jefferson County is put in my community. It's an insult to the civil rights history, to the residents, and to the legacy of Russell.

I've been fighting to counter the deterioration in my neighborhood caused by this lack of concern and disregard from investors and others outside of the Russell neighborhood.

I am rebranding Russell. I am reintroducing the Russell that my family and I have known, lived in, built, and experienced for close to a century in the same home. From this unique perspective, I am relighting the neighborhood flame. I am recalling, retelling, reintroducing, and chronicling the neighborhood's glorious and storied history. I want to burnish the luster of Russell.

In 2018, I bought a residential lot on my street and turned it into a green space for events, gatherings, and visual and performing artistic expression. I am stabilizing my block and inviting the best of Jefferson County to my home. An arts and activism group, 1619 Flux, put up two big signs that say LOVE RUSSELL. I asked an artist to create signs for the greenspace that

said VOTE in five-foot-tall letters. Things weren't going the way we needed them to go with our previous presidential election. It was important to get the vote out. The letters lit up and changed colors as they glowed in the dark. It was a bold reminder to any passerby to participate in the upcoming election.

I've hosted an assortment of events. Local light artist Francisco Cardona created a pop-up art show. He invited other artists to participate. One man put up a geodesic dome, which he lit up from the inside and filled with live butterflies. There were lasers and projected images on the outside wall of one of the houses. A woman built a closet with a light experience inside. She hung her wedding dress in the structure and played audio about her wedding day. We had a DJ and a food truck. It was all very creative and fun. The Speed Museum's artist-in-residence, Shauntrice Martin, came on site and had an art session with local children. I thought they would enjoy painting in the grass.

They could run around without getting hurt. The director of the Speed Museum at the time, Stephen Reily, came out. There's a picture of him sitting in the grass creating art, in the middle of Russell. It felt significant to me for the Speed Museum to come west of Ninth Street given the history of the way these neighborhoods were traditionally treated. The children enjoyed it. Adults were doing cartwheels in the grass. It was wonderful. The weather was perfect.

I belong to Yard Talk, a community group that formed right after Breonna Taylor was killed. Individuals get together and talk about racial injustice and what we can do about it. Professor Kristi Papailler from California State University, San Bernardino, gave a talk. She did a presentation called "Artistic Expression in the Time of Trauma." We had gone together to the Speed Museum's exhibition about Breonna Taylor called "Promise, Witness, Remembrance." I asked her to develop a presentation for the Yard Talk group. She led us in our own artistic expression around the images of Breonna Taylor. People worked in small groups, made art, and reported out about what the experience meant to them.

Russell was where David McAtee was killed by the National Guard at his barbecue stand three blocks from my house in the aftermath of Breonna Taylor's murder. That event was traumatizing for me. I wrote a post on my Facebook page that said, "I live two blocks from where David McAtee was killed. You are invited to join me on my porch, at my home, for fellowship and conversation. I'm sitting there every day it's above seventy degrees. Let me know you're coming so that I can make ice tea." Some people I worked with and went to school with came. We had frank but cordial discussions while my beagle Emma presided. Many were touched by what happened to George Floyd, Breonna Taylor, and David McAtee. I wanted Russell

to be seen as a real place. Real people live here. It's the West End of Louisville. It's not the Wild Wild West or some foreign land. I don't want your impression of Russell to be just what's in the news. I want there to be someone you know who lives in Russell. You've sat on their porch. You've talked with them.

I grew up in Russell. What has happened here is unacceptable. I am neither content nor resigned to the way things are. My charge is to restore my block. Russell must return to the grand neighborhood it is, full of history, hard work, and accomplishment that the residents are accustomed to. I want families to return to Russell. I want responsive and adequate police service. I want Russell residents to receive the respect, investment, and support from Metro government commensurate with what other residents throughout Jefferson County expect and receive. I am undeterred.

I know my noble neighborhood. It and its residents deserve respect and care. I am challenged and excited. The best is yet to come. ✦

If You Write Me a Letter, Send It Here

JOYCE WOODS

My mother Joyce Woods is the oldest person I know that's originally from her block of 19th Street. She's free-hearted, kind, and loving. She's the greatest woman that ever lived. Her little house on 19th Street is a lighthouse. She doesn't turn nobody away. If somebody come down and say, "Ms. Joyce, I ain't got no money," or, "I'm hungry," or, "I need a bath," she'll help you out any way that she can. She'll wash your clothes. That's Momma. Neighborhood momma. She ain't boastful about it; it's just what she do. She do for the undesirables just like she'd do for all of us. That's just the way she's always been. —BEN WOODS

I told my husband before he passed, "I'm gonna get that sign from Kaelin's restaurant in the Highlands, the one that says, *If you can't stop, please wave.*" Because that's what I do. I sit out here, and cars go past, and all I do is wave at them. I don't go nowhere. When the lady next door first moved in, she told me, "Woo, people just go by here and blow and blow their horn at you!" I said, "Well, I guess they would. I've been on this street seventy-nine years. Everything that done went through here, I know about it. They blow because I know 'em."

Most everybody over here call me Granny. I could take you around to the store right now, and the people in the store will say, "Hey, Granny! Where you been at, Granny? We ain't seen you in two days." And they're from Africa. If you go to 18th and Broadway, they call me Granny.

People say, "If you ever wanna find somebody, go ask Ms. Joyce. She know where they at." So people call me on the phone all the time. I've had the same telephone number since 1968. I have never changed it. By now, it's probably written on the wall all over the place, in every jailhouse. It's probably over in Iraq. People say, "Mrs. Woods! I was just calling to find out, do you know how to get in touch with so-and-so?"

Not a day go by that don't somebody stop by, sometimes just to see what I'm doing. It's good because if don't nobody stop by, you could be in there all alone. Whiney come by this morning to say hi. I told him,

"Just keep going, I don't feel good today," and he went on down that way. But it's always somebody hollering or looking for somebody. My friend Jackie Ross is from here but lives in California. Every year when he comes home, he always comes here first to find me to ask where somebody done moved to or is they still living. "Joyce, I know you know where so-and-so is. Is they still living, or is they dead?" And I'll tell him the last place I knew, and he'll go visit them.

They'll leave money for each other with me. Say somebody owes you some money. They might say, "I'm gonna leave it with Ms. Joyce for you." Or you might say, "Take my money and give it to Ms. Joyce." When they leave money with me, I count it right in front of the person, and you come and get it. I guess they trust me.

My family has been on this block for over a hundred years. My family was here when the flood came in 1937, and they came back. My mother, my sister, my brother, my cousins, and my nieces and nephews were all born in that house. I was born in that house in 1943. I've never lived off this block.

My grandparents lived at 431 S. 19th St. My grandfather was a trolley conductor, and my grandmother worked for the Heflin family. Dr. Lee Heflin was a white doctor who lived with his wife Fern out on Top Hill Road. At some point, my family bought the house the house on 19th Street from Dr. Heflin. No bank loan, just worked it out with the Heflins based on trust. Must have been a friendly price because my mom said they paid for it in just two years.

My aunt Edith worked for the Heflins from age nine until she retired, and after she retired, they paid her half her salary until the day she died. She traveled with them to Paris and everything. Ms. Heflin called us her family because they didn't have any kids. She called my auntie her daughter. We used to go to their house on Top Hill Road every Christmas. We'd slide down the banister, and they'd buy us live Christmas trees and baskets of fruit. She loved my aunt Edith, and as a wedding gift, she helped her get a house at 1303 Southwestern Pkwy. It was just a close bond. Ms. Heflin even came and had a bathroom put inside our family's house on 19th Street in 1959 so we wouldn't have to use an outhouse anymore. It was just a close bond.

My father moved to New York. He was in the service and we lost contact. My mother was a housekeeper for two wealthy families. She was a joyful person. She loved to cook. She loved life. She never put nobody out. If you were sitting there and she was cooking, and you said, "No ma'am, I don't want none," she'd say, "Here, boy. Take a piece of this chicken, shut on up, and go on and eat it." That's just the way she was. She taught me how to clean, wash, iron, and sew, and how to hem things. She taught me how to pick greens and shell beans, and she taught me how to cook. She moved down with my aunt across from Chickasaw Park around 1980. But she came up here every day. She said this is home. Then, finally, she got older, and I had to bring her here to take care of her.

I'm the same as my mother in some ways. I guess it's just in me. Don't think I don't get angry or whatever. I might tell you what I think and keep on till you come on anyway. That's the way I was brought up. My mother always said, "You don't get nothing from nothing. You have to do something. There's nothing

wrong with helping somebody, because you don't never know when you or somebody in your family is gonna be in that predicament." She always told me, "Never look down on nobody." She said it's kinda hard not to do that sometimes, but don't do it from the heart. You might say, "Go away, I don't want to be bothered today," but you don't mean it that way. You judge a person by they heart and not by they doings, and that's one thing I tried to instill in my kids.

She instilled this in me as a child. If the lady across the street was over there sweeping her porch off, and you wasn't doing nothing, Momma would say, "Go on and help her out." Or if you saw her carrying groceries, she'd just look at you, "What are you sitting there waiting on?"

I tried to do the same with my kids. Two of my boys had the job of helping the older lady across the street set her garbage out, go to the store for her, cut her grass, and different stuff. The girls was mostly trained at home: "It's your day to do the dishes, your day to clean the bathroom." But if somebody needed them to go to the store, they went. Now all of them is in healthcare, so they learned something. They learned passion for people who can't do for themselves.

When I was growing up on 19th Street, we didn't have to go out of the neighborhood to get much of nothing. We had our own little stores, pharmacies, cleaners, laundromats, and skating rinks. The Plymouth Settlement House was open for the kids to go after school. We had our library on Jefferson near 18th Street that showed movies on Fridays. We had Sheppard Park Pool on 17th Street, which was always full of people. When Eugene Gardner—Big Gene—opened a recreation program for the kids in the area at the Madison Junior High gym on 18th and Madison from five o'clock to nine o'clock every day. At 17th and Madison, we had a soda fountain called Sam Porch where we

Joyce Woods at age sixteen in front of the house where she grew up at 433 S. 19th St., Sep. 1959

From left: Joyce's brother-in-law William, Catherine, and Sissy in the neighborhood

Corner of 19th and Walnut, 1948

I was a tomboy. I'd climb a tree. I guess it's because my sister was fourteen years older than me but my brother and me was just a year apart. I built scooters out of two-by-fours, skates, and RC tops and decorated them. We rolled up and down on the streets on these scooters, and we'd park them just like you would a bicycle. Then we had some kids around here that still liked to play cowboys. One boy didn't have a scooter, so he would always take his mop and broom and ride it like a horse while we was riding our scooters.

All the girls around here were older than me, and there wasn't too many of them until a few of them moved down here when I was about ten. I was already set in my tomboy pattern by then, but I would play right along with the girls: hopscotch, jumping ropes, and playing jacks. Ladies in their twenties would be sitting out there and would show us how to drop and pick up jacks. And that's the way you learned things.

It was just always something to do. You felt safe. But we knew when the street light came on, you better be in front of your own house. If you were at another person's house, you had better have permission to be there. And then they would bring you home; they wouldn't send you home. They'd stand out there and make sure you made it down the street.

It was family-oriented, and people cared. They really did. You could do something at 19th Street and Muhammad Ali, then go to Jefferson Street, and by the time you got to Jefferson Street, your parents knew what you done. And they didn't have telephones. I don't know how they did it. Your neighbors had the right to correct you in the right way. We had to respect our neighbors and each other. You might get mad and go around the corner and say what you got to say, but you better not say it right there where somebody would tell on you.

could go after school to get hamburgers, milkshakes, and ice cream cones and hang out and listen to songs like "Rock Around the Clock" and "The Twist." When you got out of school, you'd go over and get your milkshake or ice cream cone. It was just a lot to do where you really didn't have to go past your boundaries. We didn't have too much trouble down here. It was pretty safe, and I had a good childhood.

Close to us, we had the tot lot. It was a little park with little tunnels and some swings. We all would get over there and play kickball or whatever. We'd cut across the cemetery to go to school, but coming back we came out through Paramount Pickles at 14th and Cedar. Every day we would go past there to get our pickles. When they were loading barrels off the train, pickles would fall down and they would tell us we could have them. We'd get them and wipe them off and keep going. Sometimes they would let you get some out of the barrel. Most of the time, they were going so fast with the machine loading them up they didn't want you up on the platform to get hurt. Sometimes they would just throw them to us. They hadn't put the brine to them yet, but they were good.

Then Mother's Cookies was down on 20th Street. You could smell the aroma of vanilla wafers when you come out. And Ms. Hallie had a restaurant called Ms. Hallie's on the corner of 20th and Cedar, a little teenage place on that same corner. She lived behind Mother's Cookies and her restaurant.

Mr. Gardner had a snowball stand behind the library in the little alley. You'd go in there and get you a quart of red snowball. Then there were little candy stores where you could go to. We had Harold's, and we had Saunders 5 and 10 on 19th and Muhammad Ali. Between Cedar and Jefferson, we had Sandy's Body Shop which had a candy store in it. People always called the big building on the corner of 19th and Walnut the Ice House. They'd go around back to the loading dock and buy buckets of draft beer back there. Mr. Gibson had a liquor store on the corner.

Frank Jay's first restaurant was right next to where the barber shop is now, so you had someplace to go get your hamburgers and french fries. It was called Jay's, but we always said we were going around to Frank's because that was his name. Later he built the big Jay's

Joyce Woods on Eddy Street

Cafeteria, but he started off with just a small place with a counter. We had another little place as you came down Cedar called Bud's. He was a big, red, old Irishman. He had the same pickles we were getting from Paramount, but they had been cured. You'd go in there and get a great big pickle for a dime.

We might go to the Haymarket once a week to get real fresh vegetables, but most of what we needed was right in the neighborhood. Mr. White had a hen yard in his backyard on Cedar and he sold big brown eggs. Mr. Glass, who we called Moonbeam, sold chickens.

Then we had a lady named Mrs. Virginia who starched and ironed clothes for people and did all the people's curtains. Not only for us in the neighborhood but also for rich people in the Highlands. Put those curtains on them stretchers. For two days, she might do nothing but curtains, curtains, curtains. Then she'd say, "My, I gotta go get me some rest." She'd go fishing

Neighborhood kids on Eddy Alley

Mr. Crow

and come back with a big old thing of fish, saying, "Want some bluegills? Bluegills! Bluegills!' She would take my son fishing sometimes. People took time with other people's kids. If you said you wanted to learn to do something, they would have the patience, if you had the patience to learn.

We had a lady named Ms. Molly who lived over on the corner of Eddy Alley and 19th Street, and she always made ice cream. She would tell you, "Come on over, girl! I'm gonna make some ice cream." I'd watch her churn the ice cream, then she'd tell me how many times to churn it. On Sunday, she'd have a lemon squeeze, and she'd have me squeezing lemons for her. I still have her glass lemon squeeze.

Between 19th and 20th on Walnut Street was Ben P. Wells Cleaners. Mr. Wells was about four feet tall. Because he was so short, he never had regular pants. He had to cut them off, and that made them wide-legged. If people didn't have no clothes, he'd tell them, "Come on in here, boy, and get you some clean clothes." He would give them something clean to put on. He lived behind his shop, and he'd say, "Go on around the back and my wife will give you some water to wash up." Everybody looked after everybody.

Back on a little short alley behind Cedar near 18th Street, we had a real junkyard, a *junk* junkyard. His name was Mr. Al. That's when people were selling rags, selling newspapers, selling glass. Wasn't nothing wasted. We had a man named Mr. Joe. He had a different junkyard. Horse and wagon. He used to go all up in the Highlands cleaning up for people and come back with all kind of stuff. And then we had Mr. Wright between 19th and 20th on Eddy Street. He had one arm. He had a mule and a horse, and he would go around and till the ground for people's gardens. Some people had big gardens, because if you had an empty lot next to you, you could fence it in and take care of it for a dollar a year or something like that. He kept his horse down there in a little field next to his house on Eddy Street. When he wasn't tilling the ground, he would let you ride the horse up and down the alley.

I used to watch my friend Tiny's grandmother, Ms. Whiteside, wring chicken necks on their wire clotheslines. She'd put a live chicken up there and flip it until the wire cut its neck. Then she would put it in a tub of hot water, and that was the worst smell I ever smelled in my life. They lived in the double house next door to our house.

Mr. Milton Green was our unofficial neighborhood doctor. He lived at 1924 Eddy St. He used herbs. We called him Doc Green. Once, when I was sixteen, a big piece of glass from a broken window stuck in my leg. My leg was laying wide open. My sister ran and got Doc Green and he took out the piece of glass, tied something around my leg, and put pressure on it so it would stop bleeding before they took me to the hospital to get sewed up. He would always tell you to take Father John's Medicine, an old vitamin-like liquid. If you hurt yourself, he told you what to do for it. When my uncle died, my sister sent a kid down to my house to tell me, "I think Charles is dead." I felt him and said, "Yeah, he's dead." She said, "No, I want y'all to go down there and get Doc!" He come over, took a spoon, shined it up, held it under Uncle Charles's nose, and said, "He's dead." That made it official.

Doc Green also baked pies and cakes for people, nice cakes. Made the best lemon pie in the world. And he was limber. He could do the splits, kick his leg up and touch his toes, go down with his knees in and jump right back up. He was way up in his eighties doing that. He was a joyful person. Years and years ago, he used to be the maintenance inspector at Beecher Terrace.

At 1934 Eddy St. we had a man named Mr. Melvin Pruitt. He could do anything: put a roof on, build a room on, drywall. Anything you needed done, Mr. Melvin could do it. He did a lot of work around here for people who couldn't afford a lot. If you said you needed your roof patched, and he had a piece of tar paper, he'd put it up there for twenty dollars. He'd go out further and charge other people more, but his neighbors got a

Joyce's grandson Quante on the corner of 19th and Muhammad Ali

Joyce's son Anthony with a neighbor named Howard

discount. If you said, "I've got a leak, Mr. Melvin," or, "My sink is dripping," he'd come over and fix it. He wasn't trying to make money because his regular job paid him good money. He was just helping out.

We had a man named Mr. Harrison who lived right behind us who played sax and was a music teacher. He was real nice and quiet. He played around at different churches and stuff. And then at 17th and Muhammad Ali, we had a lady that taught piano lessons. Mr. Phillip had a wood and coal shed on Eddy Alley.

He sold wood and coal, but he also did moving, roofing, and repair work. It was just things right here, so you really didn't have to go anywhere.

Everybody had a family, and something real to take care of. Mostly everybody here owned their home. Everybody in the neighborhood knew who was who. We was all poor, but we didn't know it. Some might have been a little blessed, but we was all in the same condition, and nobody made fun of anybody. People didn't move out. When they moved in, they stayed till they had no other choice but to move. You didn't move in and say, "I'm here for a month or two, then I got to go."

I went to Coleridge-Taylor Elementary School all the way to the fifth grade. That's when they started the boundary. Anybody on 20th Street could go to schools in the neighborhood, but everybody who lived on 19th had to get bused. I got bused from our side of the boundary to Charles Young between 27th and 29th on Lytle for one year. Bus fare was like ten cents. We didn't have no lunch room. If you didn't bring your lunch, the teacher sent you to the corner store with your money. We had a wood-burning stove in the classroom. I graduated at Portland Baptist Church across the street from the school. I keep telling people I was bused years and years ago, and they laugh at me. We was in the boundary. We couldn't go to Perry, we couldn't go to James Bond, and we couldn't go to Coleridge-Taylor. After elementary school, I went to Madison Junior High School and Central High School.

When we were going to school, our teachers lived in the neighborhood. Our parents knew the principal of Central High School, Mr. Wilson, who lived over on Madison between 19th and 20th. Every Thanksgiving, the Central band would march down Muhammad Ali from the school and perform a couple of songs in front of his house. Everybody would hear them coming and would come out to watch them. One of the librarians from Madison Street Junior High, Ms. Robinson, lived across the street from him.

There was a joint over on 19th and Cedar called Club Morocco. A lot of famous Black entertainers came there. The joint was on one corner, and a Holiness church was on the other. The church was a three-room shotgun house, and Elder A.T. Moore was the pastor. He blowed the saxophone. They'd go to church at six in the evening, and they might not leave till one or two o'clock in the morning. I mean, they were having *church* church. He'd blow the saxophone so good that instead of going in the joint, people would go over to the church. The music was so intense that you just had to go. The club was bopping over there; you'd see them going inside in their fine clothes, then you'd see some of them make a u-turn and go over to the church. He was blowing church sounds. I think that's how they got the money over the years to build the big church down there on 24th and Broadway.

The area was just churches and joints. In the late '60s and early '70s, a lot of soldiers was coming into the clubs. You'd see them in uniform, and they had their ladies of the night. I couldn't go through there. I was too young. When I was about eighteen years old, I used to go to the Top Hat, a bar on Walnut Street that had a lot of mirrors on the walls. My cousin's husband worked there, and he knew I wasn't old enough to be in there. He would let me and my girlfriend sit there, just as nice as can be, until it started getting crowded. Then he'd say, "I think it's time for y'all to get on up out of here." But there was also Fifth Street Baptist Church on 19th and Jefferson, a booming Black church, and a lot of other churches in the neighborhood. You were always welcome at those churches, and every church would have vacation Bible school. They would schedule them on different dates so that all the kids would have something to do all summer long.

They used to have dances up there at a place on 13th and Magazine. And you could go up there and skate. The Little Palace restaurant was our White Castle. You had places where you could go get your hat blocked. We had a Black bank, Black insurance company, the Lyric and the Grand theaters, and nightclubs like Joe's Palm Room and Charlie Moore's. We had the Piccolo Grill and the Star-Liberty cab stand right next to it. Then there was Roy and Joe's Chili parlor and Katherine's Catering where you go get them good ol' pies at.

It was a great place to grow up.

As I got older, I started to work. My first job was at the fair. I was too young to work then, but I lied about my age. I was the tallest one working there, but everybody else was older than me. After that, I worked at Spalding's laundry for a little while. Then I got married when I was sixteen, so I didn't have to work. I had my first child when I was seventeen.

I stayed married to the same man for sixty-three years. Six kids out of it. Everybody got they own home, everybody been on the job, and they learned something.

When I first got married, we moved into a three-room little cottage two doors down from the house where I grew up. Then we moved to my mother-in-law's house on Eddy Alley when she died in 1962. My husband was the oldest of her children, so we moved down there to take care of his two sisters. At the time the daddy, my mother-in-law's second husband, said he just couldn't do it right then. The owner rented us the house for thirty-five dollars a month. Five rooms, bath, and yard for thirty-five dollars a month. After a couple of years, I ended up buying the house from him for nine hundred dollars. It worked out good. We stayed down there for eighteen years.

When my oldest child was in the second grade, I started working at Perry Elementary School. They

The Rollettes Social Club
(Joyce Woods is the tallest in white), ca. 1970s

had a program called Follow Through where parents came in all day to give extra help to kids who needed it, sometimes one-on-one, or you might have three at a table that's on the same progress level. It was a learning experience for me and it was a learning experience for them. That program was real beneficial. And I could go to school with my kids and come home with my kids. You got a little stipend. After a while, I got hired as a regular behavior analysis specialist. A lot of kids came from Southwick and Cotter Homes. It was a good thing. There wasn't no kid walking off not telling you where they gone at. You better tell me where you going at, and you better be where you say you at. I worked at Perry for six years.

In the early '70s we got a color TV. My husband worked as the maintenance man in the Legal Arts Building at Seventh and Market, and a man there had it and sold it to him. We couldn't afford it no other way. Neighborhood kids—Calvin, Inky, Rodney, and Paul—would come over on Saturday mornings and I'd make ice cream or jello or something, and they'd sit in the living room and look at whatever they wanted to look at on TV with my kids.

Joyce's husband June outside of the Legal Arts Building, where he worked

People that was here stayed until the city started with Urban Renewal. Around 1959, they hung a banner on the viaduct on Walnut between 13th and 14th that said something like, "Urban Renewal will be rebuilding 15th to 21st Street." People started moving out because they didn't know whether they was gonna have a place to stay. As they say, if you know something's coming, get prepared and get ready, and that's what they did. And that's when the neighborhood started going different ways. Rental situations happening more. We had some fly-by-night people who'd move in and stay awhile and then move out. But it still basically felt the same. It didn't really bother me. But as the houses starting becoming empty and

falling down and we was still here, I just wondered why. Because they started moving out, and people was buying them up for little to nothing and making rooming houses out of them. When they took down Walnut Street, I guess it was for the good, I can't say that it wasn't, but they just scattered everything. This was a *neighborhood*.

I was born and raised on 19th Street. I stayed here the whole time. I moved a half block to Eddy Alley in 1962. In 1980, we moved from Eddy Alley back to a house on 19th Street just three doors down from the house I grew up in. We never had to get a moving van or nothing. Everybody in the neighborhood picked up a piece of furniture and moved it.

How long did I stay on 19th Street without nobody else living there? My sister and I were the onliest ones here on this block for seven or eight years. In 1998, the city wanted my land, so in return, they had to give me the land I wanted. They bought my house on 19th Street and gave me an opportunity to pick what lot I wanted. I got two lots right down the street for a dollar apiece: 433 and 435 19th St.

I've seen them tear down every house around here at one time or another, including the one I grew up in. That was the very last one they tore down. They say every house has a story, but all of those houses are gone now. I miss all the people who lived in those houses. We really knew each other. The people here now in these newer houses are friendly, but we don't know each other as well as we knew our neighbors back in the day.

My old house had big rooms, so my furniture was bought for big rooms. But all the builders were building with smaller rooms. They were coming down with the Urban Renewal stuff and all the new houses you see around here now were being built.

One day I was on the church bus coming back from a trip to Bowling Green, and I looked out the window in Bullitt County and saw a sign for a builder: $59,500, brand new brick house, all the luxuries." I said, "That ain't right." After I came home, we rode out there and got the plan, and that was right in our range. And they came and built my current house on 19th Street. I was the first house on this side of the block to be built, and that was in 1998. What the city gave us paid for the house.

The new Quinn Chapel was built across the street from me around 2002. I sat here on this porch and watched them build it. I sat here for four or five years by myself before they started building other houses on this block.

They're building up houses, true enough. But if you're not a driver or don't have a way to get around,

Joyce's last house on 19th street before building current house on the same block

Joyce's daughter and granddaughter on 19th St. The house behind them is where Ms. Joyce grew up.

you have to just about get everything you want while you're out. Whereas in my time, there was Betty's place, The Fruit Stand, at 18th and Jefferson, where you could get fresh vegetables, fresh greens, fresh anything. There was a Kroger at 18th and Jefferson. We had Gill's Fish Market. We had corner store groceries at 21st and Cedar and at 20th and Chestnut. You could walk and get what you want. But now there is nothing in walking distance at all. The closest grocery store we have is Kroger on 28th Street or Save-a-Lot on Portland Avenue between 26th and 27th.

I was always a caregiver. I ended up taking care of my mother and my husband. My husband had congestive heart failure in 1982. He had his three main arteries unclogged. They gave him eight years to live. At the time the VA didn't have all the modern stuff. He had a leaky valve and that's what kept him going down. But he lived till '07. My mother stayed with me

almost fifteen years before she passed in '06. She was ninety-eight. She had diabetes and was in a wheelchair and was losing her sight because, for a whole year, she was taking vitamin D instead of insulin. Her doctor called and said she hadn't ordered her medicine in a year. Her body just started deteriorating.

There's a dude who comes on my porch and I feed him. His social worker called me today and asked me had I seen him. I said, "He's supposed to come today to clean himself up. I went and got him a couple pairs of pants and a shirt. You might not believe this, but he came and spent the whole day with me till twelve o'clock last night! He came at six o'clock in the morning. When my grandson was going to work, he was sitting on the porch." The social worker told me, "Ms. Joyce, you know I have to check where he stays at. And Ms. Joyce, *everybody* knows you!" I said, "Everybody who?" She said, "I was talking with the man at the house where he lives at. I told him, 'A lady on 19th Street, Ms. Joyce, feeds him.' And the first thing the man said was, 'Mama Joyce!'"

People help me out, too. Mr. Manuel Hays has a lawn service and he comes over and cuts my grass for free. He says, "Ms. Joyce, you ain't got no business trying to cut that grass. Get out the way, I'll cut it." Paul Mitchell, who was one of the kids who would watch Saturday morning cartoons at our house with my kids, stops by all the time. He calls me Mama Woods. He lives out in Fern Creek these days, but he'll bring me vegetables out of his garden: tomatoes, cucumbers, okra.

Muhammad Ali Park was on the corner of 19th and Cedar. The park was still there when I built my house. The whole thing has been gone close to twenty years now. Since then, you see people under the tree where the park used to be. All of them was born around here. If they wasn't born around here, the majority of their life as a kid was around here. They got married, had

Painting of Joyce Woods, her daughter Andrea, and her granddaughter Ce'Onna

families, and wanted it better, so they moved away over the years. But they come back and hang out under that tree where Muhammad Ali Park used to be. I call it the meeting hall. I ask them, "You at the reunion hall today?" They just meet and sit and laugh and talk and picnic and stuff. Just coming together. They didn't have no place else to go. Everybody's scattered out. Some's out in Shively, some's way down and way over. And they just found a common ground back in the neighborhood under that tree. Because this neighborhood is where they had a lot of their enjoyment. I was the only nut that stayed here, and I'm glad I did. This is my permanent address. Been on the street seventy-nine years. I've never had an address that didn't have a "19" in it. I never lived across Muhammad Ali Boulevard.

As a kid, I saw everything I wanted right here—love and friendship. And then when I started having a family, when I had to go somewhere, I was able to ask my neighbors, "Will you watch my kids?" and they would say, "Yeah." I never had to really leave here for nothing. Everything was right here. And I always had enough room. In each house I had, the girls had they room, the boys had they room—they may have had to share, but they weren't in my room. So I was blessed on that part. I always figured that wherever you're happy at, that's where you stay. You can't run and find happiness. A lot of my friends have moved and moved and moved, but I stayed in my circle. I tell everyone, "This will be my last known address. If you write me a letter, send it here." ✦

Rosa Macklin grew up on Eddy Street, and we are as close as family. Her father, Milton "Doc" Green, was always taking pictures in the neighborhood. Below are some of her father's photographs, and some of her memories of her family and our neighborhood. —JOYCE WOODS

ROSA MACKLIN

My dad was born in May of 1899. His brother was born in 1896. They were raised at 1937 Eddy St. in a house owned by his grandmother, Amanda. My siblings and I grew up in that same house, and my father sold the property in 1996. It had been in our family for one hundred years. My great-grandmother had made sure her children and grandchildren had a roof over their heads, and laid the groundwork for the generational wealth of our family. From the sale of that house, I was able to buy my first and second investment properties.

My father passed away in 1997 three weeks before his 98th birthday. He was an icon in that neighborhood. Being Black during that time, we did not have the same opportunity to get good healthcare. My dad filled that gap. We did not run to the hospital when we had a cough or cold, stepped on a nail, or were injured all the way to the white meat. We learned about different remedies that could heal naturally. There was a plant, bug, or a mixture my dad would make to help you feel better.

My dad took a lot of pictures, but most of them he gave away. The pictures he took were like gifts to the people. He really just liked taking pictures just to show off his skills and his latest camera.

From 22nd Street to 15th Street, from Jefferson Street to Broadway, if you lived in that square, we knew you. This was our stomping ground. We knew the neighborhood and the neighborhood knew us. Our riches were in our relationships. No one was going to be hungry or naked. Our doors were open to strangers. We were a community! ✦

Rosa and her siblings on Easter

Doc Green's wife in front of their home on Eddy Alley

Guys playing dominoes in Cedar Park

Son of Rosa Macklin and two second cousins of Joyce Woods

Rosa and her brother Leonard on 19th Street

Doc Green and his oldest son George

Come On Up. Find You a Chair.

The front porches of Russell

WALT SMITH
CO-FOUNDER, WEST OF NINTH BLOG

Growing up, the porch was where it all started. My parents' house in Shawnee was built with a simple concrete stoop. Over the years, they added onto it until they had a full-sized porch, a space where our family could relax and converse with our neighbors. It was an extension of our home, more like a second living room. When the adults were on the porch, they had first dibs on the chairs, and the kids had to find a seat on the steps where we cooled off between games of 21 or riding bikes all afternoon. I couldn't invite all the neighborhood kids inside my house, so the porch was the best option. Neighborhood-wide, throughout the West, the porch was the universal hangout spot.

Some of the best times spent on the porch were amongst family members on what we call "Soul Food Sundays." Whenever my aunts and uncles were on the porch, they shared stories about my family moving into the Chickasaw neighborhood on Dearborn Avenue in 1960, during the white flight that took place. We'd learn about my grandfather's journey owning and operating his paving company, Smith & Sons, and being one of the first Black contractors to land jobs with white clients. He was proud to have paved the trails and the parking lot at Shawnee Golf Course, as well as doing concrete work at Churchill Downs and at the Louisville Zoo.

My father, a retired JCPS educator and pastor of thirty-seven years, once told me that when they were starting the church, they couldn't get a loan from the bank for much needed construction of the building. It was Mammoth Life, a Black-owned insurance company located in Russell, that gave them the loan for the building on 27th and Elliott. Learning how my family's history is parallel to the historical events that took place in west Louisville gave me a sense of identity and a reason to be proud of the place I call home. It also led me to become curious about how it fits into the history of the city as a whole.

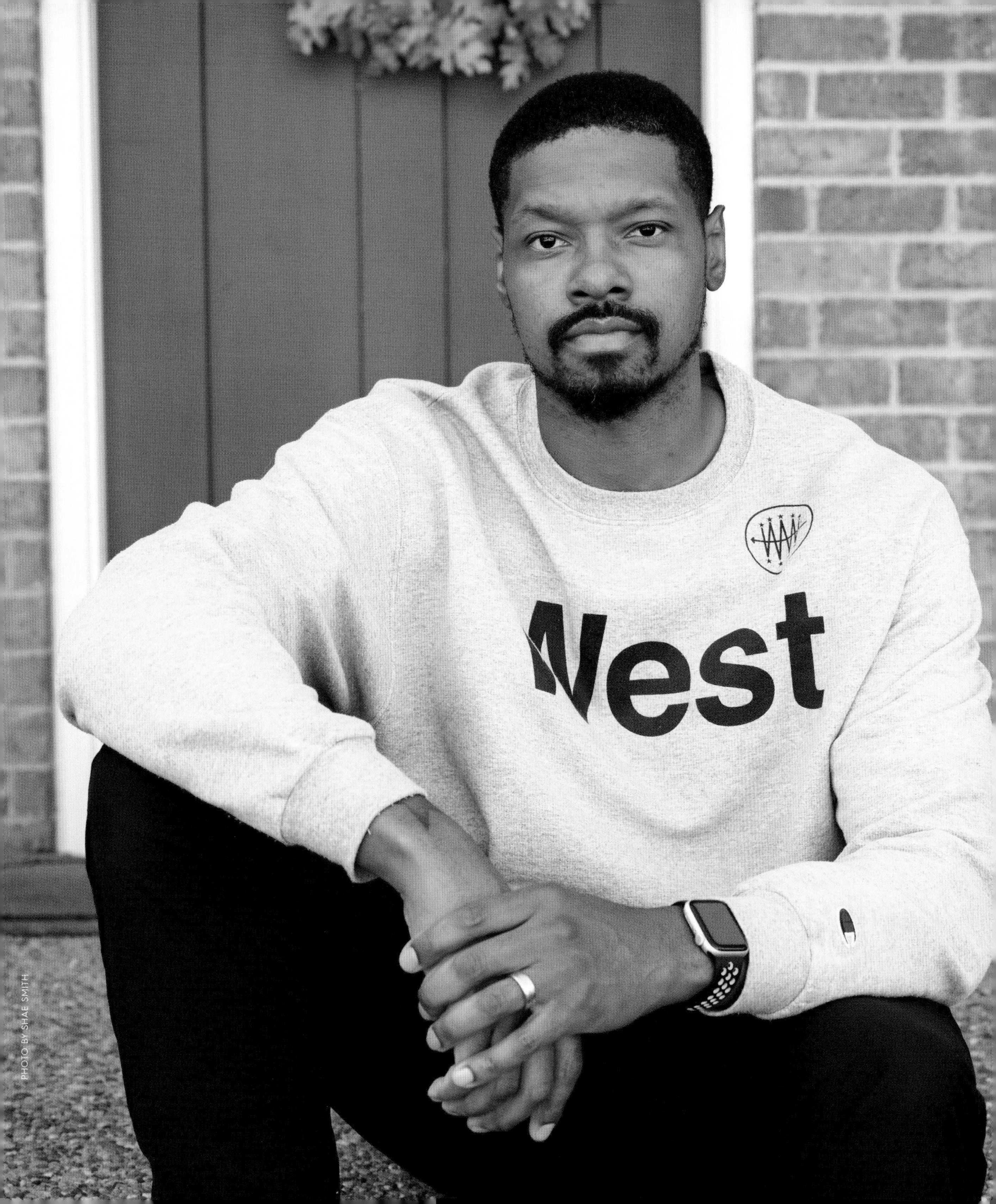

PHOTO BY SHAE SMITH

Not that long ago, I walked on my parents' porch wearing a T-shirt with an image of Fontaine Ferry Park, the former Shawnee neighborhood amusement park from back in the day. In my mind, I really thought this was something nostalgic and well-celebrated. As soon as I stepped on the porch, my father and godfather questioned me and asked, "What do *you* know about Fontaine Ferry?" I said, "It was this amusement park down in Shawnee by where the baseball diamonds are, right?" I immediately got schooled on how Fontaine Ferry was originally for whites only until integration took place, which allowed Blacks to visit only once a week. I haven't worn the shirt since.

The full history of west Louisville was never taught in school. This history is something I learned on the many porches I sat on. I found the lack of physical artifacts and photography telling the story of west Louisville upsetting, and I sometimes held onto this narrative that the city excludes our community from the conversation. I eventually shifted my perspective and asked myself, *Should it be a responsibility of someone from outside my community to take interest in the people within my community?* When I couldn't find what I was looking for, it inspired me to set out and create it.

One night in 2016, while driving to our home in Park DuValle, my wife Shae and I were talking about how what people see on the news shifts their overall perspective of west Louisville. It was sad to see how news coverage persuaded people who have never stepped foot in west Louisville that it is dangerous. We recalled the times we were met with initial shock when telling people what part of town we lived in. They'd say stuff like, "How do y'all feel about all of the crime happening down there?" or "Do y'all really feel safe raising your family there?" We talked about how this negative outlook on west Louisville affects those living within our community. When you see nothing but negative news about your community, you begin to internalize that you can't trust the people living around you. It makes it hard for people to step out of their four walls and get to know one another. So we sat in the car, and West of Ninth came to life.

Shae and I always took pride in calling west Louisville home. And while we were aware of the bad things that occurred in our neighborhood, we also knew that we were surrounded by hard-working families and great neighbors. The idea of West of Ninth is to create a platform for the voices of the West End that have been unheard for far too long. The best way for us to do so would be to meet people where they're at and allow them to share their stories.

So we took an old Nikon DSLR and our cell phones. We hit the streets of every neighborhood in west Louisville, interviewing one neighbor at a time, keeping it as informal as possible, and capturing the moment in real-time. We began publishing the blog in August of 2017, the same year that we became first-time homeowners and moved to the heart of Russell. If there's anything that we've learned over the years, it is that everyone is interesting. Whether it's turning tragedy into triumph or sharing their personal experience and providing their perspective on life, everyone has a story. We should allow each other to grow and evolve to change it.

With West of Ninth, one of the main objectives is to meet people where they're at. We're meeting them at bus stops, parks, businesses, and a whole lot of porches. I had never done any interviewing before we started the blog, and I had to learn some skills as I went. We got better as we kept going. We learned when to interject with another question to bring an interview where it could go and when to let an elder with a life-long story just keep talking. I had to learn how to ask more open-ended questions to keep the story going.

When you meet someone at the bus stop, they have a little bit of time, and they don't have the opportunity to go in depth. When someone invites you up on their porch and shares their space, you're going to get that person as they really are. They're not worried about saying the right thing. They're calling it like they see it. This is their house, their kingdom. You're a guest.

The front porch is this unique space that shares the public with the private. It's an environment that you create. It's more than just a concrete slab with a few steps and a roof. In the West End, just about every house has some type of front porch. From the spacious brick build-outs painted with bright colors and enclosed with hanging plants to the walk-up stoops beautifully landscaped with rose bushes and mulch to the makeshift stoop with one chair right outside the door. No matter how it's designed, the porch is an extension of the home. It's meant to be comfortable and relaxing. The conversations are never formal. You can let your guard down and share.

Throughout the West, it's just an unspoken understanding that you can let it all out on the porch. You chill out with family and neighbors and speak to the people passing by. It's where we connect with ourselves and the people around us. Both physically and figuratively, it's the foundation of where community takes place. It's an informal classroom where you learn manners, where you learn how to speak to people, how to respect other people's property, and how and when to express unpopular opinions. It's a safe space to vent and the most iconic stage for storytelling. It has the same kind of vibe as a barber shop, but instead of being just for guys, everybody's welcome. When people are on the porch, they're going to share and sometimes perform, play spades or dominoes for hours on end, shoot the breeze, and be reckless, serious, and funny. The porch is where it can all happen, and we won't be judged for it.

The message of the porch is, "Yeah, come on up. Find you a chair." ✦

Porch Stories

I spent a little time with Russell residents to find out what the front porch means to them. Here are some excerpts of our conversations. —WALT SMITH

MS. GRACE

I always have a nice yard. It turns heads. I'm old fashioned that way. I have people stop and take pictures. I think it's good for the neighborhood because if you start doing something, your neighbors will start doing something. Like the guy down here. He just painted his house red and put his flowers out. Another guy down the street liked the look of our porch and paid us to paint his. We had it done for the Fourth of July. We let it set for three days with nobody walking on it. "Use side door, please. Wet paint."

I'm known as a good neighbor, a nice neighbor. I will help anybody. I'm always feeding everybody because I cook a lot. You got to feed your neighbors. I have company on the porch over here all the time. My friends. Not newcomers. I always have good gatherings here. We grill. Sit and drink. Music on the porch. We have good times here.

What I want for my neighborhood is to keep it clean, and just help people when they need help. We got a lot of homeless people walking through here. I can see them coming up the street. When I see somebody walking in the hot sun, I run in to get them a water bottle or a sandwich. I buy those little fruit cups. Just everybody look after one another. Everybody show some love. And put God first. That's my mindset.

BROTHER ED

You might *think* nobody can hear you on your porch, but you probably louder than a motherfucker. All things get exposed on a front porch.

I'm always on the porch. It's hot as hell out here, but I'm on the porch because it's my refuge. I come here to escape everything. The world. The kids. Everybody. That's why I'm always on the damn porch. I'm doin' me. I ain't out here to judge nobody or point fingers. I'm just chillin'. I got my fan. Got my leg up. I got my beer. I got my boys. I'm Gucci. A1. Only people you trust come on the front porch. That's what the front porch represents.

PHOTOS BY WALT SMITH

MOOGA

Before I step out and go somewhere, it starts with the porch. I'm comfortable. I'm still at home. I might come outside with my shirt off. No shoes, no shirt, no sir.

It's therapy, for real. The porch is where I get my peace of mind. It's just a vibe. Just chillin' in your own lane. Ain't hurtin' nobody. It's a brotherhood bond. It's locked in. Damn near like the barber shop. It's good conversation, a little gossip. It's always played a role for me, my parents, my grandparents, my OG's. On the porch, you're gonna see a little bit of everything, and didn't nobody *see you* see it.

You can't forget where you came from, and a lot of us came from the porch. Gettin' our hair cut, hair braided. I love where I'm from. If I'm in Atlanta, Tennessee, Cincinnati, I'm like, "Oooh. I can't *wait* to get home." Might not be much, but it's enough for us.

MARCUS

I lived on the porch growing up. The family would sit back, and it was just a free range of open conversation and bonding. It was just a pillar. Families coming together almost like coming to the dinner table. But it was a sense of peace. It's where you can just come and just be at ease. Everybody's interacting with one another. The porch is like a big community. You get to meddle with what's going on without *mettlin'*, you know? People lift weights. Get their hair cut. Me, I play dominoes.

My family been in this house for seventy or eighty years, you dig? My family has been around. Back in the day, the Russell area used to be the shit. There used to be million-dollar people down the street. Back in the day, that was here. During the recession in the early 2000s, there started to be a lot of abandoned houses around here. I guess we just got to go through a transition. My moms instilled in me earlier that real estate is the biggest piece of value that you can hold on to. Having that sense of ownership means a lot. You can do a lot with it.

Let's put some Black owners in these homes, man. Like this couple that bought the mansion next door. Let's keep these roads intact. Put more good business here for us. Yeah, we got Lyles Mall, but we want a strip like Shelbyville Road or Hurstbourne Lane has. To hell with the liquor stores, the clubs. We got enough of them and—excuse me—we got enough churches, too. Give us some good biz. They're revising downtown. Why not here?

MIKE

I always say, nonfiction is better than fiction. This is real out here. You get to see everything. Live it. Breathe it. Everything is real. It ain't like being in the house watching TV. You can feel the wind blowing on your face, and I'm feeling the same wind as my neighbor. We got the same experiences going on. There's a camaraderie with the neighbors. Ain't no filter in between. You can't get that sitting in a house.

Hangin' on the porch is like a frame of mind. It's just a way to calm your nerves, get away, be by yourself, or around like-minded people who are striving for the same goals you are. The input you hear from them might help you in your day, might help you heal what you're going through in life. It's like going to the doctor or the psychiatrist, man. So you can deal with the other stuff that goes on out here and provide for your family. Real life.

I come on and sit by myself and don't need to talk to nobody. Just need to be out here, feel the breeze. Just be happy and see what you're helping to build just by doing little things like cutting the grass, getting the fence fixed. My brother started putting a Kroger bag on his fence. So now everybody got in the habit of throwing their trash in that bag instead of on his walkway. Things like that and being on this porch go a long way to playing a part in communicating with the neighbors. I feel like this block is a leader for all the blocks in the West. They all look out for each other.

You can help your community. You can make it better. If we start getting more of us buying houses down here, people wouldn't let their places get run down. You're gonna let somebody know, "Hey, man.

Don't throw trash on my side of the street." They helped build this, and nobody wants to see it get run down. If you got more people out here on the porch, I feel like you'd see less violence and people gonna be more willing to take care of their spots.

Just gotta look in the mirror, man. We could change all this stuff, man. We could change all this stuff. ✦

They called it West Downtown

JOE PAGE MCNEALY

I started a farmer's market at Ninth and Chestnut at the old Quinn Chapel on Chestnut in 2006. I bought produce from Kentucky farmers in a ten-county region around Louisville and sold it in the West End. Farmers were scared to come into the West End because they thought they were going to get killed or whatever. So, I said, "Okay, sell me your stuff, and I'll sell it at my market." I sold boxes full of produce, apples, plums, nectarines, and peppers.

I had been going to Community Farm Alliance meetings, listening to people talk about what was going on and how African Americans could be involved. Cassia Herron was working for them, but there were no Black farmers or Black people selling any kind of agriculture in the West End. That piqued my interest. I knew about the food business; I had run bakeries and restaurants. So I said, "Well, let me fill that void."

I was the first African American to get any money from the state through the Kentucky tobacco settlement fund. Between the fund and Spencer, Bullitt, and Jefferson County Cooperative Extension Councils, I got $25,000 to start a farmer's market in the West End. We wanted to build a permanent market like Findlay Market in Cincinnati and Eastern Market in Detroit. We were looking at 30th and Broadway where TARC has a maintenance facility across from the Nia Center. I was talking to the director of TARC at the time about donating that property to us, but that fell through.

I was driving down the street one day and saw the parking lot at the old Quinn Chapel. I found out that the YMCA owned it. The Y is supposed to promote fitness and health, so I went to their CEO, Steve Tarver, and said, "I want to put a farmer's market in the parking lot of Quinn Chapel. It fits with the YMCA's profile." He said, "Okay, let's do it." I drew up a contract, submitted it to him, and did a farmer's market there.

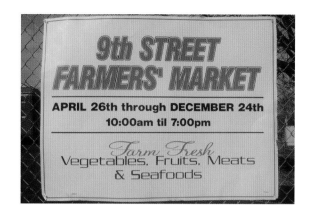

The Quinn Chapel site was a good location. You have seniors from J.O. Blanton House and Avenue Plaza. Then, we had a lot of young people that lived in Village West, now known as City View Apartments. It was a pretty good spot. We weren't really trying to make money. We just wanted to get food into the West End for people who didn't have anywhere to shop. They closed the Village West grocery store, which was

owned by African Americans, and people had to walk or take the bus to buy groceries. When I did the feasibility study, I found out that kids didn't know where food came from. They thought corn came from a can. So we wanted to educate young people and get them involved and interested in agriculture. It was more than just setting up a farmer's market.

We had a nonprofit, the Russell Neighborhood Development Corporation. We were looking to set up a larger market with value-added products—jams, jellies, prepared food, stuff you'd find in a grocery—and everything associated with them. We developed our own bottled water that neighborhood kids would sell along with the produce. We taught them salesmanship. We took them on farm trips. For example, we'd go to Taylorsville to the Berry Farm and pick blackberries and grapes. To this day, those kids will come up to me and say, "Man, we had the time of our lives." They didn't realize how much fun it was picking their own produce.

In 2007 the Community Farm Alliance commissioned a study with the Pan-African Studies Department at the University of Louisville. Before then, people were talking about the food desert and its effects in the West End, but nobody really had laid it out like Dr. Yvonne Jones, who chaired Pan-African Studies at UofL. She talked about how the demise of Walnut Street, 12th Street, and 28th Street paved the way for this food desert. All of that had an impact on why food companies didn't want to relocate to the West End. She talked about how, when whites moved out and Urban Renewal hit the West End, all the small groceries, butchers, and greengrocers left with them. Those that were left put up bulletproof glass and stopped carrying fresh fruits and vegetables. Just canned goods, snacks, beer, soda, and lottery tickets. By the 1990s it was just the Kroger on 28th and Broadway and a bunch of fast-food restaurants. The study also showed that people in the West End had to pay more for healthy food than people in more affluent zip codes. The corner stores sold cheap food at a premium. What we were trying to do at our farmer's market was to sell high-quality, healthy food at a discount.

Kroger and those big stores can sell products as loss leaders. They throw away a bunch of food. It's hard to compete with that. Metro Council put up three and a half million dollars in 2020 for a community grocery store that they still haven't allocated. They said, "We want to have it in the right location," which I can understand. If you want to open a grocery store or a market, you need a place with high visibility on a main thoroughfare. If you can't do that, the chances of getting customers are slim to none.

My family's business was right at the intersection of 12th and Chestnut, catty-corner to Central High School in the Old Walnut Street days. My uncle, Colin Page, moved to Louisville after World War I and opened an ice cream parlor called Page's Confectionery. He was in business from 1922 to 1969. He learned ice cream making at the old Vienna Restaurant and catering at Kline Caterers. Page's included a restaurant, ice cream parlor, and an ice cream manufacturing plant. People still talk about his tutti frutti ice cream and the party sherbert with three different flavors in one, like a Neopolitan. People bought it for sherbert punch. Aunt Milton was a baker and she was famous for her caramel cake.

Russell was a place where Black businesses could thrive, and Uncle Page did well for himself. Page's was small when it started, but by the time it ended, it covered almost a quarter of a block. The place was immaculate. They had a banquet hall that was all crystal chandeliers, fine china, silver, and this long dining table. It was as nice as any ice cream parlor of the time. They would hardly ever let us go up there. My father's auntie started a bridge club upstairs. There was no other place where you could have a major event that was really nice. Page's was *the* place. I have a picture of Bill "Bojangles" Robinson—the guy who did that famous dance routine with Shirley Temple—just hanging out in his suit cracking jokes on the ice cream parlor stool. The guy who they named Cotter Homes for, Joseph Cotter, his son Joseph Cotter Jr. used to bring in all the Harlem Renaissance writers and artists from New York around Derby time. Joseph Cotter Jr. was writing plays at the time and had an affection for writing poetry.

Comic Actor Bill Robinson at Pages, 1940

Aunt Milton at Page's

Mural in the viaduct on Muhammad Ali Boulevard west of 13th Street

They were always interacting with each other's work. The house is torn down now, but they stayed at 2030 Magazine. At Derby time, people slept on the floor or in chairs because they wanted to be around Walnut Street and be part of the festivities.

People don't realize that a lot of people wanted to come to Louisville because of its size and all the activities going on in the first half of the twentieth century. Louisville was bigger than Atlanta, and a lot of Black professionals descended on Louisville. The Housing Authority built Beecher Terrace in 1939 specifically for Black professionals; it wasn't a low-income housing project. Black professionals with a little cash who wanted to get a foothold in Louisville moved to apartments in Beecher Terrace which were like condos to them.

Also, some of the streets within Beecher Terrace were named after HBCUs these professionals attended.

The median income was tremendous at that time for Blacks living in the Russell neighborhood. That's why Black businesses in Russell flourished. You had low-income families who lived on the alleys and worked for people in the "big homes." But at that time, two-thirds of Russell was skilled tradesmen or professionals, and when they established their businesses and practices, they had enough cash to start buying property.

Up until 1910 or 1920, Russell—which was known as West Downtown—was predominantly white. In the first white flight out of the city, a lot of those individuals built big homes in the lower Highlands and the Crescent Hill area. There's been a lot of talk about redlining, about how the banks wouldn't lend African Americans any money to buy a home. That might have been true, but African Americans were still able to purchase homes, and I've heard that in some cases, it was the white property owners who financed or carried the note for the property that African Americans were purchasing from them.

I've heard that white property owners, who knew the Blacks couldn't get mortgages from the banks, would sometimes seller-finance the homes to the buyers who were mostly Black professionals who graduated from college and had professional degrees, like doctors and lawyers. The white property owners were professionals too, so it was like doctors talking to doctors; even though they were different races, they could talk to each other. So, even with redlining, they were still able to survive and strive.

With the big influx of African Americans, Mammoth Life and Accident Insurance Company—a Black-owned insurance company—got into mortgages. At one time, Mammoth Life had business in eight states, and between the 1920s and the 1960s, they had assets of over $30 million.

The outer edge of Russell was predominantly white. The businesses along Broadway were mostly white businesses until around 1960. There were like seven white-owned car dealerships on Broadway between Sixth and 15th at one time. So Blacks were buying cars from white business owners. Then Market Street was pretty much a Jewish community. They had department stores, furniture stores, and appliance stores. And they were situated from Sixth Street to 15th as well. There were a few Black restaurants, but most of the businesses were owned by Jewish people. The interior streets, like Jefferson and Magazine, were predominantly Black from Sixth to 15th.

I was born in the Russell neighborhood in 1954, and was raised at 20th and Chestnut until I was about six or seven years old. That house is torn down now. Uncle Page gave my mother and father the house where I was born as a wedding present. Free and clear. They didn't have any mortgage. He just bought it and said, "Here, this is a wedding present."

Their marriage didn't last, though, because my father was abusive to my mother. He'd get drunk and want to come home and beat my mother up. My mother got tired of it when I was about six or seven years old and moved us to my granddaddy's house at 32nd and Young. Seven little kids running around Granddady's house wasn't going to last too long, so Momma got an apartment in Southwick, and we lived there for seventeen years.

Daddy stayed at the house at 20th and Chestnut and worked for Page's. He never learned how to drive a car. Judge Ben Shobe used to drive him around. When Ben graduated from law school, he used to come around and hang out at Page's where he and Daddy became friends. He represented a lot of Blacks before he became the first African American since Reconstruction to be a circuit court judge in Kentucky. He'd bring Daddy to Southwick or they'd take us to Page's for ice cream. If Uncle Page needed something done around the house, we would help cut the grass or rake the leaves and that kind of stuff, and then we'd come back to Southwick.

My father used to tell us some stories while he was drunk. He would tell us about his exploits in World War II, how they wouldn't let Black and white soldiers mix even in the military at that time. He would tell us that the women in Germany and France liked the Black soldiers more than the white guys, and the soldiers would fight about that. He would tell us how they would engage the enemy, how they would get in the trucks and go out and fight, then go back, and regroup and get more ammunition. I was so fascinated hearing that stuff as a child. It was like sitting at the knee of a storyteller, but his stories were all real. It was like he was talking to you about a faraway land they didn't even show on TV. He was describing it so vividly that it was like you were there. Daddy was a hell of a storyteller, and he was drunk doing this.

When he sobered up, he loved to cook just like I do. If he stayed sober a week or so, we ate good. We used to say, "Daddy makes beans taste like steak." When my mother was with my father, she also learned how to cook. She did a lot of the parties at Page's. I used to go in there and watch her cook Sunday dinners starting when I was about six, just taking it all in.

One time, this lady named Ms. Margaret moved in down the street. I decided to make a welcome cake for her, so I made a coconut cake: white cake, coconut icing, and coconut topping. I toasted some of the coconut in the oven and sprinkled it on top. It was real pretty. I gave it to her and said, "Ms. Margaret, welcome to the neighborhood." She said, "Oh, this is so wonderful! Thank you!" What she didn't say was that she was allergic to coconut. She didn't tell me until I was older. Her kids ate it, but she couldn't eat any of it.

I stopped messing with baking when I was nine years old because I got a job working on the racetrack at Miles Park. My best friend David Franklin—who we called Tight—was working over there, and I followed him one day. If you want to be with horses, you gotta learn everything, so they started me out filling up the buckets of water, then mucking some stalls. I had a way with the horses and started getting real friendly with them. The real mean horses that people were scared of became my friends.

I worked there for six years. I was the only one in the family besides Momma that was making money,

and I was almost making as much as she was. But I was always late to school. I went to school, but I just wasn't making it to homeroom because I was working at the track in the mornings. They counted you absent if you didn't go to homeroom whether you came to school or not. At that time, they had truant officers, and if they didn't catch you, they'd lock up your parents. Well, when I was thirteen, they locked up my mother. I saw them putting her in the police car. When I went in the house, my brothers and sisters screamed at me about how they locked Momma up because of me. To get her out, I had to turn myself in. She just stayed overnight. A couple of days later, I'm in juvenile court, and she signed me over to the state.

I got sent to a youth correctional facility called Ormsby Village. I had heard about Ormsby Village because a couple years earlier my brother had been sent to Ridgewood, a maximum security lockdown for teenagers next to Ormsby Village. He was sent there for acting crazy. We used to go visit him. I never dreamed that I was going to be sent anywhere like that.

When I showed up, they took me to the administration building. The director, psychologists, and social workers were there looking at me like I was an alien or something. They said, "You've been arrested for playing hooky from school. Other kids around here, they've got more serious offenses." They didn't want to put me in with them, so they put me in the cottage with the orphan kids. I was the only one who wasn't an orphan. There were about a dozen of us in the cottage. I knew some of those other kids from the hood and from just being around the West End. I met the cottage mother, Ms. Bussell, who greeted me and had the kids greet me. Everything was real cordial. Even though I was arrested, and in custody, I was in this environment that looked like a resort. All the dormitories were little cottages with nice furniture, chandeliers, wainscoting, little antique whatnots on the shelves. There were bunk beds and kids' artwork on the walls.

I went to school there and got interested in the woodworking shop. The teacher showed me how to make lamps out of wood. I made a set of these lamps for Ms. Bussell and decorated them real nice. She was blown away because nobody had ever done that for her, and that's how we became good friends. I kept up with her in the years after I got away from Ormsby Village. I would go over and knock on her door, give her a card for the holidays, and ask if she needed anything because her husband had died and she was living by herself.

The cottage in the back at Ormsby was a lock-down cottage. If you got in trouble, that's where they sent you to be disciplined. I was sent there one time for mouthing off to a substitute when Ms. Bussell took a couple of days off to take care of her husband. The cell had a steel bed, no mattress, steel toilet, steel sink, no mirror, and no drain for the water. The guy said, "I'll be back." He came back with a fireman's hose and sprayed me at full blast. After that, he had me run around the cottage for half an hour, just constantly running. Then he made me give him fifty pushups. I'm soaking wet with sweat now. Then he said, "Take your hand, grab your leg, and stand on one leg." I did that same routine until Ms. Bussell came back and found out that I was in lockdown. She was pissed off and she got me out of there.

This was in March, and I told her in May that they couldn't keep me any longer because I got arrested for playing hooky from school. School was going to be out in May, so why should I be here? The director of Ormsby Village said, "Okay, you got a point there. You can go home."

I came back home to Southwick when I got out. I didn't get into too much more trouble at that time in my life. I mean, you had to fight and stand your ground

Bellevoire House at Ormsby Village

back in those days, but once people figured out that they couldn't bully you, they left you alone. One time when I was fourteen years old or so, these guys started roughing up my friend Paul at the roller rink at 12th and Broadway. One guy had Paul on the floor and was beating the stuffing out of him, so my girlfriend Vicki slid Paul a knife on the floor and said, "Here, let's make this even-Steven. You got a knife. Now he's got a knife." But before they could start fighting with the knives, the manager of the skating rink told them to take it outside, and they didn't fight anymore. They went separate ways. Vicki lived in Beecher Terrace, so Paul had the Beecher Terrace contingent around him, and that kind of insulated him from those guys.

People were stealing cars and all that kind of stuff too. Some friends of mine came and picked me up in a stolen car one time. I didn't know it was stolen until the police started chasing us. I said to my friend who was driving, "What's going on, man?" He said, "Hold on, man, this car is hot." And I was like, "What?" We kept going, and had a block and a half on them. We stopped the car at Beech Street and Southern, and there were two apartment buildings there that had some bushes between them. My friends ran down the alley, and I thought, *I'm not going to follow them. I'm going to dive through the bushes and hide.* I dived in there and *bam!* A wrought iron fence split my head wide open. Then the police finally came, and the officer shone the flashlight in my face, laughed, and said, "You ain't going nowhere." I was bleeding like a bloody hog. But then they started chasing my friends down the alley and left me alone. I just got up and walked over to a friend's house. Danny Boy—who later changed his name to Yusef—lived on Beech Street. His dad, Mr. Dan White, opened the door. He said, "Boy, what happened to you?" I said, "A man hit me in the head with a brick." He said, "Come on in here," and he doctored me up. I still got the scar. Mr. White was the head coach of Central High School's football team and later became the school's principal.

In 1969, I decided that if I was going to get out of Southwick, I had to do something drastic, so I joined the Job Corps. My brother had gone to Job Corps before I did and he had a pretty good experience. He said I might as well go too. So when I was fifteen, I took a sixteen-hour bus ride to San Marcos, Texas, with no money in my pocket.

In Job Corps, you learned a trade. You got three hots and a cot and fourteen dollars every two weeks for spending change. I was into carpentry because I'd learned to work with wood at Ormsby Village. I stayed down there for about six months before they opened up a Job Corps closer to home in Simpsonville. The Lincoln Institute was a Booker T. Washington-era training school for African Americans. My father had gone there. They'd changed it to Whitney M. Young Job Corps Center, and I was in the inaugural class.

I didn't start at Whitney Young immediately after I came back from Texas because it was going to be a couple of weeks for the paperwork to go through. So I went home to Southwick, but when I got there, everybody and everything was gone. Nobody there. I opened the door, and all the furniture was gone. I was like, *Where in the hell?* I was shocked. That night, I stayed in my bedroom. The next day, I went down to see Ms. Margaret, the lady I made the coconut cake for when I was kid. She knew that Momma had left because they were good friends. She told me that my mother and sister had moved in with this soldier over in Shelby Park. She just left without taking any of my belongings. I didn't have contact with my mother again until I got out of the military when I was twenty-one.

Ms. Margaret told me I could stay with her for a little while. She had a bunch of kids, and I felt like I was in the way, so I left after a couple weeks. That was my first time being homeless. Fifteen years old, walking around the streets, really homeless. I had to eat Snickers candy bars for dinner.

I was kicking it with this girl, Janice, and her grandmother said, "Well, you need a place to stay. You can stay here with us." So, I moved in with them on 32nd and Kentucky and lived there until I got placed at Whitney Young and started staying in the dorm. When I'd come home on the weekend from Job Corps, I would stay at Janice's grandmother's house.

I'd bring my buddies to 28th Street because that was where everybody hung at. After the 1968 riots, 28th Street along Dumesnil and Virginia was all messed up, but the section from Hale to Garland was still lively. At that time, if you wanted to be seen, you went to 28th Street. People were dressing real nice. They weren't wearing blue jeans. They had on alligator shoes and nice clothes. We'd shoot pool at Zeke's Pool Room at 28th and Greenwood. Senator Georgia Davis

Powers had a restaurant across the street from the pool room called Senator's Burger and that's where we'd go to eat. Man, I miss that Senator Burger. It was the best burger I ever had in my life. If you needed to wash clothes, you had Senator's Laundromat next to the restaurant. Ken Clay had a head shop and record store right there. You had an ice cream parlor, a juke joint, and a liquor store across the street.

I didn't have a permanent place to live. I wasn't thinking about having a damn career or anything like that. We were just running up and down 28th Street, having fun, doing drugs, hanging out, and acting wild. Janice and I were hanging out and I was going with this other girl named Jamilah. Her nickname was Flip. Janice was kind of wild like me. She had a daughter when I met her. Her daughter's name was Sherrie and we all called her Winkie. Jamilah was more down to earth. Jamilah encouraged me to go to the military. She said, "I know Vietnam is going on, but you need to get away from here, man." She went into the military too, did twenty years and retired from the Navy. We're still in touch today.

I would have married Jamilah, but she said she didn't want to at that time. So, I went to Janice and said, "Hey, look. Let's get married. I'm ready to go into the military, and I get more money being a married military person than being a single one. I can send you and Winkie a check every month." And she was like, "Sure." So, we went down to Granddaddy's house on Southwestern Parkway by Shawnee Park. We knocked on the door and said, "Granddaddy, we wanna get married." He had been a minister at Centennial Olivet Baptist Church on 16th and Oak. He said, "All right, come on. You got a marriage license?" He married us right inside his living room and charged me fifty dollars. Granddaddy didn't care if you were family or not: you were going to pay him the money for his services.

Joe in the service

I left in 1973 and was stationed in Fort Ord, California. I had an apartment in Marina, a small town a couple miles outside of Fort Ord. It took me six months to get that apartment because the white people didn't want to rent to a Black soldier.

I had stopped cooking about three years earlier, but I started getting interested in culinary stuff again. The first place I ate in California was an Italian restaurant above a beach full of sea lions, and I still can taste the freshness of the sandwich I ate. I have never had a sandwich like that since.

I would ride around Salinas and see hundreds and hundreds of acres of produce with migrant workers

The Mack

in a studio is lonely. You might be talking to tens of thousands of people but you sitting there by yourself, controlling these buttons and queueing up records and advertisements and stuff, so he invited me to keep him company. I started watching him closely and after a while he said, "You really want to learn this stuff? We got a practice booth. It's the same equipment I got here. You can go back there and practice." So I went back there. I started playing around with the stuff and really getting down, and the lady who owned the radio station had been standing there for about fifteen minutes just looking at me. I turned around, and she said, "You really like doing this, huh? Well, I have an 11:00 p.m. to 6:00 a.m. opening."

You had to pass a test to have a radio broadcast license, so I got my license. My radio call name was The Mack, like the movie *The Mack,* which was out then. My sign-off at the end of the show was a little panto-mime: me telling my girlfriend Debra to leave a candle in the window and blow it out when I get there. I didn't talk much on the show, though, I just played music. I knew how to put music together and how songs fit with each other or didn't. I had one of the best 11:00 p.m. to 6:00 a.m. shows around. All the people doing all-nighters got used to my show and loved it.

When I was transferred to Germany, I started disc jockeying in the clubs there and ended up auditioning for the Armed Forces Network. I got on the train to Nuremberg, which was about fifty miles away from Bamberg where I was stationed, and went to their radio booth. They were shocked. "Where'd you learn this at?" they asked. I said, "I was a disc jockey at one of the top stations in Seaside, California." They said, "You know what you're doing. You handled the board real well." Back then, it wasn't digitized like it is now. You had to queue it up, and actually do all the work. They let me come in on the weekends and deejay. The show got

out there harvesting it. That was a hell of a sight. That fascinated me.

And so I started getting excited about cooking again. I started inviting my friends over and started cooking for them. I would go to Cannery Row and get fresh fish, meat, and produce, then come back home and cook it. People would come to the crib on weekends and we'd eat and listen to music and have a good time.

You have time on your hands when you're in the service, and I started disc jockeying too. This soldier from Chicago named Kenny had a radio program and he said, "Come and hang out with me, man." Being

to be real popular, and I became a little celebrity from Nuremberg to Bamberg. I was still The Mack. I kept the Mack persona and dressed in platform shoes and gangsta hats.

In Germany, you can ride the train to anywhere in Europe. One time, this young lady friend of mine, Uta, said, "Come on, let's go to the UK." I had a jacket I'd bought in California at Saks Fifth Avenue department store—rawhide with lambswool lining inside—but in Germany, it's so cold, you can't just wear a jacket and be warm. So we go to London and we were walking down the street and there was a tailor shop. I jumped into the tailor shop and said, "I want a cashmere coat. I want it in two tone: one side black and one side brown, and I want it to be a maxi." The guy said, "I can do that. Come back in about four hours, I'll have it ready for you." So we hung around downtown and looked at the sights, then we were getting ready to catch the train. I said, "Let's go and get my coat." It fit me to a tee. I paid about four hundred dollars for a tailor-made maxicoat. That was really my look when I went to the club. I'd have a big hat on with my maxicoat and my platform shoes. I had a three-turntable box that I could fold up and it looked like I was carrying a guitar. I'd come into the club and set up on the stage, open up the top and hook it into the PA system. I started spinning records and everybody got up and danced until the place closed.

I'd signed up for three years in the service and when it was up, I left. I didn't do a lot of disc jockeying when I came back to Louisville. I started getting into food. I'd been seeing all this culinary stuff in Europe and California and I wanted to get back into making food here in Louisville.

Two guys I knew were making this bean pie and so I got with them and started helping them make bean pies. A bean pie tastes just like a sweet potato pie. You use the same flavorings and seasonings and spices.

These guys was doing it like a hobby, but I wanted to make something out of it. So they said, "Well, you just go ahead and take it." One guy moved to Connecticut another guy moved out to California. I took that pie and started putting it in every corner store in the West End.

I wanted to open up a storefront for the business, so I worked with a guy named John Greenbaum. I'd helped John when he sold the Westend Theatre to the owners of a Burger Queen franchise, and we struck up a friendship in the process. John wanted to help me out. He asked what I was doing and what I hoped to do. I said, "Well, I got this bean pie that I'm making and distributing. And I really want to open up Page's again at its last location, 38th and Broadway." John said, "Well, go and see if the building's still there. If the building's still there, I'll give you the money to buy the building and enough money to fix it up and buy the equipment. And you can put a full-fledged bakery there."

That's what I did. I went to the guy who owned it—a slumlord type of real estate guy—and I told him I wanted to buy the building which he sold to us for $16,000. It was in terrible shape. At closing, we're sitting there and I'm excited about it all. The lawyers are handling all the paperwork. John Greenbaum says, "Hey Joe, I want you to read something." He hands me some paperwork to read. It was the old deed. The property had been owned by the Doerhoefer family. They used to have a flower shop in that building. In the deed, it said something like, "This property can never be sold to a Negro." And here I am a Black person, buying the property. I read that stuff and said, "I still want the property." My family hadn't owned the property. They were renting. They probably never seen this language in the deed.

I got the property, spent $25,000 fixing it up, and started a full-fledged bakery instead of just baking bean

pies. There was a bakery at 36th and Broadway called Wohleb's. They were the Heitzman's of their time. People were used to going to Wohleb's. They would walk past my bakery and keep going to Wohleb's. So I stopped them and said, "Why y'all going to him?" They said, "His donuts are better." I said, "Well, we buy from the same vendors, we use the same mix, we use the same grease." I said, "As a matter of fact, I've got five master bakers baking for me." They were all white guys from the South End and their daddies were master bakers. I was paying them three hundred dollars a week and my wife and I weren't even taking a salary. We just had enough money to buy something to drink to chill out at the end of the day.

Sales were good when we first started. It's what we call "the ninety day newness." When you open up people run in there, but after ninety days it kind of dies

down. About six months into it, I called John and said, "Look, I'm going to change the concept. I'm going to try the wholesale business. I got five guys who can bake anything." Nobody was doing that except big companies like Linker's and Rainbo bakeries. John said, "I own French Lick Resort. I'll introduce you to the chef up there, and that'll be your first account." That got me in every door I went to. I told every potential new account, "I service French Lick Resort." And they were like, *What? This Black guy got French Lick Resort?* I said, "My reference is Chef Maurice Boone if you want to call him up." So I got all the hospitals, I got the penitentiaries in Pewee Valley and La Grange. I had damn near every fine dining restaurant in Louisville including the Bristol Bar & Grille. As a matter of fact, the Bristol's best selling pie was the bean pie; they called it "custard pie." We were sending 3500 pieces of baked goods out the back door per week to wholesale accounts.

Then we also started an all-you-can-eat buffet. We had people from New Albany, Jeffersonville, and the East End coming to Page's Bakery and Deli at 38th and Broadway, and they were coming to *eat*. We had an all-you-can-eat buffet with leg of lamb on Saturdays, and we had all-you-can-eat fish on Fridays. And then on Sundays, people would come after church and buy out everything. We wouldn't have a cookie in the pastry case after all the church folks came.

In 1983, I went into business with this lawyer who owned some property at Second and Main. He'd come to me at 38th and Broadway and over dinner one night, he offered me $300,000. That was pretty good money in 1983. He said, "We got this building that used to be the old Galt House building at Second and Main. We want you to come and put your operation there." He offered me good money.

He says, "You'll be the first Black person that ever put a restaurant east of Fourth Street." I was young and naive and thought that would be a hell of a thing. He said, "I'm putting up all the money. What do you have to lose?"

So I closed my business down to go and fix up his place on Second Street. The old slave pens had been across the street. It took me about nine months to fix it up because we had to do the mechanicals for the whole building. About a month into the project, building materials started going missing. We'd buy materials one day and come back the next day, and they'd be gone. The lawyer started accusing me of stealing the materials. I said, "Why the hell would I steal materials from my own restaurant that I'm trying to open up?" Come to find out it was the property manager who was taking the materials to build a bingo hall on Dixie Highway. They didn't suspect it was him because he was white.

The menu for Joe's Main Street restaurant, which never opened

I was accused because I was Black. That's when the relationship between me and the lawyer started to sour.

We got almost a hundred percent finished. The only thing left to do was stuff like picking out the silverware, china and the glassware, and that's what we fell out about. I had this idea about these thick-bottomed glasses that looked like you were getting more to drink than you actually were. The lawyer said, "No, we're going to do it my way." I said, "Wait a minute. This is my restaurant. I closed my business to come up here and develop this place. Now you're telling me we're going to use the silverware you want, or else?" We argued about that for thirty minutes and it got heated. I said, "You can take this damn place and stick it up your old dead grand-mammy's ass." I left there and I had fifty-six cents in my pocket.

Joe and his wife Darlene on their wedding day, 1987

That fiasco messed me up for a long time. I started attending Jefferson Community College around the same time, and I remember writing an essay called, "All That Glitters Ain't Gold" about everything that had happened. I wrote it to get some of those emotions off my chest. It was very emotional for me because that was the end of Page's Bakery, the family business that was baked into my DNA. It was like losing a child. It's something I'm probably still suffering from today. I took all these psychology courses at JCC, and that's how I got into the Human Services field. I realize now that I got that degree to help myself and to keep from going crazy.

I married my current wife, Darlene, in 1987, and we started a family and had seven children together. By the late 1980s I was working at Bridgehaven teaching mentally challenged individuals everyday living skills. School really became like therapy to me. I just kept going back, and I'm still going. I ended up getting a master's degree in 2004 from the Kent School of Social Work. My final research project was about developing the farmer's market at the old Quinn Chapel Baptist Church property. Metro United Way and the Agriculture Development Board gave me a grant to do the research for that paper. That's also how I was introduced to the idea of getting funding through the tobacco settlement fund to start the farmer's market and get fresh local food into the West End.

I know the community. There are people constantly trying to help the community and make change who can never get more than a five thousand dollar grant, whereas developers can come in and get millions of dollars. There's a lot of money being funneled into the West End right now, and it's going to the dysfunction of the West End. We're paying for this dysfunction. The people that stopped the biodigester get kicked to the curb. People like Martina

Joe with his son Mikal and wife Darlene

Kunnecke who want to save all the old historic buildings get kicked to the curb. And then the dysfunction comes in, and the developers get all the money. And when all the money's gone, they're gone, and the dysfunction continues and gets worse.

There are organizations who care about the community and live in the community who can't get that kind of money to do anything. Their projects are just as smart, and they are more invested because they live here. As long as people are coming in from the outside to "save" the community, it will remain dysfunctional, and outside developers will continue to get the money. That's the game.

Outside developers don't give a damn about the West End. They want to make a buck. They have thrown so much money into the West End, and the problems are worse. Where does the money go? That is the question we should be asking. Nobody else will say that. Everybody else is dancing around this because it goes against their interests and what's in it for them. They aren't going to say that because they're getting their piece of the action. They look the other way to keep their standing. I'm not like that. I will always try to help my fellow West-Enders succeed. I don't look the other way. ✦

"A Proud Russell Resident"

JACKIE FLOYD

My parents are both from Alabama. My mother grew up in a Black farming community, and my father grew up in a town dominated by white folks. He couldn't be as free as my mother was, and I think that since he couldn't do things, he made sure his daughters were independent. He always encouraged me to try things, to step out there, and to voice my opinion as long as I did it in a respectable manner. That's what I do now—I talk so much, and I advocate. I'm the only one of the five that has the mouth. I like to say I'm assertive; some say aggressive. Whichever gets the job done.

I was born on Thanksgiving in Louisville in 1952. I am the second of five girls. We lived on 12th and Zane, then we moved to Fort Hill. We moved down to Victory Park in 1962 when I was ten years old, and that's where I spent the rest of my childhood.

Growing up, my mother worked at Children's Hospital and my father was a construction worker. I had a typical mother-and-daughter relationship with Mama, but my relationship with my father was unconditional. He allowed me to make my mistakes and grow. I never doubted that he had my back. I think that's one of the reasons I'm strong-willed. I don't fear making a mistake; it's a learning experience.

We attended Greater Friendship Baptist Church on 12th and Zane. Mama worked night shifts, so she would come home, get us breakfast and get us ready, and then go to bed. Daddy would take us to Sunday school. He would go with the men over to my uncle's garage, where they would work on cars and argue and fuss with each other. Then he would come back, get us from church, and take us home, where Mama had dinner ready. We might even have to go back to church.

One thing that has kept me straight is my love for gospel singing. Just about every Sunday, I was in church. I love church the way we used to do it. The

Jackie's parents Almonia and Willie English

choir used to march in, and then four or five deacons would kneel down for their devotions. I really miss the choir's marching because they would get you ready for the sermon.

I love the gospel music from back in my mother's day. I love James Cleveland. I just listen to his music all the time. Every year the *Louisville Defender* would have the Black Expo with all kinds of vendors who would give away free things. My favorite part was always on Sunday night when all the church choirs and gospel groups would have their singing contest.

I went to the old Brandeis Elementary on 26th and Kentucky and then to Parkland Junior High School. All my friends went to Central High School, but I knew if I wanted to finish high school, I needed to go to another school because I was "creative in my behavior." I went to Male High School because I knew I could graduate. I was a rule-tester, and if I could drag somebody else into my stuff, that made it even better. My best friend went to Central, and I could talk her

Jackie and her eldest Stefannie Dotson, November 2017

into everything. If I wanted to cut school, she'd be right there with me.

When I entered my senior year, I was pregnant. When school started that fall, I attended Male until I started showing in November, and I switched to the TAPP school for pregnant teens. Back then, it was at the YWCA on Third Street. When a girl got pregnant, she could continue her education at TAPP. I had my baby on March 5, 1971. TAPP had classes for mothers once they had the baby. My goal was to get back to Male so I could walk down the aisle at graduation, and I did.

Before I got pregnant, my dream was to get the hell out of Louisville. I was going to go to the University of Buffalo to major in nursing. Then I got pregnant, and self-doubt came into my life. I didn't know what I was gonna do or even how to do it. I was still with my child's father, trying to figure out where I fit in. He was playing on me, and my self-esteem was really low. That was a really difficult time for me. By the time I was twenty, I had a second baby by him. People were pushing me to get married, especially my mom and sister. My mom and sister were old school and believed no matter what a man does, you stay with him. I said to hell with that. I'm glad I had enough sense not to marry him.

From the time I had my first baby to my second baby, I was taking a course through the welfare program. My second baby was really sick, and I couldn't work because daycare wouldn't take her. But when I was twenty-three or so, I was able to go back to work. I got hired on as a machine operator making aluminum foil at Reynolds. I was making good money, but by the time I'd save up money, they would lay me off. When that money ran out, they would call me back. That cycle kept repeating, so when they laid me off for the third time, I said, "It's a wrap." Working at the factory taught me that I can work with my hands, but I'm a more mental person.

One of my neighbors told me about a job at Central State Hospital. This white man named Steve May interviewed me for the psych unit working with teenage boys. I knew nothing about working with kids, nothing at all, but he saw something in me and hired me. When I got home, I called him and said, "Steve, we didn't talk about salary."

"Well, you'll be making four hundred and twenty dollars a month."

I said, "Excuse me?!" I was making four hundred and twenty dollars *in half a week* at Reynolds. I cried the first couple of times adjusting to that, but because I was a single mom, I understood a half a loaf is better than no loaf. It was my start in the field of social services.

When I started at Central State, it was like I had walked into a different world. I worked with boys twelve to seventeen who had killed their father or mother or raped someone. I didn't even know that type of thing existed, and while I had no previous experience, it didn't scare me. It just felt right. When I worked with kids, my motto was to give them all the love I had when I was with them, and when they left, I prayed they would be alright.

I learned about child abuse and sexual and physical abuse. It was so overwhelming, but I was thirsty for knowledge. The kids and staff taught me so much. I loved the kids with the most "creative behavior." There was this kid that I loved dearly. He was fifteen or sixteen and the only kid in Kentucky who had a mental inquest warrant for a whole year. Troubled people like troubled people, so me and him hooked up immediately. At the time, kids could smoke, and I was the only one who would take him out for a cigarette. He had seizures and was on fifteen different medications. He was very aggressive, and it took six or seven people to restrain him, so they kept him in seclusion most of the day. They let him go when he turned eighteen. I saw him on the bus a couple of times because his therapist was at Central State. He had terrible seizures, and when he hit twenty, he died.

I really enjoyed working with and learning about the kids. No matter what charge they had against them, the bottom line is they were still kids and wanted to be loved and cared for. I had a twelve-year-old kid from the mountains. His mother was thirty-something, and his father was in his seventies. The mother took off and left this man with the child. The boy was what we called "slow" back then. He committed a crime and was kicked out of the county. They sent him to Central State for a psych evaluation. He would cry at night, so I brought in some books for bedtime. I would read him

Jackie's mother Almonia English and her sister

a story, tuck him in, kiss him on his forehead, tell him I love him, and he'd go on to sleep. Meanwhile, I didn't know he was telling his father I was doing this.

His father loved him but couldn't drive and depended on social security. So, he would come down once a month with a friend when he got his check to see his son. On one visit, the father said,

"You the nigra that my son's been talking about?"

My co-worker was like, *Say what?* But I grabbed his hand because I knew the man was trying to say "Negro." He's from up in the mountains. He's probably never seen a Black woman before. I took it as a compliment because I was taking care of his child, and he was happy about that. I knew he and his friend didn't have anything to eat, so I always made sure they had something to eat before they took that long trip back home.

From Left: Semonia Cooksey, Stefannie Doston, Jackie and ShaTanya English

Jackie and her son William

By this time, I was in my early thirties and had become a supervisor. I learned I never want to supervise people again in my whole life. In my eyes, we're all adults and know the difference between right and wrong and what we should be doing. I was working full-time with Central State and part-time at the Home of the Innocents. I eventually went full-time at HOI and told them, "I do not want to supervise; I'm a staff person." That lasted every bit of three weeks.

While at Central State, I met and married my first husband. It was not a love thing. I was living in the projects, working for the state, and not making no money. He came along and was giving me money, being a good provider, and so I thought, "What the hell." I married him and had a baby by him. Biggest mistake of my life. I always tell the guys I'm involved with my three concrete rules: "Don't hit me, don't cuss me, and don't play on me. If you hit me, I'll kill you. If you cuss me, we're going round and round. If you play on me, you got to go." I told him, but he didn't believe me. We divorced, and I ended up going to Wayside Christian Mission. That's where I learned about the reasons women become homeless. I grew up in a very middle-income environment, so I had to learn a lot regarding social services. I came to understand people weren't simply homeless because of being lazy or addicted to drugs and alcohol. It had a really positive impact on my life.

I had an on-again-off-again relationship with the man who became the father of two children. Over the course of fifteen years, we both got married to other people, and then each separated. He was strong-willed and hard-headed like me, but at the same time, I knew he had my back. We could only go for a few months before we started sniping at each other. The relationship ended when I married my second husband.

After eight years at Central State, I went full-time

at Home of the Innocents in 1988. That's where I met my second husband, Sam Floyd. He worked in dietary, and we couldn't stand each other at first. We were complete opposites. I grew up in Victory Park, and he grew up in the California neighborhood, but we knew a lot of the same people. Our first date was a boxing match that he refereed. I dressed up because when my father went to see Muhammad Ali, he dressed up. So I was looking nice and sweet with my hair and makeup done. We went to Macklin Gym on 26th Street. When he pulled up to the gym, he kept circling the block, and I asked why. He said, "I'm trying to find a close spot because we might have to run up out of there." I thought he was joking, but when some of the guys didn't like the decision during the boxing match, they started cussing at him, and then I understood. I don't know what it was, but that night I knew this was the man I was gonna spend the rest of my life with. And I did for over twenty years until he passed in 2013.

When I had my last baby in 1989, I moved to 23rd and Jefferson in Russell. After Sam and I started dating and getting closer, I moved in with him at 27th and Broadway. From there, we went to 24th and Elliot, where our kids could play up and down the block. I had five kids, and he had three; we were a blended family. He was good with the kids; it wasn't his kids and my kids; it was *our* kids. Eventually, we lived in a house in the middle of Chestnut Street, and in 2002, we bought a new house on the end of that same street. It became the place my family would come to. My sisters lived in Shively and Pleasure Ridge Park, so my house was the center. If you need to meet somebody, come to Jackie's house.

I always cooked a big pot of chili on Saturdays no matter the season. I always had that chili on the stove. One Saturday, this guy knocked on the door asking for my sons.

From left: Jackie's grandson David, great-grandson David Jr., great-grandson LeTaz, granddaughter Dayona, and great-granddaughter Yona

Sisters Carolyn Johnson, Jackie and Beverly Robinson, November 2017

Jackie and her husband Sam Floyd

Jackie with Charles Booker

Jackie and Mayor Greg Fischer holding a plaque dedicated to Russell: A Place of Promise and the Russell Neighborhood, September 2022

"Is Rob home?"

"No," I said.

"Is William home?"

"No." And he just stood there. "Do you wanna come in? Are you hungry?" I said.

He said, "Yes, ma'am." So, I gave him something to eat, and he went upstairs to the boys' room and played their games. I created my house to be the house people wanted to come to because that's how I was raised.

We went to St. Stephen Baptist Church, where Sam grew up. He loved the Lord. We both grew up in the church. It was very important to both of us that we went to church together as a family. Every Sunday after church for about five years, my family came to my house for dinner. Sometimes I would have fifty people at the house; some would be in the basement, upstairs, in the living room, or on the back deck. I have high blood pressure, so I stopped using salt and didn't fry anything. I would bake it or steam it and use other seasonings. Even though I would cook dinner and have this big spread, my older sister would bring her own dinner, some unhealthy chicken. As her health started to go downhill and she couldn't get up and down the steps, we hosted Sunday dinner less often.

My sister stayed sick for three years. I always went to bed with my phone on, clean clothes laid out, and gas in my car because there were too many times her kids would call in the middle of the night to say, "She's been rushed to the hospital, and we don't know if she'll make it or not." The year after she died, I was diagnosed with cancer. People think I'm crazy to say this, but having cancer was the best thing that ever happened to me because I don't sweat the small stuff anymore. The doctors got all the cancer. I had to go through chemo and radiation, but I didn't lose my hair or throw up; I just lost weight. What got me through it all was my faith.

After working at Central State and the Home of the Innocents for so long, I was really curious about what happens to those eighteen-year-olds. Where do they go? The lack of services for kids coming out of foster care was really surprising. They were not prepared to enter the adult world. That was the state's fantasy. As soon as they turn eighteen, they want to go back to the relatives who abused them. They have that honeymoon period of four or five weeks, and then they are on the streets. It's sad because homeless youth become homeless adults.

My mother instilled in me the desire to involve myself in the community. I became an advocate for the homeless at the Coalition for the Homeless, the main advocacy group in Louisville for the homeless. One reason I do advocacy work is to partner with people in the community to guide them on how to use their collective voice and what methods they can use to get what they want and need. The people most impacted by the situation should be out front.

After the Coalition, I started working at the Healing Place, which provides food and shelter through its addiction recovery program. Sitting at home is never good for me, so it was good to have that to go back to. They were very supportive. While at the Healing Place, I was also working part-time for St. John Center, another shelter for homeless men. Sam and I started having problems because he didn't know how to be supportive. But I didn't give him the opportunity, either. I didn't really allow people to be there for me.

Sam and I separated for a minute until he got sick with colon cancer. He was never the same after his colon cancer surgery. He was later diagnosed with Parkinson's and then Lewy body dementia. Although I was now full-time at St. John, Sam needed full-time supervision, and I had to reduce my income so he could

Jackie and Harvey C. Russell III, grandson of Russell's namesake Harvey C. Russell Sr., February 2022

Jackie at a RPOP press conference, November 2022

Jackie with her granddaughter Dayona

Jackie and her daughters Stefannie Dotson, Semonia Cooksey, and ShaTanya English

get benefits, so I went home for a couple of months. He had one medicine that was five hundred dollars a week, and there was no way we could pay that.

Sam was sick for about three years and eventually went into a nursing facility as his health declined. I began to work in various low-income jobs in order for him to still receive his benefits. During this time, my mother was also diagnosed with dementia. It was one thing after another: *bam, bam, bam!* I was like, *Okay, God. If you think I'm this strong, I got you. I'm gonna work with you.* My children and sisters were my support system, along with my faith in God. I even took a job working in a nursing home as an activity director with folks who had dementia, which gave me a great understanding of what my husband and mother were experiencing.

I started working in the Russell community after Sam passed. I saw an ad in the paper that New Directions was looking for outreach workers in Russell. I knew Lisa Thompson from New Directions from my work at the Coalition for the Homeless, so I reached out and got the position doing community outreach for Vision Russell. I was also involved with Kentucky Jobs with Justice, which advocates for workers' rights. I participated in their various trainings and started developing my organizing skills and learning how to really advocate for people. I realized not everyone knew how to work in our community. Monday morning meetings are fine for some people, but flexibility is important in community organizing. Ideally, you should offer two options —one during the week and one on the weekend—with food and childcare. Most of all, you need to knock on people's doors and be available to answer questions.

Vision Russell hired people with deep roots in the Russell community, and I started to learn about the players in the community and started using my voice. I knocked on doors and said, "This is our community, our choice, our voice. And this is how you could use your voice, by saying what you want in your community."

The first time I started saying, "I'm a proud Russell resident," I was in a Vision Russell meeting. I say that all the time now, but I wanted people to know I *chose* to live in Russell. It's not that I have to be here because of the low rent or something. I choose to live here because I love the community. I go that extra mile with people in my community.

Around 2018, I started hearing about Russell: A Place of Promise. I had doubts. "Hell, here we go again. Another program talking about what they can do in our community." They had an event with funders from around the country to stimulate potential interest and investment in Russell, but that's not always productive for the residents. You need to engage and include residents in these conversations, especially if you're strategizing about the future of their neighborhood. With all the physical changes and financial investments happening in Russell, people keep saying, "We're coming down here because we want to empower the people." Hell, we already have the power. You need to step back and let us use our power. We don't need saviors; we can save ourselves. You need to step back and give us the tools we need.

I reached out to Anthony Smith at Cities United and Theresa Zawacki with Louisville Metro Government, who were co-leading the RPOP initiative, and grilled them like a cheeseburger. They understood my concerns, and later that year, when they formed the RPOP Advisory Board, they invited me to join. I eventually became the lead community outreach specialist for Russell: A Place of Promise. This job allows me to build relationships with the residents and encourage them to use their voices and power. I can be involved, not just engaged, with the community.

Attica Scott, Jackie, and Shameka Parish Wright

Jackie leading a walking tour of Russell, May 2021

Jackie's son and his family: William Robinson, Gina Robinson, Amelia Hinton, Aiden Hinton, Millie Hinton

It's more than knocking on the door to let someone know about an event. It's knocking on the door to check on Mrs. Jones because I know she has diabetes.

What I'm most proud of about Russell is the people. No matter what has been thrown their way—disinvestment, crime—they have still survived. They work hard every day to give their children the lifestyle they want them to have. They're putting values and morals in their children. They're still doing that no matter what comes their way. They're still checking on their neighbors, still able to laugh, and still have that positive image of their community. They sit on their front porches, and when you walk down the street, people ask you, "How you doing?" Russell is like family. Everybody in the family don't get along, but we have each other's backs.

My grandson told me one time, "Ms. Jackie, we're going to Kroger's to get groceries, okay? I don't wanna hear nothing about Russell: A Place of Promise. I don't wanna hear nothing about the Russell Neighborhood Association. We're going to get groceries, okay? You speak, and you keep it moving."

I am retiring at the end of this year. People have tried to talk me into getting into politics and running for office. Now, TV cameras love me! I got a reputation, but my interest is strategy and organizing. I'm not on Instagram and Twitter; that's too confusing. Facebook is my thing, and people follow me there. I enjoy sitting down with candidates like Charles Booker, Attica Scott, and Shameka Parrish-Wright, and strategizing on the next move in the campaign. I really love that.

My main focus when I retire is to build up the Russell Neighborhood Association. I started it while I was still at Vision Russell. It was informal, and our goals were no more liquor stores or halfway houses. My goal is to take the Neighborhood Association to the next level, formalize it, and turn it over to other people.

Jackie and the RPOP team, October 2022

I want it to be a political powerhouse so that anyone who runs for anything knows they have to get the support of the Russell Neighborhood Association because we will turn out and vote.

We need to have organizing training for the young folks. Our older generation needs to make room. I do this because somebody did it for me. When I was too busy raising my kids with my husband, advocates were out there fighting for the community. Now, I have the time. I've gotta return the favor and be out there, but I'm also allowing enough room for the next generation. I tell the young people on my RPOP team these gray hairs on my head represent streaks of wisdom. I'm going to drop a piece of wisdom on you. Sometimes you can drop enough that a seed is planted, and somewhere down the road, months or years later, that seed might sprout.

As parents, we teach our children to make their own decisions because we want them to be independent and free thinkers. So, when the young people start using what we've taught them, why do we, as parents and residents of the community, get pissed off because

Jackie during the annual RPOP Homecoming, September 2022

they're not doing it our way? Instead of telling them, "You need to do it like this," we need to step back and say, "What are your ideas? These are my ideas." When Christian Butler started working at RPOP, we bumped heads. I called her one day and said, "We need to figure out a way to work together." Ever since then, she's been trying, and so have I. Now, we have a very tight relationship. She's hungry and creative. I tell her I want her to become a Metro councilperson. I tell her, "Go to press conferences or wherever there are people because you will learn and make community connections. That's how I got where I am. I didn't know what was going on half the time, but I knew I needed to make connections."

It is our responsibility to educate people and inform them about the beauty we have in Russell. I don't say nothing negative about Russell. You cannot talk negative about my community that I live in, where I raise my children. Yes, we have problems, but doesn't your community have problems? We can work together to solve the problems. Let's sit down, meet, and figure out how neighborhoods could work together. You come down here and work on a project with us, and we'll come out there and work on a project with your residents.

I'm very aware that people try to use me to make their stuff legit, but people always underestimate me. I am not dumb. I am a thinker, and I only do something impulsive if it's an emergency. I'm good in a crisis, but other than that, I will sit back and think. I'm a night owl, so I'm up thinking and strategizing when most people are asleep. You can't fool me into something. If I do something, it's because I want to.

Russell deserves what every other neighborhood deserves. I love to read, and I want a bookstore. Attica Scott and I always go out to eat; we have to leave Russell to go eat. How come we can't have a Mediterranean restaurant or a soul food vegan restaurant in Russell? How come we can't have a coffee shop in Russell? I want in Russell the same things my tax dollars are paying for in other communities.

I want people to look at Russell through my eyes. It is beautiful in the springtime. You've got all these mansions—and if they could talk! We have the Western Branch Library, the first library in the country for African Americans, right here in Russell, and it's still in use today. I love the library. I walk in there and see the future attorneys, mayors, and governors. If you go down Muhammad Ali Boulevard, you see Black men, young and old, sitting on their front porches—it's intergenerational. When I walk through there, I speak to everybody. It's just something about seeing these men hanging on the corner that reminds me of my father and his buddies.

At Sheppard Park, you see mothers sitting out with their children at the splash pad. There's this group of men who sit along the front of Elliot Park on 28th Street. They're doing their thing, but you better not mess with any of those kids on those swings; they got their eye on them. Then you got the older men down here who are riding the bicycles, or the guys in the back on 29th Street who pull up in their cars with lawn chairs, just sitting and talking. They're all looking out for each other. The men of the community might not be doing what society says they should be doing, but they still take care of their community.

You have to inform people. You have to brag on your community, like you brag on your shoes and your purse. I always introduce myself, "I'm Jackie Floyd. I'm a proud Russell resident." This lady in Shelby Park once said, "Jackie, I started saying that! I started saying I'm a proud Shelby Park resident." When people know that you're excited about your community, it's infectious. ✦

Acknowledgments

Many hands are needed to tell the story of a place in an in-depth, long-term documentary project like this one. Louisville Story Program's mission to generate and support thoughtful and compassionate discourse would be impossible without the immense support of the community which we serve. We offer our deep gratitude to the people and institutions who have supported this work.

Beginning with the authors, whose voices ring out so clearly in these pages. Thank you for believing in this project and this process, for your honesty, and your time. There could not be a more important moment for your neighbors to read your stories. They are so vital and necessary, and are now a part of the historic record of our city and of Russell.

Thank you to Jeana Dunlap, whose vision and leadership sparked this project and made it possible, and to Louisville Metro Housing Authority for providing the anchor funding that allowed us to proceed. Thanks also to the Community Foundation of Louisville Historic Preservation Fund for supporting this project.

To our major supporters who make all of our work possible: the Fund for the Arts, Ted & Mary Nixon, Mary Gwen Wheeler & David Jones Jr., Brooke Brown Barzun and Matthew Barzun, Owsley Brown III, South Arts, the National Book Foundation, the Owsley Brown II Philanthropic Foundation, the Kentucky Arts Council, and the Arthur K. Smith Family Foundation.

To Spalding University for providing us office space, administrative support, and endless collegiality.

To Shellee Marie Jones for translating all of the text and photos into a beautifully-designed book. We are so grateful for your brilliance and dependability.

To Nathaniel Spencer and the good folks at WeCU Productions for producing the project video. Thank you for throwing yourselves so fully into the work.

To the good folks who provided introductions to some of the authors: Ravon Churchill, Mariel Gardner, Alice Houston, Martina Kunnecke, Barbara Sexton Smith, Ben Woods, and the staff of Russell: A Place of Promise.

To Tony Woods for bringing his car out for the back cover photo shoot, and to Manuel Hayes, Joe-Nika Irvin, Daicha Williams, Andre Woods, and Dasha Woods for bringing their kids.

To Savannah Darr, John Hawkins, and Tom Owen for their help with fact-checking.

To Deborah Mitchell-Johnson for her support in tracking down photos.

To our volunteer transcriptionists M.A. Allgeier, Jerusha Beebe, Dana Frank, Parker Hobson, Jane Kennedy, Mary Kate Lindsey, Noelle Maxwell, Sally Rother, Cat Sar, Samuel Schrier, Whitney Soergel, Ryan Speight, and Brooke Zimmerman. And to Joel Luna Shafer for always being there to assist with our printing and shipping needs.

To the University of North Carolina's Southern Oral History Program, whose archived June 6, 2006 David Cline interview with Manfred G. Reid Sr. supplied excerpts for Mr. Reid's chapter.

Thanks also to everyone else who provided funding for this project or general operating support, including: Susan Bentley, the Gheens Foundation, the Kentucky Oral History Commission, the Sociable Weaver Foundation, Emily Bingham & Stephen Reily, Porter Watkins, Clarese Fuller, the Snowy Owl Foundation, Gladys & John Lopez, Smith Rodes, Cornelia W. Bonnie, Rose Cooper & Allen Bush, Claudia Gentile, Valle Jones & Ann Coffey, Phil & Landis Thompson, Mimi Zinniel, Dr. Fred & Judy Look, Rick & Corie Neumayer, Elizabeth Matera, Ellen Sears, Michael & Amy Washburn, Anne McKune, John H. Clark IV, James & Vandy Chisholm, Amber Booker Duke, the LG&E Foundation, Will Oldham, Anthony Smith, David Tachau, Jennie Jean Davidson, David Henry & Clare Hirn, Roy & Julie Elis, Tom & Jenny Sawyer, Lynn Wilkinson, L'Tanya Williamson, Beth & Doug Peabody, Terri Phelps, Carolin Washburn, Carmichael's Bookstore, Cassie Blausey, Kate & Jason Crosby, Glenn & Therese Flood, Mary Grissom, Gene & Peggy Hoffman, Kristen Lucas, Alyssa & Doc Manning, Bob & Bo Manning, Colin McDonald-Smith, Christine Payne, Jake Allgeier, Martha Neal & Graham Cooke, Gary & Carol George, Clark Johnson & Diane Pecknold, Jane Kennedy, Cecilia Omdal & Mark Murdock, George Poling, C.J. Pressma, Janice Pullen, Robert & Felice Sachs, Sue & David Vislisel, and Bronwyn Williams.

And thank you, reader, for your commitment to knowing your neighbors with greater clarity. In both the telling and the receiving of these stories, we are offered common dignity and a greater stake in our claim to the city that we love.

—Althea Allen Dryden, Christine Gosney, Joe Manning, and Darcy Thompson
LOUISVILLE STORY PROGRAM

LOUISVILLE STORY PROGRAM

Our lives as they really are.

This book was published by Louisville Story Program, a non-profit organization committed to strengthening the bonds of community by amplifying unheard voices and untold stories.

Through rigorous writing and oral history workshops, and with professional editorial support, participating Louisville Story Program authors from historically underrepresented communities document the richness of lived experience in Louisville communities from the inside out, and in their own words. Their work is published in professionally designed books, exhibits, and radio programs that promote dialogue across the community and increase awareness of overlooked aspects of Louisville's culture and history. Our authors are paid for their work, and we leverage their achievements into as many additional professional, educational, cultural, and social opportunities for them as possible.

Find the full catalogue of Louisville Story Program titles as well as audio stories, videos, and information on upcoming projects at

louisvillestoryprogram.org